Bede
and Anglo-Saxon England

Papers in honour of the 1300th
anniversary of the birth of Bede,
given at Cornell University
in 1973 and 1974

edited by

Robert T. Farrell

British Archaeological Reports 46
1978

British Archaeological Reports

122, Banbury Road, Oxford OX2 7BP, England

Details of all issues of British Archaeological Reports will be sent free of charge and without any obligation to purchase, on request from the above address.

B.A.R. 46, 1978: "Bede and Anglo-Saxon England."
© The Individual Authors.
Price £3.50 post free throughout the world. Payments made in currency other than sterling must be calculated at the current rate of exchange and an extra 10% added to cover the cost of bank charges. ISBN 0 86054 005 7.

Cheques and postal orders should be made payable to "British Archaeological Reports" and sent to the above address.

For a list of other B.A.R. publications, please see the last page.

Printed in Great Britain

CONTENTS

LIST OF FIGURES

LIST OF PLATES

PREFACE

The studies in this volume are limited in two ways. All originated during the Bede celebrations at Cornell, and all deal with some aspect of Bede's life, his works, or the cultural _milieu_ in which he flourished.[1] The Bede observances at Cornell extended through the academic years 1972-3 and 1973-4, in commemoration of the thirteen hundredth anniversary of the birth of Bede in 673 and the founding of his monastery at Monkwearmouth in 674. In addition to formal lectures by visiting scholars during both academic years, a seminar was held in 1973 under the auspices of the Society for the Humanities and a special seminar on the art history and archaeology of the Anglo-Saxon period was given during the spring of 1974. The annual meeting of the Medieval Academy of America took place at Cornell in May 1973, when two major lectures were given by Professors Rosemary Cramp and David Wilson, whose papers served as bases for their contributions to this volume.

Apart from Professor Ó Carragaín's contribution, which is included for the further information it provides on the Ruthwell cross, all the papers in this volume were given at Cornell during the years of the Bede celebrations. Despite this common origin, the papers are widely variant in scope and subject; many of the writers had to travel long distances, and they were deeply engaged in teaching and administration at their own universities. They were not all at Cornell at the same time. The common factor is that they were all given to the same group, the Cornell community, and it is hoped that their appearance in the present format will allow a wider circle of readers to make use of what was given to Cornell over the course of several years.

The papers have been grouped to some extent by similarity of topic. First are those of Dr. Wilson and Professor Wetherbee, dealing respectively with advances in our knowledge of Bede's culture since 1935, and the question of Bede's Latin style. Next come the archaeological and art historical papers of Professors, Cramp, Farrell, and Ó Carragaín, all concerned with objects and concepts related to what can be called the age of Bede rather than to his own corpus of writings and the relations of that corpus to other traditions. Professor Calkins' paper is a kind of coda, appropriately placed in this collection because the Romano-British and Anglo-Saxon artifacts from an early English cemetery were rediscovered at Cornell by felicitous and fortunate circumstances during the course of the Bede commemoration. These objects were put on display for the latter half of the series of events, and served as a point of interest for the members of the Medieval Academy of America who assembled at Ithaca in the spring of 1973.

In the first paper, Dr. David Wilson surveys advances in the study of the archaeology and culture of Bede's time, and outlines some of the fundamental changes in attitude which have come about since 1935, when Thompson edited a collection to commemorate the anniversary of Bede's death.[2] Unless new evidence is put forward, we must now view the Picts as a major force in the culture of Northumbria, contributing much to the rich amalgam which is distinctive of that area in the age of Bede. The exchange was not limited to borrowing a kind of technology at one remove, as when Nechtan sought workers from Bede's monastery to help him build churches juxta more Romanorum. Wilson also follows through on the new and more general localisation for a whole range of "insular" manuscripts first proposed by Masai in a long-ignored work,[3] and more recently supported by the research of Professor Julian Brown.[4] The Lindisfarne Gospels, Durham Gospels, and the Book of Durrow show eclectic taste, and even Kells itself may well have come into being in an eastern Scottish centre, subject to Northumbrian influence. Perhaps the most significant aspect of Professor Wilson's survey is the clear evidence he adduces for the strong influences English tradition in art had on such clearly European artifacts as the Tassilo chalice, the Rupertus cross and the Franco-Saxon manuscript of c. 800. All of these are material evidence for the impact of the cultural aspects of the English missionary schools which had Northumbrian, and ultimately Bedean, traditions as their base. Professor Wetherbee has a simple but useful purpose, to show that while Bede did not indulge in the excesses of the so-called Hisperic mode of Latin style, his prose was a fully eloquent instrument. Bede wrote clearly, but elegantly; directly, but with restrained skill rather than the plainness of one incapable of greater art. If Professor Wetherbee's analysis is accepted, Bede's style constitutes a "positive contribution to the development of a medieval Christian Humanism." In his study, Professor Wetherbee calls on aspects of the styles of both Vergil and Gregory as points of comparison, but holds that Bede's accomplishments in the Historia Ecclesiastica are still sui generis. Mr. Wormald's paper surveys a very broad field that cannot easily be summarized. His material certainly provides practitioners of both disciplines with a careful survey of major trends in both fields. In addition to providing the basis for evaluation of what Bede accomplished, Wormald gives us a detailed notion of what Bede did not record in the Historia and why he did not record it. This is perhaps the most useful aspect of his work. Mr. Wormald presents further evidence to show that we can make some fairly sound assumptions about the lay Germanic audience as it developed in England through and beyond the age of Bede on lines parallel to those in continental manifestations of German aristocratic society. In Wormald's words we have an apparent paradox in that heroic literature in England was preserved "essentially because the early medieval church was an Adelskirche." Wormald also considers in passing the impact of Celtic or Insular Christianity.

In two closely related papers, Professor Cramp and I deal with aspects of the iconography of the Ruthwell cross. This splendid but enigmatic monument has been the subject of intense study for a long time; hopefully, we have made it possible to understand it better, and to see more clearly the tradition of which it was the most complex and accomplished product. We survey parallels for the iconographic sequence from a broad range of areas —liturgy, sculpture, sculptural commentary and literature among them. The cross is a rich indication of a splendid age, and the iconography is an outstanding cultural achievement in which Early Christian tradition is used with a full understanding of the modes of association of icons. It is our contention that Ruthwell is to be associated both with Wearmouth-Jarrow, Bede's own monastery, and a range of sculptures elsewhere.

Professor Ó Carragáin's brief paper provides a larger, theological, intellectual and liturgical context for the tradition which underlies the crosses. Bede and his monastic superiors were all very much aware of what was going on in the Christian world. Bede's attitudes toward the Saracens develop as the tide of Islam washed over large areas of Christian Europe, and Benedict Biscop made repeated trips to Rome and other Christian centres in order to enrich the spiritual and intellectual life of Wearmouth-Jarrow.[5] It is therefore not unlikely that new feasts and observances would be incorporated into the liturgy of the Northumbrian church. Pope Sergius was known to Benedict Biscop, Ceolfrith, Hwaetberht and Wilfrid, and Bede mentions him in the Historia Abbatum. Sergius, perhaps because such rites and feasts were part of the Eastern tradition from which he came, firmly established the feasts of the Annunciation and the Exaltation of the cross, and also the chant "Agnus Dei, qui Tollis peccata Mundi, Miserere nobis" as part of the Ordinary of the Mass. Professor Ó Carragain shows how these recent changes are reflected in the iconographical programme of the Ruthwell cross.

The final essay in the volume, Professor Calkins' study of the Frilford grave-goods, deals with materials which though Anglo-Saxon almost certainly pre-date Bede by more than a century. They were rediscovered by chance, in the course of moving collections from the old University museum to the splendid new Herbert F. Johnson Museum of Art at Cornell. The bronze brooches and iron objects which were dug up in the late nineteenth-century at Frilford, Berks. were clearly a source of perplexity for a long-dead curator, who had them wrapped in tissue, piled into a shoe box and thrust into the back of a cupboard. Professor Calkins and I had a series of adventures working both with the objects themselves and with their history. After I had completed primary conservation and provisional reconstruction, I had to fly with the pieces to London so that they could be properly conserved by the staff of the British Museum Conservation Laboratory. Since the capture of airplanes for political and pecuniary gain was a minor industry at the time, several tense hours were spent convincing very dubious airport security officials and later the FBI that though a sixth-century spearhead was technically a weapon, it could not, and indeed would not, be used in an attempt to "skyjack" the aircraft. Later in the same academic year, Professor Calkins had an equally entertaining time tracing down the origins of the pieces in written evidence both here at Cornell, and later in England. It seems fitting that this collection of essays should close with an account of rediscovery.

There are many acknowledgements, since many contributed to the making of this book. The American Council of Learned Societies and the American Philosophical Society provided funding for me to work on the art history and archaeology of the Anglo-Saxon period, and more particularly on the study and recording in photographs of the crosses at Ruthwell and Bewcastle. Funding for the study and conservation of the Frilford objects was generously provided by the Cornell Humanities Research Fund, and later by the National Endowment for the Humanities of Washington, D.C. (a federal agency). Mrs. Leslie Webster was a great help in placing the pieces in the British Museum laboratory for conservation; the English department at Cornell provided small grants for photographs and illustrations, and secretarial assistance for typing. The assistance of Mss. Sheila Bonde and Susan Kruse was invaluable, for their painstaking work in compiling and checking materials made the pleasant task of composing this volume less time consuming than it would otherwise have been. Mrs. Janet Godden did a thorough check of the manuscript for errors in form and content, and made many suggestions for the betterment of the book. I most gratefully acknowledge the generous aid of these persons, and claim remaining faults as my own.

Robert T. Farrell
Village of Lansing
June, 1976

FOOTNOTES

1. The papers of Professors Calkins and Ó Carragaín are both lacking in one of these respects; see below.

2. Bede, his Life, Times and Writings, ed. A. Hamilton Thompson (Oxford, 1935).

3. Francois Masai, Essai sur les origines de la miniature dite Irlandaise (Brussels, 1947).

4. "Northumbria and the Book of Kells", Anglo-Saxon England 1 (1972), 219-46.

5. For Bede's views on the Saracens and his change in stance towards them, see J. M. Wallace-Hadrill Bede's Europe, Jarrow Lecture (1962).

I. THE ART AND ARCHAEOLOGY OF BEDAN NORTHUMBRIA

David M. Wilson

Bede's manhood coincided with a time of peace and, although peace is
not necessarily conducive to cultural growth, Bede's lifetime was one of the
most intellectually stimulating and original periods in the history of Britain.
The artistic products of that period — the Book of Durrow, the Lindisfarne
Gospels, the Codex Amiatinus, the Ardagh chalice, the Ruthwell cross, the
church at Hexham and the monastery of Jarrow — are great and influential
intellectual achievements. In this relatively quiet and prosperous period
the kingdom of Northumbria received inspiration from the whole of the known
world and was the donor of considerable cultural riches to the rest of
Christianity.

It is my purpose in this contribution to survey the nature and influence
of Northumbria in the age of Bede, and to outline the changes in scholarly
perspective on that age which have come about in the forty-odd years, since
the commemoration of Bede's death in the volume Thompson edited in 1935.
As an archaeologist I must study the period primarily on the basis of its material culture, and confine myself to the analysis of stylistic and art historical
evidence. The field is broad, for discoveries in the past forty years have
added greatly to our primary evidence. The excavation of major monastic
centres such as Wearmouth and Jarrow, the Sutton Hoo ship and the St.
Ninian's Isle treasure are but a few spectacular high points in a much larger
context of informative but less exciting discoveries. It has become increa-
singly clear that Northumbria was a major centre with a tradition in art of
a very high standard. What is more, Northumbria was the meeting place for
productive interchange with the art of two Celtic traditions, the Irish, and the
Picts to the north. As I will show in the course of this paper, this Northumbrian art, itself the product of several cultures, had an influence on the
continent of Europe as well. These facets of Northumbrian culture form the
major burden of this chapter together with a summary of the few archaeological
finds of a secular nature in Northumbria which can be dated to within Bede's
lifetime.

Perhaps the most important British archaeological find of recent years
is the treasure discovered during excavations on a tiny peninsula, St Ninian's
Isle, off the mainland of Shetland. The treasure, which I consider to be a
secular hoard, was buried in the nave of a small church, probably in the face
of Viking attack, at the end of the eighth century or at the beginning of the
ninth. All the objects in the hoard are of silver and all but one are of Pictish
manufacture.[1]

The treasure was originally enclosed in a larch-wood box together with
the jaw-bone of a porpoise. It consisted of twenty-eight silver objects, the

majority of them gilt. Seven shallow bowls, usually with an omphalos in the base but in one case of semi-hemispherical shape, are decorated in pointillé technique. Five have geometric or interlace patterns, but two are embellished with elaborate animal ornament (Pl. I). With these bowls was the only piece in the hoard which might have been imported — a silver hanging-bowl (Pl. II) of a well-known type, presumably of Northumbrian origin and possibly made during Bede's lifetime. It is an elaborate object, ribbed externally with moulded features in the form of a displayed boar, and with mounts inside and outside, one of which is ornamented with trumpet spirals and the other with animal ornament. A silver spoon, with a modelled animal head at the junction of stem and bowl, and a strange hooked-like object, which might quite accurately be described as a winkle-picker, are charming but rather meaningless ornaments of a type probably worn on a woman's chatelaine. A sword pommel is intricately decorated with chip-carved animal ornament; with it are a pair of scabbard chapes (one possibly unused) carved with elaborate interlaced animals and having animal-headed terminals. One chape (Pl. III) bears an inscription which Kenneth Jackson has interpreted as Pictish: on one face it reads Resad filli Spuscio, on the other in nomine d[ei] s[ummi]. Jackson sees the two names (Resad and Spucio) as Pictish, and this identification helps to place these objects against their cultural background. Three silver-gilt objects, shaped like pepper-pots, are almost certainly elaborate buttons — their base plates are very similar in form and size to bone buttons from other sites in Orkney and Shetland. They are elaborately decorated with animal interlace and spiral ornaments.

There were thirteen penannular brooches in the hoard. The largest (Pl. IV) is nearly 11cm in diameter and (without its pin) weighs nearly 150 grammes. These brooches are truly penannular and have pins with a hook-like head. They are decorated with interlace ornament and most of them have lobed terminals and rising cusps at the terminals and at the ends of the panels on the hoop. Such features — the truly penannular form and the cusped terminals — distinguish them from their Irish contemporaries, which I have termed "pseudo-penannular." If brooches of this type are plotted on a distribution map it is clear that their distribution is largely confined to the Pictish area of Scotland and we may now begin to consider the possibility of defining a Pictish school of metal work of the eighth century. The Pictish identity of this type of brooch is further supported by the recent re-discovery by Mrs Curle of clay bi-valve moulds for such brooches from the Pictish levels at the Broch of Birsay in Orkney. [2]

The most striking parallels to the art of the St Ninian's Isle treasure are naturally with the art of the late Pictish stones. The animals with looped necks and spiralled hind-quarters encountered on the bowls and "pepper-pots" of the St Ninian's hoard are distinctive, and are clearly paralleled on a few pieces of sculpture such as the Aberlemno stone. [3] But the most interesting parallels outside Scotland are to be found in the art of the Anglo-Saxon manuscripts and particularly in the art of such objects as the Lindisfarne Gospels, for here are animals drawn in pointillé technique exactly analogous to those found in the St Ninian's Isle corpus. On fol. 95r of the Lindisfarne Gospels, for example, tucked between the legs of the monogram of the initial letter of the word Initium, is an animal (Fig. I,1) in all respects similar to that on one of the St Ninian's bowls. The Gospels provide many such

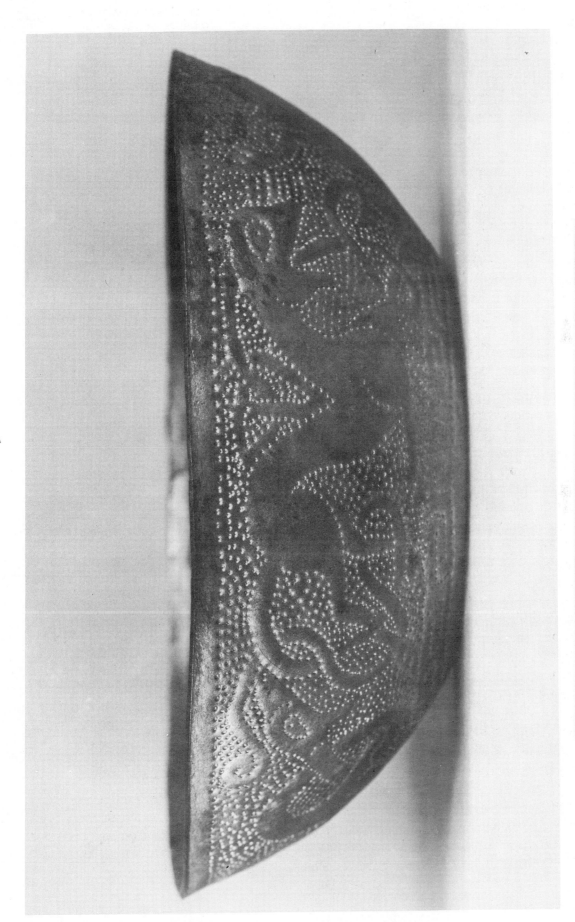

Plate I   Animal ornamented bowl from the St Ninian's Isle treasure. Copyright British Museum.

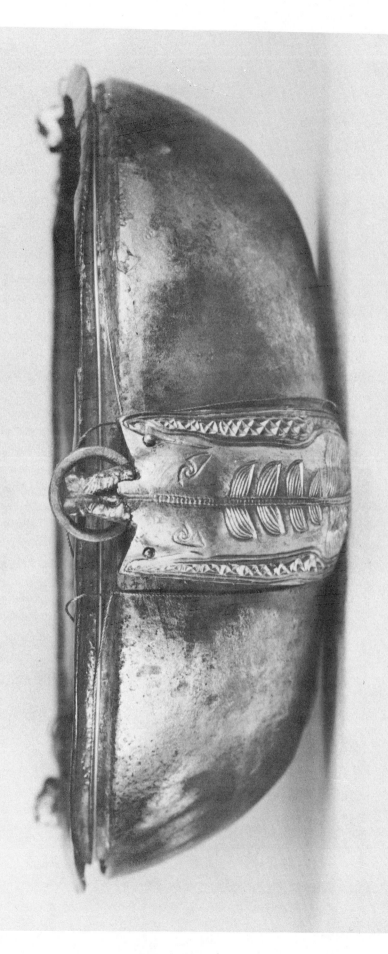

Plate II   Hanging bowl from the St Ninian's Isle treasure.
Copyright British Museum.

Plate III   Inscribed chape from the St Ninian's Isle treasure.

Plate IV   The largest penannular brooch from the St Ninian's Isle treasure.
Copyright British Museum.

Fig. 1   Animals from the St Ninian's hanging bowl no. 2 compared with
(bottom) animal from the Lindisfarne Gospels. Copyright E. Wilson.

parallels but certain features carry the art into the eighth century, to years beyond 698 when the Lindisfarne Gospels were written and decorated. Parallels with the Rome Gospels (Vatican, Barberini lat. 520) and the Book of Cerne in the University Library, Cambridge, are close and significant, and would suggest a date for these objects in the latish eighth century.[4]

Other parallels occur with manuscript art and particularly with the Book of Kells. The extraordinary trick of separating the head and hindquarters of an animal by a neck or body composed of a series of loops, seen on the pommel and the "buttons," occurs clearly in the art of the Book of Kells.[5] This is the most significant of the parallels with this great manuscript, but others do occur.

Parallels with Irish art are rare in the St Ninian's Isle corpus, but attention should be drawn to the feature, seen on the sword pommel, for example, where the hind legs of the animal are reversed in their spiral contortion. This detail is encountered on the Tara brooch[6] — an almost certainly Irish object of the eighth century — but, to my knowledge, it occurs in no other place in the corpus of Irish metalwork or manuscripts — although relatively common in Scotland and Northumbria.[7]

The St Ninian's Isle hoard can be seen, therefore, as a depository of a highly individual art, clearly native to the kingdom in which it was found but drawing its inspiration from external traditions elsewhere in the British Isles. That Pictish art was so influenced has been clear for a long time. Past studies of stone sculpture have drawn attention to the close correspondence between Pictish and Northumbrian styles.[8] The Hilton of Cadboll stone (pl. V), for example, demonstrates in its borders an undeniable relationship with the inhabited vine-scroll of Northumbrian sculpture, seen in classical form, for example, on the Ruthwell cross (pl. VI).

A number of significant breakthroughs have been made in the course of the last twenty years in the field of Pictish-Northumbrian archaeology and style history, stimulated first by the late F. T. Wainwright's summer school entitled "The Problem of the Picts," the lectures to which were published in 1955.[9] Articles and books (in which Isabel Henderson,[10] Robert Stevenson,[11] Charles Thomas,[12] Julian Brown,[13] Kathleen Hughes[14] and myself[15] have been the main protagonists) have provided a basis for a reappraisal of stylistic problems. Charles Thomas's ingenious study of Pictish sculpture has not stood up to critical examination of the chronological and art-historical basis which he used, but there does now seem to be some basic understanding of the relationship between Pictland and Northumbria and a closer definition of the material culture and style-historical influences which made up this fascinating and almost forgotten culture.

Bede was well aware of the Picts — the neighbours of the Northumbrians — and every study of the Pictish problem in the eighth century has started from the introduction to his long account of Ceolfrith's letter to Nechtan, the king of the Picts.

> Nechtan, king of the Picts, who live in the northern parts of Britain, having been convinced by assidious study of ecclesiastical writings, renounced the error which he and his race had until then

Plate V   Sculptured stone from Hilton of Cadboll, Easter Ross, Scotland.
Copyright National Museum of Antiquities.

Plate VI   Ruthwell cross, Dumfriesshire: Inhabited vine-scroll.

held about the observance of Easter, and led all his people to celebrate with him the catholic time of keeping the Lord's resurrection
... sought help from the English ... So he sent messengers to the
venerable Ceolfrith, abbot of the monastery of the apostles St Peter
and St Paul [at Monkwearmouth and Jarrow] ... The king asked the
abbot to send him information by letter to enable him to confute...
those...who presumed to celebrate Easter at the wrong time; also
[information] about the shape and method of tonsure by which it was
fitting that clerics should be distinguished...He also asked for
builders to be sent to build a church of stone in their country after
Roman fashion ... Abbot Ceolfrith complied with his pious wishes
and requests, sending the builders he asked for and also a letter.[16]

Thus, at the beginning of the eighth century there was a direct ecclesiastical contact and, in view of the builders sent by Ceolfrith, direct cultural
contact between Northumbrians and Picts.

This contact affords a striking parallel to that established with Gaul by
Benedict Biscop at the time of the foundation of the joint monastery of Monk-
waremouth and Jarrow a few years earlier. The actual results of Benedict's
request for masons and other craftsmen from Gaul are easy to over-estimate
in cultural terms; but his appeal is indicative of a tendency, apparent in
seventh and eighth century England, to turn to the Continent for cultural inspiration. For welded into the fabric of English culture of this period is much
of the late classical tradition, most clearly seen in manuscript art, architecture, texts and religious observances. Similarly, Nechtan's appeal to
Ceolfrith may not have been (and almost certainly was not) the first, nor even
the most important, catalyst which introduced Northumbrian influences into
the Pictish north; but it is certainly indicative of the major sources of
Pictish inspiration, for when traces of foreign culture appear in Pictland they
seem to be impregnated with the essence of Northumbrian/Mercian influence.
The great stone slabs and the minute figures carved by jewellers show this
influence clearly. In architecture the influences are less clear. Douglas
Simpson's identification of the lower stage of the tower of Restenneth Priory
in Angus as "in all probability the remains of the porticus of the church built
more Romanorum, by masons from Wearmouth at the order of King Nectan
MacDerile, about the year 710,"[17] may be too definite, but there are undoubted Northumbrian elements in this building which certainly relate it to
influences from England.

These influences are central to the identification of one of the most important British manuscripts of the post-Bedan period — the Book of Kells.
Many have felt unhappy about placing this manuscript in an Irish scriptorium,
but Julian Brown has grasped the Irish nettle and has published a most significant paper which argues with clarity towards a conclusion so obvious that
one is left aghast at its sense. Brown's concluding paragraph reads:

The Book of Kells is the most complex and the greatest work of
Hiberno-Saxon art. If its date is between the 746 of the Leningrad
Bede and the 822 of the Macregol Gospels, then Northumbria, Pict-
land, Iona and Ireland are all possible homes for it. It is for

archaeology to settle the question. Palaeography can do little
more than tell her sister where and when to start looking: at
Lindisfarne, in the middle years of the eighth century. We can
certainly apply to Kells Mrs Henderson's words about Pictish
sculpture: 'it was ... the creation of artists freely participating
in the evolution of [the Hiberno-Saxon] style and contributing to it
some of its most daring and magnificent monuments.' My own archaeological answer to the question of origin is this: 'a great
insular centre ... subject to Northumbrian influence ... in eastern
Scotland'. Because of the vigour and freshness of the Lindisfarne
elements that they include, I cannot easily believe that either
Kells or the related antiquities from the Pictish area were made
after the end of the eighth century. If Kells were of the ninth
century, I should wonder how the style and technique of Eadfrith's
scriptorium at Lindisfarne could have been so brilliantly revived
after an interval of a century.[18]

"A great insular centre ... subject to Northumbrian influence ... in
eastern Scotland." It is becoming clearer, the more we study the art of the
British Isles in the pre-Viking Age, that the old adage that all things beautiful
come from Ireland is no longer true. This is not to deny the artistic capabi-
lity of the Irish craftsmen; one only has to look at the Tara brooch and the
Ardagh chalice to realise that there was art in Ireland. On the other hand
looking at the panorama of insular art from Sutton Hoo onwards, the great
achievements of Durrow, Lindisfarne, and Kells, the Ormside bowl, the
Ruthwell cross, and now the St Ninian's Isle treasure, it is clear that there
are many elements completely outside the experience of Ireland, and of the
Irish artist. It is difficult to find a high quality Irish manuscript before the
Macregol Gospels.[19] The Cathach,[20] the Munich sacramentary,[21] the
Bangor antiphonary,[22] the Schaffhausen Adamanan[23] and the Cadmug Gospels[24]
provide little that can restore our faith in the ability of the Irish scribe. The
Fahan Mura cross, if it is correctly dated (which I doubt),[26] is the only
major piece of Irish sculpture from the period before 800. If the south cross
at Ahenny,[27] and the Irish high crosses which are allied to it, can perhaps
be forced within the eighth century, they may (in view of the arguments of
Robert Stevenson) be derived from the area which produced the Book of Kells
and reached Ireland by way of Iona and the west of Scotland.[28]

It is in metalwork that Irish craftsmanship is best seen, but most of the
motifs (with the exception of the trumpet-spiral — a universal pattern buried
in British imagination since the early Roman Iron age) have their origin outside Ireland. The animal ornament, skilfully contorted by the Irish craftsman, is derived without question from the German menagerie, presumably
by way of the Anglo-Saxons. The use of enamel reached new heights in the
hands of the Irish masters, but archaeological work since the war has produced ample evidence for the presence of workshops capable of producing
enamel in the east of Britain.[29] The corpus of metalwork in late seventh-
and eighth-century Ireland is qualitatively impressive but in mass small —
the Ardagh chalice,[30] the Tara brooch,[31] the Moylough belt shrine,[32] the
Kilmainham brooch,[33] a handful of buckles and brooches. But the corpus

claimed for Ireland has been reduced. Work, as yet unpublished, by James Graham-Campbell[34] has demonstrated beyond peradventure that the Dalriada brooch and the Roscrea brooch, once thought to belong to this period, are in reality of ninth-century date. The Copenhagen shrine[35] could easily be as Scottish as the very similar Monymusk reliquary,[36] and who is to say where the Saint-Germain objects[37] derive from? The reaction against Françoise Henry has in the last few years been almost unfair in its vigour. In some cases some of the protagonists may overstep the mark in taking material from Ireland and establishing it in eastern Britain, but I think that Brown's work on the Book of Kells, Stevenson's study of the Iona crosses and the recent work on the St Ninian's Isle brooches, indicate that this has been done on a dispassionate basis. The arguments are convincing and have not been seriously criticised, as yet, by our Irish colleagues.

In the centre of this artistic maelstrom was Northumbria. It produced at this period great works of art of which the Lindisfarne Gospels and the Codex Amiatinus, produced during Bede's lifetime, are the undoubted master-pieces.[38] The Book of Durrow almost certainly belongs to this group, as do the Echternach Gospels and the Durham Gospels (A.II 17).[39] The position is that largely reached by Masai in 1944 in his Essai sur les origines de la miniature dites irlandaise. Now, however, we can base our arguments on detailed palaeographical comparisons impossible to a Belgian during wartime. The major insular manuscripts of the late seventh and early eighth century are Northumbrian, not Irish; the detailed work of Lowe and Brown has made it possible to see that such a position is quite tenable. Together with Verey[40] they have shown that the Durham, Echternach and Lindisfarne Gospels were produced in the Lindisfarne scriptorium between say 690 and 710. Manuscripts produced at Wearmouth/Jarrow include the Codex Amiatinius, the Middleton Leaves in the British Library,[41] the Leningrad Bede[42] and probably the British Library Bede (Cotton Tiberius A. IV).[43]

The Book of Kells has links with both Wearmouth/Jarrow and Lindisfarne and, according to Brown, must date to the middle of the eighth century; but it looks almost as though it must be considered as Pictish. Like the church of Restenneth this manuscript may not be the direct product of the contact established by Nechtan, but it is certainly well within the atmosphere which allied the cultural areas of Pictland and Northumbria. The same contact is emphasized by the St Ninian's Isle treasure and the late group of Pictish stones with their eclectic art.[44] Northumbria was a major donor to the art of the Pictish kingdom in the eighth century. Either Northumbria or Pictland, or both, were major donors to the art of Ireland. Is Iona with its carved crosses a step towards Ireland?

The importance of Iona as a stage in the transmission of ideas and of art is hard to estimate. Iona, according to its own account, was a towering centre of intellectual activity. So was Jarrow. But Lindisfarne, not a par-ticularly strong intellectual centre, was the Northumbrian centre which produced painting of the highest standard, and this we know only by the ac-cident of a single colophon. Could not some great Pictish centre have been as artistically influential as Lindisfarne, which apparently produced no great scholar?

Northumbria had influence outside Ireland and Pictland. The continental missionaries of the eighth century were frequently turning to Northumbria for aid. Boniface continually asked for English books.[45] He even asked Egbert of York for copies of the work of Bede himself, and among the books he managed to obtain was one manuscript of Capuan origin, which was bound (presumably in Northumbria) in the best quality English red leather, and mounted with silver ornaments executed in a rather run-of-the-mill English style.[46]

Wilhelm Levison defined the eighth century as one of the two periods in history in which "England ... exercised a broad, deep and lasting influence upon continental ways of thought and life."[47] The names of Wilfrid, Boniface, Willibrord, Alcuin, Lullus and so on are familiar to all medievalists, as familiar as the great monuments of the Franco-Saxon school of manuscripts. Less familiar, perhaps, is the important role that English metalworkers played in the art of the Continent. This does no more in many ways than underline the known facts, but since Günther Haseloff's important monograph, Der Tassilokelch, appeared in 1951[48] a great deal of new information has come to light which clearly demonstrates the important position held by the Anglo-Saxon artist in Europe in the Bedan period.

It is known, from the Liber Pontificalis, that members of the Schola Saxonum in Rome made altar plate for the basilica of St Peter's in this period and, while the products of this particular school cannot be recognized, the massive early ninth-century ring from the river at Bologna[49] and English objects of similar date from Pavia[50] demonstrate the penetration of Italy by objects made in English workshops. Further, although the taste of the Mediterranean people was very different from that of the Anglo-Saxons at this period, enough common Germanic heritage survived to admit such foreign taste to the centre of the Christian world. The metal mounts on the Capuan Diatesseron of the Gospels which undoubtedly belonged to St Boniface have been referred to above. These are miserable little mounts, but the impressed silver plates introduce us, for example, to the rather more splendid ornament of the same technique on the Ormside bowl.[51] The pattern on this bowl is the familiar inhabited vine-scroll, rather barbarized in respect of its animals, but well within the classical tradition imported into Northumbria by Benedict Biscop and his successors.

The same technique and pattern can be seen on the Rupertus cross, from Bischofshofen near Salzburg in Austria.[52] This cross (designed presumably at the order of, or in memory of, Bishop Rupert of Salzburg at the beginning of the eighth century, to hang in his private chapel, perhaps even over his tomb) is 158cm high. It is ornamented with a vine-scroll which has become degenerate (pl. VII), the animals merging with the plants to produce a single running motif, a feature which occurs quite frequently in eighth-century insular metalwork.[53] The glass inlays of the cross again reflect, on a very coarse scale, similar insular inlays in Britain.[54] There can be little doubt that this object was made by an English artist, presumably working in this area of the Continent, an area which has also produced that remarkable English-influenced object, the Tassilo chalice.

Plate VII   Arm of Bischofshofen, Austria, Cross.
            Copyright Bayerisches Nationalmuseum, Munich.

The Tassilo chalice was made to the order of Duke Tassilo for the monastery of Kremsmünster.[55] The abbey was founded in 777 and Tassilo was deposed by Charlemagne in 788, giving a terminus post quem and a terminus ante quem for its production. Haseloff, in his seminal study of this work, first defined the English inspiration of the animal ornament while showing the eclectic nature of the craftsman's pattern book. This style was widespread in Lotharingia in the late eighth century and objects ornamented in this fashion are found as far apart as northern Norway, southern Yugoslavia and Ireland.[56] The most splendid — but also the latest — example of the school is the famous cover of Pierpont Morgan MS 1, a gospel book connected with the monastery of Lindau by the Bodensee, but which has no history earlier than the beginning of the last century.[57]

The Tassilo chalice takes us towards the end of the eighth century, but the school which it represents was obviously a powerful one on the Continent throughout that century (indeed the same traditions survive into the tenth century). In the seventh century the quality of English metalwork was higher than that of any surviving metalwork in Christian Europe; the story which started with Sutton Hoo and reached its peak in other parts of the British Isles in the Ardagh chalice and the St Ninian's Isle treasure also influenced the Continent. The Tassilo chalice, the Bischofshofen cross and possibly the Enger reliquary,[58] stand in the same relation to the Ormside bowl and the Witham pins as does the manuscript art of the Franco-Saxon school of the end of the eighth century to the Lindisfarne Gospels and the Book of Kells. All reflect the enormous influence of the insular, and more especially the English, missions to the heathen nations of Frisia and Germany.

Pendant to this we find further English influences on the Continent in another art form — sculpture. Work in bone and ivory is particularly significant in this context. The two ivory plaques, 30cm high, from the church of St Martin at Genoels-Elderen (now in Brussels)[59] demonstrate how the humanist figural tradition of the Mediterranean is fused with the bold flight from naturalism in human portrayal which is so typical of the insular art of the eighth century, most strikingly obvious in the evangelist portraits of the Lindisfarne Gospels. The obvious insular influences (including specifically the inscription) caused no less a scholar than Bernthard Bischof, in a lecture in London, to postulate a Northumbrian origin for this piece. Peter Lasko[60] has a hint of qualitative criticism for these two panels in pointing out that they were produced away from the central court of Charlemagne. This may be due to the possibility that they belong to a period earlier than the establishment of the emperor's court school under the influence of a powerful and highly original English tradition. This is not a pale reflection of the court school's work but a Germanic attempt to come to terms with classical naturalism. Leaving emotive judgments aside, it is clear that English bone and ivory sculpture of a high standard existed at this time, although relics of it are very few and far between. The splendid English casket which made its way to the German monastery of Gandersheim and is now in the Herzog Anton Ulrich Museum in Brunswick, reflects better perhaps than the Franks Casket[62] the true quality of craftsmanship in this medium in eighth-century England.

England was a centre for stone sculpture in this period, as the hundreds of crosses, friezes and carved stone still extant clearly show. One might therefore expect to find English-influenced sculpture on the Continent. The nearest we get to this, however, is the fragment of a marble choir screen from the monastery of St Johann, Müstair, Switzerland.[63] Here the influence of the Anglo-Carolingian school of ornament which produced the Tassilo chalice is plain. The reason for the lack of sculptural material must lie in the influence of Italian sculpture in the south and the possibility that wood which perishes, was one of the main media for three-dimensional art north of the Alps.

In sum, England — and particularly Northumbria — was a major donor in the art of western and northern Europe in the period of Bede's lifetime. The art followed the missionaries and the teachers.

The material mentioned in this short essay and the ideas produced here are largely the product of archaeological activity either in the field or in the study in the last twenty-five years. As a result the influences of England outside its own boundaries have become clearer. Contacts with Pictland, Ireland and the Continent are seen more clearly and, by understanding these contacts, we are nearer to an understanding of the very complicated relations of these different areas with each other; relations in which Northumbria obviously played a leading part. The image of the learned scholar Bede should not, however, blind us to the achievement of the south of England — and particularly of Mercia and Canterbury. Nor should we forget that there were places in Northumbria other than Lindisfarne, Jarrow and Monkwear-mouth which were also centres of learning: Alcuin was a product of York.

But archaeology has a responsibility to clothe the splendid remains of culture and art in more mundane apparel. The archaeologist must provide evidence of the daily life of the people who made these splendid objects: in this we have not yet been enormously successful. Rosemary Cramp's excava-tions at Monkwearmouth and Jarrow clearly demonstrate the religious side of this splendid period, and her pupils and assistants have also been excava-ting elsewhere in Bedan Northumbria on secular sites, as at Hartlepool in county Durham, immediately outside St Hilda's monastery. Sites like this, producing secular evidence, remind us that Bede did not tell the whole story of Northumbria.

One series of excavations is however of great importance in relation to the problems discussed here. Much of the material is unpublished, but the excavations by Brian Hope-Taylor at the royal sites of Yeavering and Bam-brough, and at Old Dunbar, are central to the problem of the external re-lationships of Northumbria both before and during the Bedan period.

We know a little more about Yeavering than we do about the other sites. Bede pays passing attention to the site in a well-known passage referring to the year 627:

> So great is said to have been the fervour of the faith of the North-
> umbrians and their longing for ... salvation, that once when
> Paulinus came to the king and queen in their royal palace [villam
> regiam] at Yeavering [ad Gefrin], he spent thirty-six days there

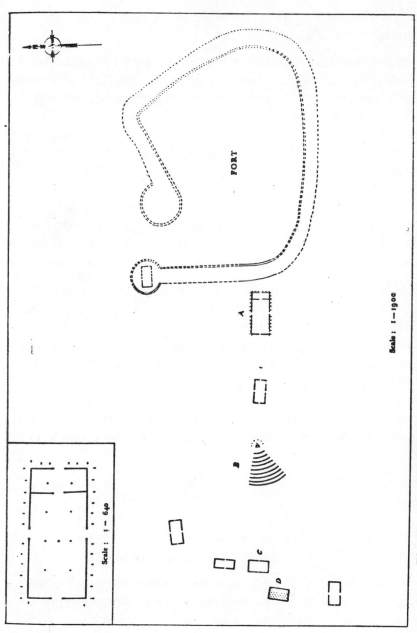

FORT

Scale: 1—1900

Scale: 1 — 640

Fig. 2 Diagrammatic plan of buildings existing in the time of King Edwin
(616-32) at Yeavering, Northumberland. A. Hall; B. Timber
'Amphitheatre'; C. Building alleged by the excavator to be a pagan
temple converted to Christian use; D. Building with a sunken floor.
The inset shows the timber hall (A) to a larger scale. (After Hope-
Taylor.) Copyright of Her Majesty's Stationery Office

occupied in the task of catechizing and baptizing ... This palace
was left deserted in the time of the kings who followed Edwin, and
another was built instead in a place called Maelmin.[64]

The site of Yeavering (fig. 2) was identified from the air by J. K. St Joseph
in 1949 and was excavated between 1953 and 1957.[65] One of the earliest features is probably the large timber-palisaded fort which may have been used
as a refuge in times of trouble; but it is the other structures on the site
which are remarkable. A series of timber halls span a period of half a
century or more at the beginning of the seventh century. The published plan
postulates the site during the reign of Edwin, the period when Paulinus
preached there. The large building (A) is presumed to be the royal hall. It
was about 27m long and its walls were built of massive upright timbers set
in a foundation-trench. Its roof was supported with the aid of external but-
tresses and its interior was aisled and had a separate room at one end. The
other buildings served ancillary purposes, perhaps as lesser halls, perhaps
as storage places. Building C may have been, according to the excavator,
a temple converted into a church, but the arguments in favour of this interpretation have not yet been published and must for the moment be treated with
extreme scepticism. An odd feature is the extraordinary structure (B), which
consists of a bank of tiered seats, clearly an assembly place. Romantics
trained to the Protestant tradition may imagine Paulinus preaching there —
although it might equally well be the equivalent of a parliament building or
Madison Square Garden — it would certainly have been very draughty for
the spectators! A recently published reconstruction of the site gives some
impression of its appearance.[66]

Excavations at Thirlings and at the royal site of Bambrough will also be
extremely important when information about them is released. We do, however, know a little more about one other site also dug by Hope-Taylor, and
this is of great interest in any discussion of this period. At Doon Hill,
Dunbar, just south of the Firth of Forth (only 25 miles from Edinburgh),[67]
Hope-Taylor excavated a defended seventh-century hall which was in many
ways similar to those found at Yeavering. The hall had two periods, the
first hall having been destroyed by fire. The units of measurement used in
the layout of the first hall were exactly the same as those used at the royal
site. It was about 23m long, a little smaller than the Yeavering halls. The
building technique is rather different from that found at Yeavering and the
gable walls are V-shaped in plan. Hope-Taylor postulates a British building
tradition behind this hall — it is certainly without parallel in the Anglo-Saxon
or Germanic world — and suggests that some of the British traditions influenced the Northumbrian kings when they built Yeavering. Such a thesis
would underline the conclusion which many scholars have put forward, that
Bernicia was largely a British kingdom with an imposed Anglian ruling element. We may see, as has Leslie Alcock, support for this idea in the extreme paucity of Anglian grave-goods of the pagan Anglo-Saxon in Bernicia.[68]
By the time of Bede, however, this part of the country must have been largely
Anglo-Saxon as regards language and also as regards culture. The normal
contacts were southwards with Canterbury and Gaul, but there can be little
doubt that the northern Northumbrians had contact northwards (contact which
is enshrined in the Pictish wars and in the mission of Nechtan) and westwards
to Iona and Ireland.

NOTES

1. A. Small, C. Thomas and D. M. Wilson, St Ninian's Isle and its Treasure, (Oxford, 1973).

2. I am grateful to Mrs Curle for allowing me to see this material before publication.

3. Small, Thomas and Wilson, St Ninian's Isle, pl. lv.

4. Ibid., pp.125ff.

5. Ibid., pp.137ff.

6. F. Henry, Irish Art in the Early Christian period (London, 1965), pl. 42.

7. Small, Thomas and Wilson, St Ninian's Isle, pp.126ff.

8. I. Henderson, The Picts (London, 1967), p.115ff.

9. F. T. Wainwright, The Problem of the Picts (Edinburgh, 1955).

10. Henderson, The Picts.

11. R. B. K. Stevenson, "Pictish art," Wainwright, Problem of the Picts, pp.97-128, and idem, "Sculpture in Scotland in the 6th-9th Centuries A.D.," in Kolloquium über spätantike und frühmittelalterliche Skulptur, (ed. V. Milojcić), (Mainz, 1971), pp.65-74.

12. A. C. Thomas, "The animal art of the Scottish Iron Age and its origins," The Archaeological Journal, 118 (1961), 14-64.

13. T. J. Brown, "Northumbria and the Book of Kells," Anglo-Saxon England il (1972), 219-46.

14. K. Hughes, Early Christianity in Pictland (Jarrow Lecture, 1970).

15. In Small, Thomas and Wilson, St Ninian's Isle.

16. Trans. B. Colgrave and R. A. B. Mynors, Bede's Ecclesiastical History of the English People (Oxford, 1969), pp.533ff.

17. W. D. Simpson, "The early Romanesque tower at Restenneth Priory" The Antiquaries Journal 43 (1963), 283.

18. Brown, "Northumbria and the Book of Kells," p.243.

19. Henry, Irish Art, pls. 110 and N.

20. Ibid., pls. 9 and 12.

21. Codices Latini Antiquiores, ed. E. A. Lowe, 12 pts (Oxford, 1934-71), IX, no. 1298.

22. F. E. Warren, The Antiphonary of Bangor (London, 1893-5).

23. Henry, Irish Art, pl. vii.

24. CLA VIII, no. 1198.

25. Henry, Irish Art, pl. 54.

26. R. B. K. Stevenson, "The chronology and relationship of some Irish and Scottish crosses," Journal of the Royal Society of Antiquaries of Ireland, 86 (1956), 94.

27. Henry, Irish Art, pls. 76-7.

28. Stevenson, "Chronology."

29. Small, Thomas and Wilson, St Ninian's Isle, pp.108f.

30. Henry, Irish Art, pls 33, 39, C and D.

31. Ibid., pls. 28, 38, and 40-42.

32. Ibid., pls. 34-5.

33. A. Mahr, Christian Art in Ancient Ireland (Dublin, 1932), pl. 22, 2.

34. J. Graham-Campbell, in Ulster Journal of Archaeology, forthcoming.

35. Mahr, Christian Art, pl. 16.

36. Small, Thomas and Wilson, St Ninian's Isle, fig. 41.

37. Henry, Irish Art, pl. 66.

38. R. L. S. Bruce-Mitford, "The art of the Codex Amiatinus," Journal of the British Archaeological Association 3rd ser. 32 (1969), 1-25.

39. Brown, "Northumbria and the Book of Kells," passim.

40. Ibid., pp.243-5.

41. E. A. Lowe, English Uncial (Oxford, 1960), p.19, pl. x.

42. E. A. Lowe, "A key to Bede's scriptorium" Scriptorium 12 (1958), 182-90.

43. Ibid., p.189 and pl. 21 a-b.

44. Small, Thomas and Wilson, St Ninian's Isle.

45. These requests are conveniently listed by G. W. Greenaway (Saint Boniface (London 1955), pp.64f.).

46. D. M. Wilson, "An Anglo-Saxon bookbinding at Fulda (Codex Bonifatianus I), Antiquaries Journal 41 (1961), 199-217.

47. W. Levison, England and the Continent in the eighth century (Oxford, 1946), p.1.

48. Munich, 1951.

49. A. Peroni, Oreficiere e metalli lavorati tardoantichi e altomedievale del territorio di Pavia (Spoleto, 1967), fig. 37.

50. Ibid., pl. iii, 24.

51. T. D. Kendrick, Anglo-Saxon Art to A.D. 900 (London, 1938), pl. lx.

52. Karl der Grosse, Werk und Wirkung (Aachen, 1965), fig. 107.

53. E.g. D. M. Wilson, Anglo-Saxon Ornamental Metalwork, 700-1100, in the British Museum (London, 1964), pl. xviii.

54. Henry, Irish Art, pl. D.

55. G. Haseloff, Der Tassilokelch.

56. Listed in D. M. Wilson, "The Fejø cup" Acta Archaeologica 31 (1960) 172f.

57. M. Harrsen, Central European Manuscripts in the Pierpont Morgan Library (New York, 1958), pp.6ff.

58. V. H. Elbern, "Ein frankisches Reliquiarfragment in Oviedo, die Engerer Burse in Berlin und ihr Umkreis", Madrider Mitteilungen 2 (1961), 187ff.

59. P. Lasko, Ars Sacra 800-1200 (Harmondsworth, 1972), pl. 11.

60. Ibid., p.13.

61. C. Scherer, Die braunschweiger Elfenbeinsammlung (Leipzig, 1931), pl. I.

62. British Museum Guide to Anglo-Saxon and Foreign Teutonic Antiquities (London, 1923), pl. viii.

63. J. Werner, "Frühkarolingische Silberohrringe von Rastede," Germania 37 (1959), pl. 26.

64. Trans. Colgrave and Mynors, Bede's Ecclesiastical History, p. 189.

65. The best short account of these excavations occurs in D. M. Wilson and J. G. Hurst, "Medieval Britain in 1956," Medieval Archaeology, 1 (1957), 149f. The full report of the excavations is promised for 1975.

66. T. H. Rowland, Anglo-Saxon Northumbria (Newcastle upon Tyne), p. 40f.

67. D. M. Wilson and D. G. Hurst, "Medieval Britain in 1965", Medieval Archaeology 10 (1966), 175f.

68. L. Alcock, Arthur's Britain (Pelican edition) (Harmondsworth, 1973), p.310.

II. SOME IMPLICATIONS OF BEDE'S LATIN STYLE

Winthrop Wetherbee

There is general agreement about the special qualities of Bede's Latin:
it is pure, simple and efficient, and commentators have differed chiefly in
the aspects of Bede's larger achievement to which they have chosen to relate
these qualities. His style may be viewed as the mirror of that process of
selection and distillation in which so much of his work as educator and trans-
mittor of the classical heritage consisted; it can be seen to mark the decisive
emergence of a new Christian Latin, wholly emancipated from the constraints
of late-classical and "Hisperic" rhetoric and with its own Christian equiva-
lents for the more strictly classical norms of purity and decorum; and it is
hard to avoid seeing in Bede's achievement of gravitas through the pursuit of
simplicity the triumph of a saintly personality, a singular blend of humane
sensitivity and humilitas.

The primary purpose of this paper is to point out some implications of
Bede's accomplishment as a writer of Latin and a preceptor of Latin style.
I would like to suggest that in addition to the extraordinary efficiency of Bede's
Latin in transmitting and exemplifying the essentials of literacy, its simplicity and purity and its freedom from stylistic self-consciousness constitute
in themselves a positive contribution to the development of a medieval
Christian humanism. The very acuteness with which Bede recognised the
educational needs of his place and time and his clearsighted, unembarrassed
indifference to superficial graces of style were qualities which made it possible for him to adopt a relaxed and familiar attitude toward classical and
pagan culture and aesthetic values without that traditional fear of contamina-
tion of which the best known exemplum is St. Jerome's Ciceronian dream.
Bede was unusually sensitive to these values: we need only think of his account of the singing of Cædmon and ask ourselves how many early medieval
educators would have been so ready to concede to vernacular poetry on
Christian themes a decor and dignitas uncapturable in Latin.[1] But we never
question his perspective, or the sureness of touch with which he handles such
materials: Christianus est, non Vergilianus .

This sureness of touch is everywhere in Bede's work, on the level of
literary intention and in the clear conceptions of his educational program.
It appears in the care with which he culled from a wide range of grammarians,
and made accessible to people for whom Latin was necessarily a textbook
subject, the principles of a serviceable Latinity, including the remarkably
classical syntax of his own prose.[2] It informs his consistent concern to
stress the pedagogically effective at the expense of received standards of
fine writing. This is most obvious in his freedom from the Hisperic manner-
isms which encrust the prose of Aldhelm and survive in an occasional purple

patch in Boniface;[3] but it is present also in his measured response to stylistic traits which he clearly appreciated. He could admire the effect of homoioteleuton in the Preacher and in earlier Christian Latin poetry, yet gently deplores its excesses in the works of his beloved Gregory and avoids it in his own.[4] His De arte metrica is among other things a quite convincing demonstration of the virtues of Prudentius, Sedulius and the Christian Latin poets, and his discussion of versification in particular shows unusual discrimination: he is at pains to point out the various capacities of the hexameter and its adaptibility to the development of sustained effects over several lines.[5] He is, moreover, capable of rising to this standard in his own verse, as in the lines which climax his account of the spread of the Christian revelation in the Proem to his metrical life of Cuthbert:[6]

> Nec iam orbis contenta sinu trans aequora lampas
> Spargitur effulgens, huiusque Britannia consors
> Temporibus genuit fulgur venerabile nostris,
> Aurea qua Cuthbertus agens per sidera vitam
> Scandere celsa suis docuit iam passibus Anglos.

But for the most part Bede's verse adheres to the simpler patterns of school-verse, with its regular caesurae and its tendency to make each line or half-line a syntactic unit.[7] Such verse was more readily imitated and easier to commit to memory, values which for Bede the teacher took priority over heroic style.[8] In limiting and simplifying the range of poetic effects Bede helped to provide a starting point, an attainable standard from which medieval Latin poetry could develop effects of its own. The De arte metrica itself contributes to this purpose, asserting in a matter-of-fact way the Christian poet's prerogative of suspending the strict laws of quantity in the interests of the Spirit,[9] and the treatise has been seen as a significant harbinger of the shift from quantitative toward accentual verse.[10]

All of these effects of Bede's teaching and writing must of course be seen as subordinate to the single great task of synthesizing and transmitting that portion of classical learning essential to the preservation and dissemination of Christian knowledge. The importance of this work and Bede's success in accomplishing it have led historians quite naturally to dwell on his efficiency, his ability, in R. B. Palmer's words, "to select, adapt, digest, and rework his sources — his excellence in short as a textbook writer."[11] But there are other significant features of his writing as such, closely related to his pedagogical activity and in certain respects as far-reaching in implication, which this understandable emphasis has tended to obscure. I will try to characterize some of these as they appear in the Historia Ecclesiastica and the metrical life of Cuthbert.

It would be impossible to characterize in any uniform way the "style" even of those portions of the Historia which represent most simply Bede's own contribution, for they tend to the same diversity as the older material, the hagiographical and historical writings, ecclesiastical records and correspondence, incorporated into the work. There are, however, certain moments, some of them among the most remarkable in the Historia, when Bede brings us dramatically so close to a particular scene that his characteristic hagiographer's perspective on the relations of persons and events

does not wholly govern our sense of what is taking place. At such moments
the lucidity and economy of his style, together with the sense of decorum and
the responsiveness to different cultural and aesthetic values cited earlier in
connection with his textbooks, are made to do in a subtler way what is done
on a larger scale in the Historia by the shifts of focus between chronicle,
hagiography, theological dispute and the records of church councils. We are
shown, from an imaginary perspective which complements the religious perspective provided by Bede's sources and by his own larger purpose in the
Historia, how men of a particular place and time responded to the religious
influence at work in their national life. The account of the council at which
Edwin and his retainers accept Christianity is probably the best-known passage of this sort, centered as it is around the haunting image of the sparrow
fleeing de hieme in hiemem through the Northumbrian banquet-hall;[12] an
equally effective example for our purposes is the episode precipitated by
Bishop Aidan's giving away of a fine horse bestowed upon him by King Oswine,
a passage which I would like to consider in detail.[13]

> Donauerat [rex] equum optimum antistiti Aidano, in quo ille,
> quamuis ambulare solitus, vel amnium fluenta transire, uel si
> alia quaelibet necessitas insisteret, uiam peragere posset. Cui
> cum paruo interiecto tempore pauper quidam occurreret elimosy-
> nam petens, desiliens ille praecepit equum, ita ut erat stratus
> regaliter, pauperi dari; erat enim multum misericors, et cultor
> pauperum, ac uelut pater miserorum. Hoc cum regi esset rela-
> tum, dicebat episcopo, cum forte ingressuri essent ad prandium:
> 'Quid uoluisti, domine antistes, equum regium, quem te conueniebat
> proprium habere, pauperi dare? Numquid non habuimus equos
> uiliores plurimos, uel alias species, quae ad pauperum dona suf-
> ficerent, quamuis illum eis equum non dares, quem tibi specialiter
> possidendum elegi?' Cui statim episcopus: 'Quid loqueris,' inquit,
> 'rex? Numquid tibi carior est ille filius equae, quam ille filius
> Dei?' Quibus dictis intrabant ad prandendum. Et episcopus
> quidem residebat in suo loco. Porro rex, uenerat enim de uenatu,
> coepit consistens ad focum calefieri cum ministris; et repente inter
> calefaciendum recordans uerbum, quod dixerat illi antistes, dis-
> cinxit se gladio suo, et dedit illum ministro, festinusque accedens
> ante pedes episcopi conruit, postulans, ut sibi placatus esset,
> 'quia numquam', inquit, 'deinceps aliquid loquar de hoc aut iudicabo,
> quid uel quantum de pecunia nostra filliis Dei tribuas.' Quod uidens
> episcopus, multum pertimuit, ac statim exsurgens leuauit eum,
> promittens se multum illi esse placatum, dum modo ille residens
> ad epulas tristitiam deponeret. Dumque rex, iubente ac postulante
> episcopo, laetitiam reciperet, coepit e contra episcopus tristis usque
> ad lacrimarum profusionem effici. Quem dum presbyter suus lingua
> patria, quam rex et domestici eius non nouerant, quare lacrimaretur,
> interrogasset: 'Scio', inquit, 'quia non multo tempore uicturus est
> rex; numquam enim ante haec uidi humilem regem. Unde ani-
> maduerto illum citius ex hac uita rapiendum; non enim digna est
> haec gens talem habere rectorem.' Nec multo post dira antistitis
> praesagia tristi regis funere, de quo supra diximus, impleta sunt.

The readiness with which the large-spirited bishop, whom we may imagine as embarrassed and constrained by the king's largesse, over-reacts to a poor man's appeal for alms is suggested by the abrupt rattle of Bede's description of the act: "praecepit equum/ita ut erat/stratus regaliter/pauperi dari." This is at once balanced by the slow, sonorous, rhythmical phrases which gloss Aidan's action in spiritual terms: "erat enim multum misericors, et cultor pauperum, ac uelut pater miserorum." The humour of Oswine's indignation at Aidan's having squandered, not just a horse, but an equum regium on the poor man, when any number of equos uiliores would have done as well, is caught rhetorically in Aidan's rejoinder: "Numquid tibi carior est ille filius equae quam ille filius Dei?" Then the flamboyant alliteration of "coepit consistens...calefieri...caleficiendum..." sets off the process by which, in the course of a single long sentence, the heat of the fire at which the king is warming himself after hunting seems to generate the sudden impulse to contrition which makes him throw himself at the feet of Aidan and place all of his treasury at the bishop's disposal.[14] Then follow in rapid succession Aidan's initial fright at Oswine's action and his hasty promise that he bears the king no ill will "if only he will sit down to dinner and cast off his sadness"; but no sooner is the king's unhappiness eased than Aidan himself bursts into tears. The scene ends with the bishop, as if withdrawn to another plane, uttering his dira praesagia (expressed in his native Irish, and hence obscure to Oswine and his court) that so humble a king must be destined for an early death.[15]

There is nothing particularly Christian about the series of sweeping emotional gestures which constitute the movement of the scene, but the tolerance, indeed the obvious sympathy with which Bede dramatizes the excesses and inconsistencies of a society adapting itself to Christianity are as effective, and in their way as appropriate to the purposes of the Historia, as a more hagiographically stylized rendering might have been. There was indeed no conventional means whereby he might have suggested so well the complex relations between king and bishop, social and religious values, or the workings of a religious sensibility in which wholly pagan attitudes coexist with an imperfectly assimilated Christian eschatology.

But the point I most wish to emphasize is Bede's unobtrusive but complete linguistic control over the tone and movement of the scene. Gregory of Tours frequently shifts from one perspective to another in a manner similar to Bede's, representing the Frankish kings now as agents in the spiritual conquest of Europe, now as human beings to be judged by their inner response to their role. I am certain that Bede's sense of history and historiography owes a good deal more to Gregory than scholarship has so far demonstrated.[16] But to compare with the technique of the passage just considered the array of stylistic eccentricities, contradictions and ambiguities by which Gregory seeks to manipulate his different points of view is to appreciate the great advantage Bede enjoyed in the possession, among other gifts, of a flexible and uncoercive prose, capable of remaining wholly coherent while making itself wholly available to the task of reflecting nuance and irony in the behaviour of his human subjects.

Of course the Historia Ecclesiastica remains largely sui generis Though it had considerable influence as a model for early medieval historiography,[17] the implications of its more strictly literary qualities were realized only in the long course of the evolution of medieval narrative literature, and I am conscious that my attempt to consider them in the context of Bede's attitude toward style is at best impressionistic. An aspect of Bede's stylistic practice which can be discussed with more precision is his use of classical material. His refinement of a Christian curriculum from the silva of late classical pedagogy is sometimes considered to have involved the elimination of any contaminating trace of ancient sources, and it is true that an important feature of the treatises on metre and rhetoric is their effective substitution of Christian for classical examples. But there is also a good deal of borrowing from classical sources in Bede's writings. Some of it is due, no doubt, to the common practice of working together phrases from standard authors in writing hexameter verse, and some is probably inadvertent or wholly accidental; but a number of instances plainly reflect deliberate allusion,[18] and I think it is possible to find operating in these the same naturalness and sureness of touch which typify Bede's syntax.

Contrasting Bede's verse with Alcuin's, Peter Dale Scott observes that in Bede's poetic diction the inevitable classical elements are "subordinated to his Puritan sensibility and moralizing purpose," leaving him "little room for rhetorical indulgence."[19] It is certainly true that Bede's writing offers nothing like the rich and occasionally enigmatic blend of pagan and Christian reference present, for example, in Fortunatus; neither does he indulge in the sort of mechanical Christianizing which will place the Tityrus of Vergil's eclogue "sub tegmine Christi." It may be said, indeed, that what typifies Bede's contacts with classical poetry is that they take place almost invariably on rhetorically neutral ground. The result is, as Scott suggests, to render Bede's materials tractable to his own purposes, but the suggestion of tension in his characterization is slightly misleading, for the peculiar effectiveness of Bede's appropriation of classical sources seems to me less a matter of rigorously subordinating them than of taking them wholly for granted.

Though many of the classical tags in Bede's verse are likely to have been drawn from quotations in the grammarians, it seems safe enough to take for granted a first-hand knowledge of Vergil.[20] Several allusions to the Aeneid in the Historia seem to imply a knowledge of the context of the line or phrase quoted, as when a man raised from the dead speaks of having passed through the other world, like Aeneas and the Sibyl, "sola sub nocte per umbras,"[21] or again when we hear how Edwin, passing an anxious night among enemies, "caeco carperetur igni" like Dido after meeting Aeneas,[22] or see the priest Coifi destroying "eas quas ipse sacrauerat aras" as a sign of his acceptance of Christianity.[23] In the metrical life of Cuthbert the borrowings are briefer and more numerous, and give a definite impression of easy and familiar reference to Vergil's text.

It is just this familiarity that seems to me significant in Bede's Vergilian echoes. There is no attempt to evade or disguise his trafficking with a pagan author, yet even the most apparently deliberate allusions seem intended to evoke the ancient text only on the most superficial level. It would perhaps be possible on the basis of the echoes from Aeneid II and VI, which Bede tends to relocate in very different contexts, to view him as allusively contrasting the discordia and uncertainty of the Vergilian universe with the stability of a world ordered by heroic sainthood;[24] but there seems to be little correspondence between the extent and vividness of the echoes and their contribution to such a potentially allusive context.[25] It seems clear that Bede is responding to Vergil's language and control of atmosphere mainly for their own sake; that he knew Vergil well and was fond of his poetry, but appropriated its effects for his own purposes with little regard to their source. Nothing in his use of the Aeneid corresponds to the complex patterns of parody and subversion in Prudentius or the fifth-century poets' adaptations of Vergil's heroic idiom to the glorification of Christian heroism. He exploits the vividness, conciseness and familiarity of his author, and the effect of his use of Vergil's words is finally, as it were, to domesticate them.

I think, however, that precisely this domestication of Vergil can be seen as a characteristic and important achievement of Bede as stylist. As in dealing with the intractable elements in the culture of his own day, his approach to the most influential of classical authors is one of clearsighted tolerance, and enables him to establish a modus vivendi in which the potentially disruptive force of Vergil's eloquence is neutralized. It also offers a striking illustration of Bede's role in transmitting and shaping medieval literary culture. Vergilian language sets off the simplicity of his style as it sets off the purity of the hymns of Ambrose, while the disarming straightforwardness of his borrowing anticipates the modest classicism of Alcuin's poetic reflections on monastic otium. But Bede's appropriation of Vergil is neither programmatic nor simply recreational. It has neither the polemical intensity of Ambrose nor Alcuin's tendency to treat Vergil as a cultural symbol, though it constitutes an important stage in the process of redefinition which made possible the celebrated "humanism" of the Carolingians. Bede simply makes use of Vergil's words, accepting them with respect, but at the same time with a confidence and unpretentiosness such that their distractingly evocative powers become in his hands sine viribus ignes. It is one more example of his unique ability to recognize value in the product of an alien culture and make it serve his own sure Christian purpose.

NOTES

*   Leisure to prepare the present version of this essay has been provided by a fellowship granted by the John Simon Guggenheim Memorial Foundation.

1. "Hic est sensus, non autem ordo ipse uerborum, quae dormiens ille canebat; neque enim possunt carmina, quamuis optime composita, ex alia in aliam linguam ad uerbum sine detrimento sui decoris ac dignitatis transferri." Historia Ecclesiastica IV.22. The text for this and all subsequent quotations from HE is that of Charles Plummer (Oxford, 1896). Bruno Luiselli ("Beda e l'inno di Caedmon," Studi Medievali 14 (1973), 1013-36), sees Bede's divergences from the wording of the Old English as dictated by theological considerations. Several adjustments, for example, seem intended to achieve a more consistent focus on God as Creator, and such a phrase as "filiis hominum" may be deliberately substituted for the "eordu bearnum" or "sons of earth" which he may

28

have found in his Northumbrian original. However Luiselli's analysis
does not seem to me to justify his assertions (pp. 1018 and 1033) that in
the passage I have just quoted Bede is claiming to have achieved by his
adjustments an equivalent to the decor or dignitas of the Old English
original.

2. On Bede's modus operandi in compiling his textbooks see the careful
   analysis of the section de littera of the De arte metrica by R. B. Palmer,
   "Bede as textbook writer: a study of his De arte metrica," Speculum 34
   (1959), 573-84. More general is Bronislas Gladysz, "Eléments classiques
   et post-classiques de l'oeuvre de Bède 'De arte metrica,' " Eos (Commentarii Societatis Philologae Polonorum) 34 (1933), 319-43. On Bede's
   syntax see D. R. Druhan (The Syntax of Bede's 'Historia Ecclesiastica,'
   Catholic University Studies in Medieval and Renaissance Latin 8
   (Washington D.C., 1938), who shows convincingly that Bede's Latinity
   was in many respects closer to Augustan standards than that of Gregory,
   Cassiodorus and other Christian authors.

3. Palmer notes in passing Bede's evident neglect of Aldhelm and Virgilius
   Maro, among others, in compiling his textbooks ("Bede as textbook
   writer," p. 575, n. 13), but has not to my knowledge published the
   further study promised on this subject. On Hisperic Latin in England
   see W. F. Bolton, A History of Anglo-Latin Literature 597-1066 I
   (Princeton, 1967), pp. 46-8. However Bolton's list of examples of
   "Hisperic" diction in the metrical life of Cuthbert (ibid., p. 139) is misleading, as all the words given are found in the Christian Latin poets of
   the fourth and fifth centuries, who were Bede's preferred examples of
   "classical" eloquence. For the Hisperic and pre-Hisperic background
   of the English tradition of "hermeneutic" Latin which begins with Aldhelm,
   and for the later history of this tradition, see the important article of
   Michael Lapidge, "The hermeneutic style in tenth-century Anglo-Latin
   literature," Anglo-Saxon England 4 (1975), pp. 67-111.

4. See De schematibus et tropis (ed. Karl Halm, Rhetores latini minores,
   Leipzig, 1863, p. 610), where Bede quotes the Moralia in Iob and
   comments: "Et huiusmodi orationes esse reor, quas Hieronymus
   concinnas rhetorum declamationes appellat." See also Paul Meyvaert,
   Bede and Gregory the Great (Jarrow Lecture, 1964), p. 12.

5. De arte metrica (ed. Heinrich Keil, Grammatici latini VII (Leipzig,
   1878), pp. 242ff.

6. Vita sancti Cuthberti, lines 25-9, ed. Werner Jaager, Palaestra 198 (Leipzig
   1935 p. 60 . The high style of the passage of which these lines are the
   culmination seems to have been meant as a form of homage to the saint
   and a way of dignifying and promoting his cult. For more strictly
   educational purposes Bede elsewhere reduces to straightforward prose
   a number of Paulinus' classically ornate poems on St Felix; see Wilhelm
   Levison, "Bede as historian," in Bede, his Life, Times and Writings,
   ed. A. Hamilton Thompson (Oxford, 1935), pp. 115-16.

7. See Alistair Campbell, "Some linguistic features of early Anglo-Latin
   verse and its use of classical models," Transactions of the Philological
   Society (1953), pp. 15-16.

8. On the importance of formal structure, numerical patterns and symbolism as mnemonic devices in Bede see Charles W. Jones, "Bede as early medieval historian," Medievalia et Humanistica 4 (1946), 26-36.

9. See De arte metrica, pp. 251-2, where Bede discusses the difficulty of adapting certain Christian terms to classical metre; he notes in Sedulius the irregular line "Cum sancto spiritu gloria magna patri," and remarks that the poet "in order to sing clearly the glory of the sacred and undivided Trinity has neglected the rules of correct disposition."

10. See Gladysz, "Elements classiques et post-classiques," pp. 320 and 343.

11. "Bede as textbook writer," p. 575.

12. HE II.13.

13. Ibid., III.14.

14. As Druhan points out (Syntax of Bede's "Historia Ecclesiastica," p. xxii), anacolouthon is very rare in Bede; but in the effect of Oswine's outburst, which intrudes upon the Syntax of the sentence and gives it a somewhat elliptical movement, as in the heavy reliance on participles in the famous "sparrow" passage (HE II.13), we may see a willingness to take small liberties with syntax to achieve a special effect.

15. Bede uses differences of language for dramatic or symbolic effect at several points. With Aidan's reversion to Irish here cf. the emphasis on the special qualities of Cædmon's English (HE IV.22, quoted above, n. 1), and the pulcherrimum spectaculum of Oswald translating the preaching of Aidan from Irish into English for the benefit of his court (ibid., III.4).

16. There has been no serious attempt, so far as I know, to determine the extent of Bede's knowledge of and debt to Gregory. See the suggestive comment of J. N. Wallace-Hadrill (The Long-Haired Kings (London, 1962), pp. 61-2). Like Paul Meyvaert's tentative comparisons between Bede and Gregory the Great, however, these serve finally to indicate how much work is still to be done on Bede's literary relations.

17. See Levison, "Bede as historian," pp. 149-50.

18. Not all scholars would agree. Peter Hunter Blair, The World of Bede (London, 1970), pp. 288-89, suggests that Bede deliberately avoided contact with ancient literature and that "we need very strong evidence before we can admit that any of the works of classical antiquity were known to Bede at first hand." See also the remarks of my fellow contributor to this volume, Patrick Wormald (below, p. 60, n. 134).

19. "Alcuin as a poet: rhetoric and belief in his Latin verse," University of Toronto Quarterly 33 (1963-4), 236, an article which provides an excellent introduction to the Latin culture of the eighth and ninth centuries in its literary aspect.

20. Alistair Campbell, "Some linguistic features of early Anglo-Latin verse," p. 5, suggests that Vergil's stature in this period was such that a phrase used by him which appeared in an Anglo-Latin poem would probably have been taken as a Vergilian echo.

21. HE V.12; Aeneid 6.268.

22. HE II.12; Aeneid 4.2.

23. HE II.13; Aeneid 2.501-2. Here Bede may have been struck by the suggestion in the words themselves, though not their Vergilian context, of some such conversion formula as the "adora quod incendisti, incende quod adorasti" used by Gregory of Tours, Historia Francorum 2.29 (31) of the conversion of Clovis.

24. See. e.g. "venerabile donum," Vita Cuthberti 282, Aeneid 6.408; "ignis edax," VC 322, Aen. 2.758; "summa fastigia," VC 556, Aen. 2.302, 758; "corpus exsangue," VC 892, Aen. 2.542; "moribunda...membra," VC 934-935, Aen. 6.732. As Jaager's generous critical apparatus makes plain, Vergilian language may often have been "laundered" through such intermediaries as Juvencus or Sedulius. See also Campbell's remarks on the limits and abuses of such source study ("Some linguistic features of early Anglo-Latin verse," p. 4).

25. The two most elaborate borrowings occur at VC 302: "Dumque iter inceptum peragunt, venere sub amnem" (cf. Aen. 6.384: "Ergo iter inceptum peragunt fluvioque propinquant "); and VC 403: "Vix quae bis terni cervice subire potentes" (cf. Aen. 12.899: "Vix illud lecti bis sex cervice subirent"). Neither seems to reflect anything more than fortuitous reminiscence triggered by a coincidence of detail. Cf. the insertion of Aen. 2.1, "Conticuere omnes, intentique ora tenebant," in HE III.11.

III. BEDE, "BEOWULF" AND THE CONVERSION OF THE ANGLO-SAXON ARISTOCRACY

Patrick Wormald

I

Introduction: Bede versus "Beowulf"

The Venerable Bede did not believe in birthdays. He preferred men to
be commemorated on the anniversary of their deaths. It is entirely in keeping with his own priorities that we should know much more about his last
hours than about all the rest of his life put together. It is therefore most
unlikely that, quite apart from his famous humility, he would have endorsed
a Festschrift, designed to commemorate the thirteenth century of his birth.
It is as well to begin by making this point, as this is not the only respect in
which Bede's priorities will have differed from those of modern historians.
Perhaps the major trend in the historical study of Bede since the last anniversary in 1935, which was marked by a mass of celebratory literature, in
which A. Hamilton Thompson's Bede, his Life, Times and Writings formed
the centrepiece and to which Cornell's M. L.W. Laistner made so memorable
a contribution, has been the growing awareness that Bede was not a historian
like ourselves, and that he differed in more than just his faith in miracles.
In this paper, reflecting the trend, I wish to argue that, if a modern historian
wishes to understand the conversion of the Anglo-Saxon aristocracy, he has less
to learn from Bede, than from other sources, some of which are not works of
history at all. This might perhaps seem a strange way of paying tribute to a
master of the historian's craft, yet I am convinced that, even if my argument
be accepted, Bede's stature as a historian is thereby enhanced, rather than
diminished.[1]

Until recently, and certainly still in 1935, commentators were mainly
concerned to emphasize, and to praise, the many respects in which Bede came
up to their own exacting standards, whether of religious orthodoxy in the six-
teenth century, or of historical accuracy in the twentieth. For example, Sir
Frank Stenton's fine paragraph on Bede is, in some ways, a fairer portrait
of his own great book than of Bede's:

> [Bede's] critical faculty was always alert; his narrative never de-
> generates into a tissue of ill-attested wonders, and in regard to all
> the normal substance of history his work can be judged as strictly
> as any historical writing of any time. His preface, in which he
> acknowledged the help received from learned friends, reads like
> the introduction to a modern work of scholarship. But the quality

which makes his work great is not his scholarship, nor the faculty
of narrative which he shared with many contemporaries, but his
astonishing power of co-ordinating the fragments of information
which came to him through tradition, the relation of friends, or
documentary evidence....[2]

That Bede did indeed possess these qualities is not disputed. The Ecclesiastical
History of the English People is so excellent a source of knowledge for the
period it concerns that it would scarcely be an exaggeration to say that we
know more about the conversion of the English than about any series of events
in British History until the twelfth century. Yet it is possible that the book's
very excellence is one of its drawbacks, in that it conceals from view, as
lesser medieval historians do not, that Bede's conception of the nature and
purposes of history will have been very different from ours. Since 1935
scholars have made massive advances in the edition and study of Bede's non-
historical works, fields into which it is not possible to follow him with the
same sense of familiarity, and which remind us more of what distinguishes us
from Bede than of what we have in common with him.[3] Recently, too, students
of Bede have become more conscious that Bede's History was itself a member
of a particular historiographical tradition, which was that of the Christian
early Middle Ages, and not that of the Victorian university.[4] This has not
entailed a decline in respect for Bede's authority. So far as facts are concerned, his chronology of the Kentish conversion has withstood critical examination more successfully than has that of Gregory of Tours for the baptism
of Clovis.[5] But it has meant a new tendency to recognize that what Bede will
have considered appropriate ad instructionem posteritatis is not necessarily
what we should wish to know if we are to understand the events that he is
describing.

Hence, changing attitudes to Bede have been accomplished by the asking
of new questions about the age that he describes, and the search for other
angles of approach to it, whether historical or, more particularly, archaeological and art-historical. At its crudest, the Ecclesiastical History's main
theme could be reduced to: "At this time the A people received the Faith from
Saint B under the rule of King C". Historians are nowadays keen to know not
only that this was so, but also how and why. In the process, histories of the
early English church have largely ceased to be catenae of the astonishing
series of immortal stories with which Bede adorns his theme, and Henry
Mayr-Harting's Coming of Christianity to Anglo-Saxon England has become
perhaps the first treatment of the subject to give Wilfrid, Aldhelm and
Guthlac, all of whom suffer in different ways from Bede's dominant perspectives, the same weight as is given to Aidan, Chad and Cuthbert, who are, of
course, Bede's special heroes.[6] The connection between the reinvestiga-
tion of Bede's historical work and fresh approaches to his age is also made
in the work of James Campbell, who has followed two surveys of Bede's place
in the historiographical tradition of the early medieval West with a reassess-
ment of the "First Century of English Christianity" in the light of factors
which Bede's History largely ignores: the growth of ecclesiastical wealth,
the expansion of monasticism, and the very close contemporary links between
England and Gaul.[7] In this essay, I intend to continue the search for alternative perspectives. Specifically, I wish to suggest that we can supplement and

modify Bede's portrait of the conversion of the early English nobility by consideration of its vernacular literature, and above all by investigating further the the other major masterpiece of early English literary culture, Beowulf.

In 1935 it would have seemed outrageous to most scholars, and to many it may still seem extraordinary today, to suggest that a unique, anonymous and scarcely datable poem, concerned almost wholly with real and legendary events in Scandinavia at least a hundred years before the conversion of the English really got under way, might in some ways tell us more about the realities of seventh- and eighth-century England than a historian who is universally recognized, and who has been almost from the start, to be among the greatest that have ever lived. But it is not only the study of Bede that has changed. Recent directions of research into Beowulf, and associated "heroic" literature, have done much to enhance its historical relevance. Two directions may be distinguished in particular, the historical, and the literary.

That Anglo-Saxon poetry should have something to tell us about early English society has been accepted since the days of J. M. Kemble, and, in the hands of H. M. Chadwick, this literature became, for a time, a devastating instrument of historical, and even sociological, assault upon the nineteenth-century school of early Germanic studies.[8] But it was in 1935 itself that Ritchie Girvan in his Beowulf and the Seventh Century presented closer parallels than had ever before been noticed between the world of the poem and that of seventh-century England. Like W. W. Lawrence who had made some of the same points in his Beowulf and the Epic Tradition (1928), Girvan was more concerned to elucidate the poem itself, than its historical background, but his arguments included profound insights, based on his knowledge of the poem, into the culture and politics of the period.[9] For example, the central figures of the poem are frequently found outside their own "national" and "tribal" contexts, serving as exiles, adventurers, retainers and leaders of warbands at the court of "foreign" kings; it was in this capacity that Beowulf himself came to the court of Hrothgar with his escort. Chadwick had shown that this was also a significant feature of early English society. The way in which King Oswine of Deira (642/4 - 51) by his "generosity" and "courtesy" caused "noblemen from almost every kingdom to flock to serve him as retainers," is closely paralleled in the poem by the way that Hrothgar's, "success in war (heresped) his glory in battle", were such that "his band of young followers grew into a mighty following (magodriht micel)"[10] Girvan's achievement was to show how the operations of this mechanism accounted for the political developments of seventh-century Britain, whereby the frontier kingdoms, Bernicia and Deira, Mercia and Wessex were continually growing stronger, whereas the older kingdoms of the south and east, notably Kent and East Anglia, were atrophying. Expanding kingships, offering prospects of rewards in loot and land, were able, like Hrothgar, to attract this class of wandering warrior to their banners, at the expense of those whose outlets were being blocked, and it was by attracting such military specialists that kings were able to continue their campaigns of expansion. It was a snowball process, in which the great grew greater, and the weak melted away.

The possible impact of Girvan's views was immeasurably increased by discoveries in a second field, that of archaeology. Two of the most famous excavations since 1935 have revealed, at Yeavering in Northumberland, a large complex of wooden halls that is irresistibly reminiscent of Heorot, and at Sutton Hoo, in Suffolk, a treasure both fabulous in quantity and venerable in age, much of it showing Scandinavian connections, which thus recalled the various heirlooms described by the Beowulf poet, and which, interred as it is within a ship, and beneath a barrow, resembles what we should achieve, if we conflated the obituary ceremonies for Scyld at the beginning, and Beowulf at the end of the poem.[11] It may be that the significance of these parallels has been exaggerated, but, at the very least, the lavish material world of the poem has now been given its counterpart in the material deposits of seventh-century Britain.

Third, and finally, Professor Dorothy Whitelock, in her celebrated Audience of Beowulf (1951) widened the possibilities for the poem's date into the later eighth century, and brought to light, mainly with the help of place-names, an audience of Anglo-Saxons to whom Grendel, his mother and the dragon, the monstrous foes of Beowulf, will have seemed every bit as real as human enemies. She also demonstrated, from external evidence, what the poem itself had already suggested to earlier scholars, that the poet's audience must have been familiar with a wide variety of similar stories, to the extent that he could afford to refer to them only in passing.[12] Beowulf might thus be seen to reflect not only the behaviour and material environment, but also the fears and literary tastes, of the early Anglo-Saxons.

To say this is not, of course, to ignore Professor Whitelock's own warning against reading "precise contemporary relevance into poetry with a preference for the typical situation with a universal application". But it was Marc Bloch's view, stunningly put into practice in his Feudal Society, that, "in every literature, society contemplates its own image," and literature can sometimes tell us a lot about the society in which it arose, precisely because it is not primarily concerned to tell us anything.[13] The general atmosphere of life as it was lived by Bede's contemporaries, give or take a couple of generations, probably is reflected in Beowulf. It now seems very likely that King Oswald of the Bernicians (633-42) was actually much more like King Hygelac of the Geatas than any reader of Bede's famous chapters would immediately appreciate, and both kings certainly met the same sort of death. The impression given by close attention to narrative sources, to archaeology and even to toponymy suggests that, unique as it is, Beowulf represents significant features of the world that Bede describes, and gives us important clues in the understanding of it.

For this there is, perhaps, one particular reason. Beowulf, Finnsburh, Waldhere and the later Battle of Maldon are literature about, for, and even by, the Anglo-Saxon aristocracy. The early law-codes establish the existence of an aristocracy of birth in Anglo-Saxon England, as they do not on the Continent.[14] But quite apart from the legal evidence, there are ample indications, as on the Continent, of a prominent de facto aristocracy. One revealing story in Bede describes how the Northumbrian thegn Imma was betrayed as a warrior, and thus liable to vengeance, by his "appearance, manner and conversation."[15] In early Anglo-Saxon charters, several beneficiaries, or witnesses are described as the "faithful" or "revered" "companion" or "minister" of the king, and it is their closeness to him that constitutes their claim on his gratitude.[16] Perhaps above all, archaeology demonstrates that early English society knew a class of wealthy specialized warriors. Certain graves are distinguished by the appearance in them of weaponry that is otherwise extremely rare — swords, helmets, coats-of-mail — and where they are found, the rest of the deposit is often extremely rich.[17] Quite apart from the whens and wherefores of the appearance of cavalry in western Europe, possession of this sophisticated equipment must already have given its owner some of the same military significance as the later mounted knight. It is thus understandable, first that kings should have sought to attract such figures to their standards; second that those kings who could do so rapidly increased their military power; and third that the warriors themselves should have developed, on the classic Weberian prescription, an awareness that they were an elite.

It is clear enough that we encounter this class in Beowulf and in associated literature. Beowulf himself is escorted and buried by the sons of noblemen, and the poem is stiff with the terminology of the retinue. The word eorl, which, in the earliest laws, signifies "noble," in contrast to ceorl — "commoner"— is used, in the poem, no less than seven times as often as ceorl, thus suggesting that the poet took the noble status of his subjects almost for granted.[18] The military equipment which archaeology reveals to have been rare and precious is virtually universal in Beowulf, Finnsburh, and Waldhere (also in the Old High German Hildesbrandslied). Beowulf himself disposes of three sets of helmet, corselet and sword, and the same combination is attributed to four other individuals, and to three groups of retainers. As Girvan said, "everything specifically indicated in the poem is gold."[19] It thus seems reasonable to use heroic literature as a window on the mentality of a warrior-aristocracy, whose existence and whose importance is reflected by other sources, historical, legal and archaeological, but whose preoccupations do not seem to be described elsewhere.

Least of all are they described in Bede. It is possible to find evidence in Bede that the world of Beowulf was the same world as that whose history Bede is telling, but Bede's is an Ecclesiastical History: secular heroes, court-life, warfare in general, had no place in the tradition, and monsters still less of one. For all that the poet and the historian share a certain loftiness of tone, it seems likely that the beginner, confronted with similar translations of each, would conclude that they came from different civilizations altogether. They are separated by what Professor Momigliano, in another, not dissimilar, context, has called a "vast zone of silence."[20] That is why Anglo-Saxon heroic poetry offers more than a complement, it offers an alternative perspective, to Bede's impression of his age, all the more important for the fact that it is a perspective to some extent representative of a powerful body in society.[21] It is the emergence of this literature in such a capacity since 1935 that encourages a historian to take a closer look at parallel developments in a more "literary" field.

In 1936, one year after the last Bede anniversary, and in the same volume of the Proceedings of the British Academy as contained a characteristic panegyric on Bede by R. W. Chambers, Professor J. R. R. Tolkien published his "Beowulf: the monsters and the critics," which it would be no exaggeration to describe as one of the most influential works of literary criticism of the century, and since which nothing in Beowulf studies has been quite the same.[22] The arguments of Tolkien's paper were not universally accepted, and some of its effects would perhaps have been disowned by the author, but its general impact could be summarized by saying that most critics have learnt to take the Beowulf poet a great deal more seriously.

To previous generations of critics, visibly obsessed with the Homeric model, there was little dignity in the hero's struggles with monsters that were at once improbable and disgusting, and the view that the poem was "cheap" or "trivial" encouraged the opinion that it was also irrelevant: the real epics of the Anglo-Saxons must have been lost.[23] Similarly, it was generally accepted by 1936 that Beowulf was largely the work of a single author, and was composed in writing, but as long as such authoritative critics as Klaeber, the poem's most distinguished editor, continued to be embarrassed by the poem's structure, it remained a serious possibility that the poem has descended in the manner of Homer, rather than that of Vergil.[24]

Tolkien argued powerfully that, for the Germanic mentality that gave birth to the myth of Ragnarok, the monsters of the poem were the only appropriate enemies for a great hero, and thus shifted Beowulf from the irrelevant fringes, to the very centre, of the Anglo-Saxon thought-world. This naturally encouraged a pre-existent tendency to square the poem with what else was known of the "serious" levels of Anglo-Saxon thought — chiefly the Latin scholarship of the church. Secondly, Tolkien went far towards vindicating the structure of the poem by arguing that it was a balance of contrasting and interlocking halves. His thesis not only convinced many critics, but inspired them to follow his example, with the result that Tolkien's own position has been outflanked. Whereas previous generations of scholars, Tolkien included, had been quite prepared to explain what they considered structural and stylistic blemishes as interpolations, modern writers seek evidence of artistic refinement in some of the poem's least promising features.[25] As Beowulf's appearance has come to seem less untidy, one of the few remaining reasons for disbelieving in a single literate authorship has been undermined. This is particularly important, because, over the same period, a determined attempt by A. B. Lord, F. P. Magoun and their pupils to prove that Beowulf and other such such literature was orally composed seems to have met with defeat, at least on points. That Anglo-Saxon poetry contains "oral formulae" such as were originally discovered by Milman Parry in Homer and the poetry of the southern Slavs is now agreed, but it has also been demonstrated that supposedly "oral" formulae appear in undeniably literate contexts elsewhere, while close study of the way in which the Beowulf poet used formulae has made oral composition seem less and less plausible. Indeed modern critics have turned the tables on the "Homeric" school. It is agreed that "formular economy" and the precise repetition of substantial passages are typical of oral verse, but Beowulf is notably lacking in either; for the late Professor Campbell, the closest analogies to Beowulf in style of composition were to be found in late classical, rather than in Homeric, epic.[26]

Few English poems have grown as much in stature over the last forty years as has Beowulf. More to our point, the development of Beowulf criticism since 1936 has made the poem seem more representative of learned culture in the age of its composition, and has strengthened the thesis that the poem was composed with pen, not harp, in hand (similar trends in the study of the other heroic poems have made it seem likely that the same is true of Waldhere and Maldon, if not Finnsburh). Both points have an immediate relevance for students of early English Christianity. If the poet belonged in any way to the mainstream of Christian Latin scholarship, as increasing numbers of critics suppose, it is obvious that he was Christian himself, and highly likely that he was some sort of priest. But the same is probably true even of an ability to write, if indeed the poet could write.[27] Since the issue of literacy has not entered the debate over Beowulf as often as, perhaps, it might have done, it is worth giving this point some emphasis. It is scarcely open to argument that literacy reached the Anglo-Saxons with the coming of Christianity, and I do not think that the evidence will allow us to postulate much in the way of literacy outside the ranks of the clergy before 900.[28] We know of one unquestionably literate king before Alfred, the Irish-educated Aldfrith of Northumbria. We also know that some lay noblemen learnt to read, apparently by being brought up in monasteries.[29] In Alfred's day, we know from Asser's Life that there were books of poems at the West Saxon court, but we do not know where, or by whom, they were written down, nor do we know what sort of poems they contained. In fact, Asser offers powerful evidence against a widespread lay literacy at least in ninth-century England. Despite what he represents as an altogether exceptional enthusiasm from an early age, Alfred did not learn to read until he was nearly forty, and Asser's description of the reaction of Alfred's judges to the royal injunction that they should all learn to read does not suggest that the West Saxon aristocracy altogether shared their ruler's enthusiasm.[30] There is nothing from early England to match the evidence for extensive lay literacy that we find in contemporary Ireland.[31] We do not even have the sort of evidence for literacy outside religious communities that is furnished on the Continent by the writing-offices of the Frankish or Lombard kings, or by the Carolingian court-schools and Hofbibliothek. There are no identifiable Anglo-Saxon court-manuscripts, even from the tenth century, and Anglo-Saxon charters were almost certainly the work of their clerical beneficiaries, or of the nearest religious house if the beneficiary were a layman at least until after Alfred's day.[32] Anglo-Saxon England was a culture of what anthropologists call "restricted literacy," and among several interesting features that it shared with African cultures under Islamic influence in the eighteenth and nineteenth centuries was an effective clerical monopoly of its educational process.[33]

If, then, Beowulf is layman's work, it is a great rarity; and provided one takes a fairly broad view of what constituted a religious community in early Anglo-Saxon England (it would have to include cathedral familiae, and several more dubious congregations, as we shall see), the historical evidence of the distribution of Anglo-Saxon literacy supports that school of critics who have felt that the leisured and expansive tone of the Old English epic argues composition in a religious community under classical, or at least biblical, inspiration.[34] At the very least, it is difficult in the circumstances to envisage a Beowulf poet who was barely tinged with Christian values, or even one who could write English, but not read Latin, and it seems reasonable to proceed on the basis that the author of Beowulf was most probably a cleric, or an associate of clergy. We shall see that, even on an old-fashioned reading of the poem, this is by no means as unlikely as it might at first look.

The historical study of Beowulf over the last forty years has greatly encouraged the view that this, and similar, poems might represent many of the interests and values of the Anglo-Saxon warrior-classes, to which Bede, for his own good reasons, does less than justice. At the same time, the critical study of the poem has brought us to the point when, for various reasons, it does look as though it may have belonged to the literary culture of early Anglo-Saxon Christianity. Meanwhile, scholars are more aware than they were that Bede's is only one impression, not necessarily the most representative, of what was going on in seventh- and eighth-century England. There are bound to be serious difficulties about suggesting that Beowulf can tell us as much about the world in which it originated as Bede, not least because we have very little direct evidence that Beowulf was considered representative of anything at the time, or even that it was much admired, whereas Bede's book was an instant best-seller. Nevertheless, in the light of the above trends in the study of Beowulf, it does look as though the poem might have important implications for our understanding of the conversion of the Anglo-Saxon aristocracy, and in the light of what has also happened to the study of Bede, the point does seem to be worth investigating at this stage. It was Tolkien who suggested that, "Beowulf is a historical document of the first order for the study of the mood and thought of the period, and one perhaps too little used by historians."[35] It is time that historians once again took up the challenge. I wish therefore to examine the relevance of heroic literature, and especially Beowulf, for students of religious change in early England. I shall need to give my own answer to the question with which every Anglo-Saxon historian is one day faced: is Beowulf sensibly described as a Christian poem? But in so doing I shall regard the nature of early English Christianity as still an open question, and one on which Beowulf itself may have as much bearing as Bede. This must not be a circular argument, but it will be one with two movable axes: the evidence of Beowulf, and that of other sources, must be taken in tandem.

II

The religious character of "Beowulf"

Even historians cannot be unaware that the religious character of Beowulf is a highly controversial subject. Despite such authoritative pronouncements as that of Professor Whitelock, the problem remains one of the most thoroughly trampled of all the critics' cabbage-patches. The published options range from the view that it is a thinly veiled illustration of sacrificial kingship, to the suggestion that it is a rather less transparent allegory of Christian baptism. It is unnecessary, and would indeed be impossible, to discuss all such interpretations, but it might, perhaps, be helpful to review the features of the poem which have driven its critics to such diverse conclusions.

The first, and perhaps the biggest, difficulty in Beowulf is that there is a discrepancy between the practices ascribed to the protagonists and the sentiments that they express. Some of the practices are unmistakably pagan.

39

Under pressure from Grendel, the Danes resort to the worship of idols. Beowulf's body is cremated; so is that of Hnaef in the Finnsburh episode, and thus, too, the Danes wished to honour AEschere. Neither practice had ever been remotely tolerable in Christian circles.[36] On the other hand both the poet himself, and his heroes, refer to the power, providence, justice, and generosity of a single God. "Let the wise God, the holy Lord, adjudge the glory to whichever party he thinks fit," says Beowulf. "It is truthfully said", adds the poet within twenty lines, "that mighty God has always ruled mankind".[37] It has been argued that there is nothing very Christian about the God being invoked, but he is a good deal more like the Judaeo-Christian deity than he is like Woden, and it is hard to see where the poet got so uncompromisingly monotheistic a Divinity, if not from the Bible.[38] The contradiction in the poem is at its most acute in the famous "Excursus", where the Danes worship idols only a hundred lines after they have been entertained by a song about God's Creation of the World. The poet goes on to condemn them for it, though not without a note of sympathy. To reject this passage as an interpolation does not, however, help matters, since it is only a microcosm of the difficulty raised by the entire poem: the poet seems to have known that his heroes were pagans, yet he was prepared to attribute to them some of the apparently Christian opinions that he held himself.[39]

Second, Beowulf can convincingly be argued to bear traces both of Christian homily and liturgy and of lingering pagan beliefs. Some of the poet's vocabulary — forscrifan, candel, non — seems clear evidence that he and his audience had been exposed to the language of Latin Christianity.[40] On the other hand the way that he uses eacen to describe both the strength of the hero, the sword in the monster's lair, the lair itself, and the dragon's treasure, suggests that he possessed a residual faith in pagan magic.[41] Wyrd in the poem is a notorious crux; at times, it seems that the poet was familiar with the Boethian concept of Fortuna; at others, as when Dryhten is described as Wigspeda gewiofu (weaver of victories), one is immediately reminded of the Germanic goddess of fate.[42]

Third, there is the paradox of the scriptural references. The references to the Bible are explicit enough, but they are confined to the early chapters of Genesis, with some possible mentions of the last judgement. Apart from the creation song, there are two references to the murder of Abel by Cain, and one to the flood. It can be argued that the poet twice finds it necessary to say that Cain killed his brother, as if knowledge of the fact could not be taken for granted, and that in the manuscript that we have Cain is confused with Cham, son of Noah. On the other hand, it has also been pointed out that the poet possesses, and assumes, a considerable knowledge of the obscure corner of Genesis describing the descent of giants and monsters from Cain and their destruction by the flood.[43] After the flood, we hear no more: no Moses, no Isaiah, no Christ and no Paul. Clark Hall's famous remark that there was little in the poem to offend a "pious Jew" has often been quoted, but so sparing are the citations even from the Old Testament, that a pious Jew must have been scarcely less dissatisfied than a pious Christian.[44] It seems almost as though there were a conscious avoidance of New Testament doctrines, like redemption. Any positive impact that the biblical references might otherwise have is therefore diminished by their limited range.

Finally, and crucially, there is a profound ambiguity in the ethical tone of the poem. It is both unquestionably "secular" and almost idealistic. No first-time reader of Beowulf could fail to be struck by the pleasure it takes in the good things of life. We hear much about drinking and singing. Twenty-five lines dwell on the presents given by Hrothgar to Beowulf after the hero's first great success. When Beowulf lies dying, and Wiglaf is ransacking the treasure in the dragon's barrow, we are told that "the messenger was in haste"; if so, the poet was not, because he devotes thirty lines to an account of what Wiglaf found.[45] Moreover, it has rightly been argued that Beowulf lacks anything like the triumphant confidence as regards death and the life after death of mainstream Anglo-Saxon Christian poetry; judgment is occasionally promised, but its outcome is either bad or uncertain. In what is perhaps the most famous passage of the entire poem, Beowulf consoles Hrothgar for the death of Aeschere. "It is better for everyone that he avenge his friend, rather than mourn him long. We must expect an end in this world; let he who can win glory before death; for a dead warrior, that is the best aftermath". This is not necessarily a heathen sentiment, but it can scarcely be described as a wholly Christian one.[46] In all these respects, Beowulf resembles heroic literature in general, whether English, Germanic or Indo-European.

Yet against all of this one must set the elevated tone of the poem, which so impressed Klaeber and Chambers. This does seem to distinguish Beowulf from the Nibelungenlied, or from what Chambers called the "wild heathenism" of the Norse. An impressive illustration of the essential "idealism" of the Anglo-Saxon epic is furnished by its very last lines. "It is right that men should honour their lord in words and cherish him in their thoughts, when he must depart from the body. Thus it was that the Geatas, his hearth-companions, mourned the fall of their Lord; they said that he was among all kings of the earth, the kindest and most gracious of men, the gentlest to his people, and the most eager for praise". Klaeber, in a much-misquoted passage, was sufficiently moved to recognize features of a type of Christ in the hero. Even critics of the poem's Christianity have confessed to finding in it a "perfect nobility that is hard to credit in pagan times".[47] Faced with this fundamental ambivalence, scholars have been inclined to react subjectively. Some have ascribed the "gentle nobility" of the poem to Christian influence, while others have credited its joy in the manly virtues to paganism. But Christianity can scarcely claim a monopoly of gentle nobility, any more than can paganism of the manly virtues. The truth is that we do not really know enough about the poetry of the pagan Anglo-Saxons to be sure that Beowulf is either similar, or dissimilar, to what had been composed before the coming of Christianity.

Not all these points are of equal weight, but they tend to balance each other out, and this is the main reason why agreement as to the religious character of Beowulf has been so difficult to reach. Instead of following critics into further controversy along these lines, historians might simply pause to consider the startling prospect which already confronts them. How is it that a presumably Christian, arguably clerical, pen has produced a work whose Christianity has been so controversial? It is, one suspects, the tension between a Christian authorship that is argued by literate composition and a seemingly less than whole-hearted religious commitment that has led several recent scholars to the view that the poem does have a Christian meaning, but that it is hidden, that Beowulf is an allegory with a Christian message. The allegorical exposition of Scripture was, after all, one of the dominant intellectual interests of the early Middle Ages, and students of Beowulf had been encouraged since 1936 to relate the poem to the more serious concerns of the age.[48]

It now seems unlikely that any allegorical solution to the problems of Beowulf will command assent, partly because it does not make adequate sense of the poem, and partly because it does not make much sense of the principles of early medieval allegory. But even if such an approach does fail, it is to the credit of its exponents that they have at least recognized the existence of a problem. Most modern scholars, like R. W. Chambers before the war, have been sufficiently influenced by the Christian features of the poem, as described above, to regard it as an acceptable Christian product. Yet the fact is that, in Beowulf, a great deal of space has been devoted to the warlike deeds of a pagan Scandinavian, in a poem which seems to be brushed, rather than suffused, by the Bible, and which is dominated, as Tolkien argued, by the sense that bygone days, however heathen or hopeless, were also noble. Much of Beowulf may edify (like Hrothgar's "sermon"), but much of it does not. It is widely agreed today that Beowulf is about the qualities of the "noble pagan"; few have remembered Chadwick's legitimate objection that a Christian poet of the period had no business to be celebrating the secular virtues of noble pagans, and the fact is that, as compared with the ninth-century Waltharius, or the thirteenth-century Nibelungenlied, the Beowulf poet is unusually explicit about the pagan rites that his heroes celebrated. There are real difficulties here, dramatically highlighted by the fact that two such acknowledged experts as Professor Whitelock and Dr Sisam can come to diametrically opposed conclusions as to the level of Christianity in the poem.[49]

III

Christianity and secular Germanic culture

What the debate perhaps calls for at this stage is something more in the way of objective criteria for scholarly judgment, some further study of what Christianity would have meant in eighth-century England, and of how the Christians of the period might have reacted to Beowulf. So far as I am aware, there has never been an extended study of the orthodox attitude to heroic literature in the vernacular, to set alongside the standard works of Marrou, Laistner and Henry Chadwick on Christianity and classical culture.[50] It is perhaps appropriate that something of the sort should be attempted in a Cornell volume. But merely to list the rules will not be enough in itself. We shall have to see whether the rules were altogether obeyed, and this is a question which historians, dazzled by the brilliance of Bede, have not always answered with much interest or sympathy. I propose to ask therefore, first of all what the orthodox position regarding literature like Beowulf was, and secondly, how orthodoxy fared in seventh- and eighth-century England.

For these purposes, there is one crucial piece of evidence, which has long been familiar to historians and critics, but whose implications have never been fully appreciated, because its historical context has not been examined. In a letter of c. 797 to Hygebald, bishop of Lindisfarne, the Northumbrian scholar, Alcuin, wrote: "Let the word of God be read at the priestly repast. There should the reader be heard, not the harpist (citharistam); the sermons of the Fathers, not the songs of pagans (carmina gentilium). What has Ingeld to do with Christ? The House is narrow, it cannot hold both. The King of Heaven wishes to have no fellowship with so-called kings, who are pagan and lost; for the eternal king reigns in Heaven, the lost pagan laments in Hell. Hear the voices of readers in your houses, not the crowd of revellers in the streets".[51] The Ingeld of this passage is easily identified. He must be the Heathobard prince, whose marriage to Freawaru, princess of his hereditary Danish enemies, resulted in further bloodshed and divided loyalties; the story is familiar to us through a garbled version in the later Danish historian, Saxo Grammaticus, as well as through the English poems, Widsith and Beowulf itself.[52] Here, then, a story which actually constitutes one of the digressions in Beowulf, and which must have involved some of the same sort of subject-matter, is roundly condemned as any concern of monks. Alcuin's remarks thus have an obvious bearing on the subject under discussion. They have been dismissed on the grounds that Alcuin was a fanatic, that he says nothing about the written composition of literature about Ingeld, and that his ban could not have extended to such a poem as Beowulf, even if it did proscribe other heroic literature, such as Finnsburh.[53] But Alcuin was not a fanatic. His letter is simply a vigorous expression of cultural currents that ran right through the church of the early medieval West. Written or unwritten, we have seen that Beowulf is substantially "secular" in much of its tone, and its concern is with pagans. It is possible, by examining the tradition which Alcuin was articulating to show that, on both counts, Beowulf would probably have been considered every bit as unsuitable as any poem about Ingeld.

In the first place, Alcuin is representing the tradition of monastic and canonical hostility to the cultivation of secular literature in ecclesiastical contexts. For example, in a seventh-century rule for nuns, which has been plausibly connected with the circle of St Columbanus, we find: "There is to be silence, so far as concerns the otiose, frivolous, scurrilous, base and evil-minded tales (fabulis)" there are to be no fabulae superfluae, and an account is to be kept of "otiose words." Similar provisions appear in most monastic rules including that of St Benedict.[54] The canons of church-councils speak the same language; thus, the enormously influential third council of Toledo (589): "Because otiose fabulae are frequently put forward at tables, a reading of the divine scriptures is to be added to all priestly repasts, for this purpose, that their souls be edified, and that superfluous tales be forbidden". The eleventh-century English canonist, Archbishop Wulfstan (1002-23), echoed these norms when he specified in his 'Canons of Edgar' that no priest was to be an eal-scop (presumably an ale-minstrel).[55]

The evidence in fact suggests that these were already the views of the earlier English churchmen, quite apart from Alcuin, though some of them have been wrongly supposed to have been sympathetic to literature such as Beowulf. The English bishops, meeting at Clovesho in 746/7 forbade priests to chatter in church in the manner of secular poets, or corrupt the sacred text by "tragic" sound; this decree hardly suggests official endorsement of traditional forms of versification.[56] Bede himself is known to have been interested in the vernacular, and in English verse, but the only piece of his that we have is exceedingly devout, and there is no evidence that the carmina that he knew were any different. Of Cædmon, the late seventh-century Whitby cowherd, and putative founder of vernacular religious poetry, Bede writes that he had received his gift from God, and hence, "he could compose no frivolous and futile poetry at all, but only those things that pertained to religion suited his pious tongue". (In Cædmon's reported list of further works, there is nothing remotely like Beowulf.) The chapter which immediately follows in Bede's History includes among the sins for which Coldingham was (in Bede's view, justly) condemned, banqueting, drinking and "fabulating". Only three chapters before, Bede had used the word fabulae of stories about runes. Twice, in his commentary on Samuel, Bede seems to condemn libri gentilium, fabulae saeculares.[57] It does not look as though he favored the cultivation of anything other than directly religious verse. Aldhelm is another whose approval of secular verse has been assumed. A famous story in William of Malmesbury, writing in the early twelfth century and quoting King Alfred as his authority, told told how this finest of English poets used to sing a poem at the bridges leading out of Malmesbury, and, by gradually introducing scriptural matter, delay his congregation's precipitate departure from church. But it has not been sufficiently emphasized that the poem in question was regarded by William certainly, and probably by Alfred, as trivial, and that both sources felt it incumbent upon themselves to explain why such "frivolous" and "ludicrous" material was necessary; that is why we have the story. Alfred's attitude tells us nothing direct about Aldhelm's general style of composition, but the whole tendency of the passage is such as to suggest that Aldhelm regarded Scripture itself as the proper subject of verse, and that he would have wished to see the edifying element more obvious than it is in Beowulf. [58]

In the nature of the evidence, none of these texts can be shown to proscribe Beowulf as such. It is not certain by any means that every fabula referred to in the canonical sources conceals an illicit fancy for secular literature, whether classical or Germanic. But these references do establish that Alcuin's remarks draw upon a recognizable tradition. It seems to go back to the original Christian attitude to the pagan classics, as unforgettably enunciated by Tertullian, Jerome and Gregory the Great. Like Dr Hunter Blair, I have the impression that "What has Ingeld to do with Christ?" is a conscious echo of, "How can Horace go with the Psalter?"[59] If these were the priorities of the religious life, it is hard to see how Beowulf could have been tolerated in its present form, for all its "Christian coloring."

It could be argued, however, that these are the standards expected of clerics, and religious commnities; they did not, perhaps, apply to laymen, or to the royal courts, which might have been expected to appreciate the poem. This argument cannot be pressed too far. A literate Beowulf is, as we have seen, likely to have been the work of someone who was at least on the fringes of clerical society and, in the Early Middle Ages, there was no independent lay ethic, such as developed later, in the thirteenth century. On the contrary laymen, and kings especially, came under increasing pressure to conform to sacerdotal norms.[60] So far as this concerns secular literature, we find

44

Gregory the Great, in his notorious letter to Desiderius of Vienne (601), writing of classical verses unfit to be recited even by a religious layman; and Jonas, Bishop of Orleans (818-43) in a work entitled De Institutione laicali uses much the same language as the canons already quoted, and cites, on this point, a sermon of Bede's, which was presumably addressed originally to clergy. He criticizes especially those whose delight in vain and obscene confabulation is nowhere greater than when they go to church.[61] The most significant illustration of this point, for our purposes, comes from the Carolingian royal family itself. In a famous passage, Einhard describes how Charlemagne (768-814) had written down and committed to memory the, "barbarian and most ancient songs, in which the deeds and wars of kings of old were sung." Yet Louis the Pious, Charlemagne's son and successor (814-40) thought otherwise. According to his biographer Thegan Louis, "never raised his voice in laughter, nor did he have themilici, clowns, actors or harpists at his table on great festivals, and he never showed his white teeth in a smile"; further, "the poetic songs of pagans (carmina gentilia), which he had learnt in his youth, he rejected, nor did he wish them to be read, learned or taught".[62] Hence if we use the evidence of Einhard to show that a Christian court might commission literature like Beowulf, we ought also to acknowledge the evidence of Thegan that, according to an influential segment of Christian opinion, it should not have done.

The second current of opinion that finds expression in Alcuin's remarks is the teaching of the early medieval western Church on unbaptized pagans. Ingeld was unbaptized, and had gone, thought Alcuin, to hell; it was for this reason, and not because he was a Dane or a coward, that Alcuin considered his story to be unsuitable material for a Christian audience. Beowulf himself, and the other heroes of the poem, were open to the same objection. St Paul had, of course, envisaged that Gentiles could appreciate moral truths by natural law, and would be judged on that basis; western writers like Augustine and Gregory were never prepared to assert that God had condemned all pagans.[63] Nevertheless, the theological tradition of the West, taking its inspiration from Augustine, discouraged sanguine speculation about the fate of the unbaptized, and emphatically opposed the indulgent celebration of pagan virtues.[64] There was no systematic case made at this stage for the redemption of the unbelieving, such as we find in association with the 'new' secular literatures of the twelfth and thirteenth centuries.[65] Bede, confronting anew the challenge of the Pelagian, Julian of Eclanum, admitted that there had been just men among the unbaptized, like Job; for Bede, however, such men were important mainly as illustrations of the independent activity of Divine Grace, not of justification by human virtue. The trouble with Beowulf, and also, apparently, with Ingeld, is that although they may, or may not, have had virtues, there was no suggestion that they had Grace.[66]

This is all the more remarkable since the conversion of the Celtic and Germanic barbarians naturally raised the problem of the condemned ancestor in an acute form. The terrible old Frisian King, Radbod stepped back from the edge of St Wulframn's font on overhearing a remark to the effect that he would not now join his ancestors in damnation, and declared that, "he could not lose the company of his predecessors, and sit with a small number in heaven".[67] Yet no evidence really suggests that the Church's teaching was modified as a matter of official policy, or that the experience made any difference to its attitude to literature like Beowulf. In his correspondence with his fellow-countrymen, St Boniface played heavily on the irony that the purity of the damned Saxons should shame the sexual licence of Christian Mercian kings, and appealed with passion for assistance in the salvation of so many lost souls, but in each case it is the fact of damnation that dominates his consciousness. There is a lot of difference between this attitude and that of Beowulf, in which pagan virtues are praised over three thousand lines, with a brief, passing, reference to their probable futility.[68]

It has in fact been suggested that the flexible missionary methods advocated for the Anglo-Saxons by Pope Gregory the Great are relevant to the survival in England of a heroic tradition, focussing upon a pagan past.[69] Just possibly, the famous suggestion that pagan shrines and festivals be converted to Christian use may have a bearing on the adaptation of scopcraeft to the teaching of the Bible, by such as Aldhelm and Cædmon, but it cannot be read as an endorsement for the honoring of pagan ancestors in poetry or anywhere else. Archbishop Theodore (669-90) was soaked in the writings of the great pope, yet his Penitential specifies that when churches are converted, the cadavera infidelium interred therein are to be flung out.[70] Another close student of Gregory's mission literature was Pope Nicholas I (858-67), the greatest canonist of the early Middle Ages, who faced a series of questions, including one on pagan ancestors, from the newly converted Bulgars. He showed typical Gregorian flexibility in, for instance, permitting the wearing of trousers, and in writing that, though jokes and profanities were to be discouraged at all times, the Bulgars could not be expected to lose their notorious sense of humor overnight, so they could make a start by being serious in Lent. But when it came to ancestors, Nicholas was firm: "As for your kinsmen who died unbelieving, one may not pray for them, because of the sin of incredulity, according to John the Apostle, who said, 'There is a sin unto death; I say that it may not be prayed for': a sin unto death is that of those who die in the same sin".[71] Thus, while individual missionaries may well have told their flocks not to despair of the salvation of their ancestors, there is, as Chadwick rightly argued, no evidence for a school of "liberal churchmen" in early medieval Europe, and such evidence as we have indicates, as we shall see, that those who indulged a taste for secular literature about pagan heroes were not so much liberal as drunk.[72] Once again, Alcuin cannot be considered unrepresentative of the mainstream tradition, and once again, it is hard to see how Beowulf can have been exempt from its provisions.

To the arguments that I have been presenting so far there are, it is true, an important set of objections. Suppose that Alcuin were consciously reflecting the conventional ecclesiastical hostility to classical letters: the work of Laistner, Leclercq, de Lubac and others has now revealed how very artificial such hostility was. Alcuin himself wrote slightingly of Vergiliaca mendacia on more than one occasion, as did his biographer, yet Alcuin was obviously extremely familiar with Vergil's works.[73] Should we not, therefore, take his strictures upon songs about Ingeld with similar measures of salt? St Augustine, in his De Doctrina Christiana had accepted the educational necessity of the classics, and, adapting a metaphor of Origen's, had taught that profane literature could have a moral significance, as the spoils of the

Egyptians had benefited the fleeing Israelites. Hraban Maur, pupil of Alcuin, and master of the school at Fulda (822-47) used the same argument in his tract on the teaching of clergy. Theodulf, bishop of Orleans (798-818), himself the most gifted poet of the Carolingian Renaissance, wrote of finding truths in the frivola...plurima of classical verse.[74] Yet I doubt whether these arguments are relevant to the case of Beowulf, or associated literature.

In the first place, even if Beowulf itself were agreed to possess a single edifying message, the secular apparatus of the poem, which we have noted above, remains excessive. Hraban wrote that whatever in gentile books, "is superfluous, concerning idols, love, the care of secular things, that we shall cut off";[75] much of Beowulf would have been disqualified under this rule. Secondly, the classics might be educationally indispensable, inasmuch as they were inextricably entangled with the whole culture of the Christian Fathers; but nothing suggests that the vernacular had any educational utility before the days of Alfred's England, and when Alfred did eventually find a use for Saxonica carmina, there was no need, as there was in Latin, to use pagan stereotypes rather than freshly composed religious poetry, which could edify while it instructed.[76] Third, and crucially, the western Fathers from Jerome to Hraban were wrestling with the problem of a pre-existent corpus of classical literature, the use and memory of which could not be blotted out. But when writers like these wrote of searching the dungheap of the classics for gold, they did not endorse the creation of more dung that more gold be dug out.[77] Thus, there is nothing to suggest that anyone in the western tradition would have approved the use of original compositions, such as Beowulf, in preference to more direct methods of instruction. Hraban Maur at Fulda was indirectly responsible for no fewer than three major monuments of Old High German verse, but all are versifications of the Gospels which make the message more accessible, rather than new gentile books, conveying it by hints. Moreover, Otfrid, the author of one, and a devoted pupil of Hraban's, actually wrote in his preface that he had written his translation as an alternative to secular literature, to "the sound of useless things", the "obscene song of laymen".[78]

The objections to any comparisons between the use made of classical literature by the western Fathers under a smokescreen of ostensible disapproval, and the cultivation of literature like Beowulf are underlined by the evidence of material survival. The libraries and scriptoria that have preserved for us most of what we know about Latin antiquity, have also bequeathed from the early period one short and truncated Old High German lay, the Hildebrandslied, and one full-length epic, albeit in Latin, the Waltharius, from the Continent.[79] From England, they have left us a single full-length vernacular epic, Beowulf, preserved in one manuscript which seems to owe its existence to the fact that it is a compendium of the monstrous. Three other fragments of "secular" poetry, Waldhere, Finnsburh, and Maldon (all, be it noted, from outside the medium of the main poetic codices); and the strange "catalogues" of the Exeter Book, Widsith and Deor.[80] In none of these cases, except perhaps the very last, is there any suggestion that "secular" themes were used to put across Christian messages. On the other hand, almost ten times as much unmistakably religious poetry has survived in England, and the proportion on the Continent is far higher. To me, these dismal proportions tell their own story, as indeed does the disappearance of Charlemagne's collection. I think

it is one of severe ideological pressures on the channels of transmission.
We cannot at least ignore the fact of disappearance, nor fail to ask why it was
so.

So much for the orthodox position. I do not pretend that theory and practice are the same thing. But, set in its ideological context, it seems that
Alcuin's famous letter may, after all, have important implications for the
study of Beowulf. Those critics who have supposed that Beowulf has comparatively little to do with Christianity have a better case, in theory, than modern
authorities have usually been willing to grant. On the other hand, the tendency
among scholars over the last thirty years to integrate the composition of the
Anglo-Saxon epic with what else is known of the learned culture of early English Christianity is open to some serious objections. The patristic works that
have been ransacked for clues to the poet's attitude to wealth, sin and judgement also contain what are (by Byzantine, or later medieval standards, for
example) surprisingly tough provisions on the cultivation of secular literature
and on the salvation of pre-Christian ancestors, and I am not sure whether
we can divorce the Augustinian hierarchy of letters, or Augustinian ecclesi-
ology, from the patristic legacy to Anglo-Saxon England. [81] Nor can it be
assumed as readily as it often has been that all these works were widely known
to the earliest English scholars. It is both dangerous to regard such centres
as Malmesbury, Jarrow and York as typical, and unsatisfactory to assume
that books known to the greatest scholars necessarily circulated widely.
Writing the preface to his Genesis commentary for Bishop Acca of Hexham,
Bede said that much had been written on the subject by Basil, Ambrose and
Augustine, but, "because all this is so copious and deep that the books can
scarcely be acquired except by the rich, and they are so profound that they can
scarcely be examined except by the learned, your holiness enjoined upon me
the task..." (of making selections). [82]

In short, it is often accepted today that Beowulf represents the work of an
Englishman with "average" patristic culture. But we know what a product of
the library at York thought of literature of this type; we may strongly suspect
that the most distinguished son of Jarrow will have shared his opinion, and we
have no reason to believe that the outstanding Malmesbury scholar thought any
differently. If we are still to believe that Beowulf belongs within the same
tradition, then two stipulations are surely necessary. First, patristic influence must be demonstrated, and not taken for granted; we must have something concrete to set against what we know of Alcuin's position. Second, if
we are to accept that there is such influence upon Beowulf, it must be admitted
that something rather extraordinary had happened to orthodox priorities in the
poet's hands, and in that case we must search not only for the Mediterranean
l :cy, but also for what it was, in the insular tradition, that had distorted
the perspective. Otherwise, Alcuin may be left in possession of the field, as
a representative member of a flexible, but not a liberal, tradition, that ran
from Augustine via Gregory, Bede and the school of York to Alcuin himself,
his pupil Hraban, and the school of Fulda. The corollary is that if we are to
understand how Beowulf, and other such literature, came to be composed by
a Christian, even a clerical, pen, the ideological heritage of western Christianity in the early Middle Ages is the wrong place to look.
as far as I am prepared to go in this direction.

That, however, is as far as I am prepared to go in this direction. Despite
the official opposition to Germanic secular literature, Beowulf did find its way
into writing in an age when literacy was largely a preserve of the clergy, and

was certainly a Christian monopoly. This anomaly, if anomaly it be, requires explanation. We now need, therefore, to ask how widely the orthodox position was in fact followed.

IV

The social and cultural context of secular Germanic literature

There have been two notable attempts in recent years to confront Chadwick's case against an early medieval "liberal Christianity" by looking at what particular classes of churchmen really thought about the noble pagans of their heroic past. Professor Donahue has sought to explain the existence of a major early English Christian poem about noble pagans, by invoking the more easy-going attitude towards the pre-Christian past that was characteristic of the Irish. Professor Donahue's evidence that the Pauline doctrine of natural law had taken root among the Irish, and flourished there more vigorously than elsewhere in the early medieval West is most convincing and can be supplemented. One of the early Irish synods, for example, declared: "If we find the judgement of the heathens good, which their good nature teaches them, and it is not displeasing to God, we shall keep them". Early Irish legend tended to lay special emphasis upon the virtues of such noble pagans as Cormac and Morand, and one might add that early Irish hagiography offers examples of the "baptism" of dead heroes; in Tirechan's seventh-century Life, St. Patric baptized the grandson of Cass, son of Glass, by raising him temporarily from a grave in which he had already spent a hundred years. In Germany, St Boniface had difficulties with an Irish heretic named Clement, who taught that Christ had freed all souls when harrowing hell, "believers and unbelievers, praisers of God and worshippers of idols". [83] Given this evidence that the early Irish made a series of efforts to reconcile their past and its heroes with the new dispensation, it is not at all surprising that during the seventh and eighth centuries they were committing the Ulster Cycle, with all its pagan heroes, to writing, and at the same time adopting the learned legacy of western Christianity. It was believed that the Tain Bo Cuailnge was exported in exchange for Isidore's Etymologiae. [84]

In view of what happened in Ireland itself, it is a very reasonable suggestion that Beowulf, like much else in early Anglo-Saxon civilization, was directly or indirectly influenced by Irish ideas, and specifically by Irish tolerance of a pagan past. The poem's restricted range of biblical allusions are like those of the "Testament of Morand"; the confusion of Cain and Cham was widespead in Ireland (though it was also made by Alcuin himself); monsters, in Celtic stories, do sometimes move freely beneath the surface of lakes, as they do in Beowulf, whereas, in the poem's Scandinavian analogues, their lair is located in a cave behind a waterfall. It is perhaps significant that Alcuin's suspicions about an interest in the deeds of Ingeld focused themselves upon Irish-founded Lindisfarne, where, as Dr Mayr-Harting has recently shown, something similar may have happened one hundred years earlier. [85] Conversion by the Irish may have made literature like Beowulf more acceptable. It is unfortunately impossible, however, to establish any connection between Celtic influence and what little we know of heroic literature on the Continent, such as Charlemagne's collection of barbara et antiquissima carmina, and plausible though Professor Donahue's case is, it might therefore be unwise to depend too heavily upon the "Irish solution."

Meanwhile, Professor Benson has argued that the outlook of the Irish was shared by the English missionaries to Germany, and that they thought of the kindred pagans of the continental mainland not with horror, but with, "interest, sympathy, occasionally even admiration." There is indeed evidence, among St Boniface's converts, as among the early Irish, of a lingering interest in heroic ancestors, and it was in St Boniface's own Fulda, a generation after his death, that our sole manuscript of the Hildebrandslied appears to have been written. [86] At the same time, we have seen that Boniface himself is unlikely to have disagreed with Alcuin about the fate of the unbaptized, or the impropriety of extolling their virtues at length; he was scandalized by Clement's excessively generous interpretation of the "Harrowing of Hell." There is really no good evidence of a theory of the noble pagan among the English missionaries, such as we find among the Irish, and such as we could use to explain the existence of Beowulf.

It thus seems unlikely that either the Irish or the continental connection will solve our problem on its own. But Professors Donahue and Benson have introduced important new elements into the debate over Beowulf. Their arguments put a new premium not upon hypothetical doctrinal foundations for a literature of pagan heroism, so much as on concrete evidence of an interest in it. In each case, this interest has a recognizable historical context, and a cultural rationale. For the Irish, the key condition was the vigorous conservatism of Celtic learned culture, preserved as it was by a powerful and priviledge class of professionals, the filid. [87] Among the English missionaries and their converts, we are confronted with an understandable determination not to be separated from a past that was closely linked to national origins (the Anglo-Saxon royal genealogies, as we shall see, offer good evidence of a surviving awareness that the northern Continent was part of the English past). Whether we agree or disagree with the arguments of these scholars, we can take our cue from them, and look again, both at the evidence for a cult of the heroic in early Anglo-Saxon England, and at the social and cultural context in which it is found.

I therefore return, once again, to Alcuin's letter. Often as this has been quoted, no significant attention has ever been paid, so far as I know, to the context in which Alcuin's strictures occur. The letter is full of forebodings of the Apocalypse, when there shall be no use for precious stones or for gold or fine clothes. Alcuin stresses that what matters is the ministry, not banquets; where is the honor in groaning tables, when Christ starves at the door? Paupers should be fed rather than actors; drunkenness and pompous vestments are insane. Alcuin wrote more than once in this vein; even the abbot of Monkwearmouth-Jarrow was given a warning similar to Hygebald's (we know that his predecessor had actually sent abroad for a citharista). The archbishop of York was rebuked for parading around the countryside with so large a number of retainers that he was severely straining the resources of the monasteries that were obliged to put him up. [88] It is not certain that any of these men were actually guilty of such excesses, but it is revealing that these criticisms should have been voiced, even in general terms, suggesting as they do that, as well as indulging a taste for worldly literature, the Northumbrian Church had adopted worldly standards.

The connection is borne out by the very similar criticisms that we find earlier in the eighth century. The Council of Clovesho (746/7), whose opposition to secular rhythms of declamation I quoted earlier, also sees the danger in a wider context. Two of its clauses refer to the conduct of secular business by churchmen, two to the wearing of secular dress, two to associations with laymen, whether within the monastery or on lay ground. Two clauses condemn drunkenness in clerical ranks, and others castigate the patronage of "ludicrous arts" in monasteries: poets, harpists, musicians and the staging of horse-races on religious festivals. The decrees of this council appear to link up with a letter from St Boniface to Archbishop Cuthbert of Canterbury, (740-61), denouncing the various abuses in the English Church that had come to his ears. They included foolish customs in dress, clerics going hunting and carrying arms, and the episcopal custom of not only getting drunk oneself, but also of forcing others to do so, as, says the saint, neither the Franks, nor the Lombards, nor the Romans, nor the Greeks, but only the English do. [89]   As early as 679-80, a council in Rome on the affairs of the English Church prohibited the bearing of arms by clergymen, jokes, games and the patronage of harpists and symphoniaca; while Archbishop Theodore's Penitential actually begins with a complex statute on the rights, as well as the wrongs, of drunken vomiting among the clergy. [90]

Into this context I would like to bring a further piece of crucial evidence as to the state of affairs in the eighth-century English Church: the letter which Bede wrote in the last year of his life (734) to his pupil, Archbishop Egbert of York. Like Boniface and Alcuin, Bede was bitterly dissatisfied and it looks as though he was objecting to some of the same things. In particular, he felt that there were too few bishops and too many monasteries. The large size of the Northumbrian dioceses guaranteed a healthy episcopal bank-balance, but it did nothing to help the souls of the faithful, who saw their bishop once a year, if then. "Moreover it is rumoured abroad about certain bishops that they serve Christ in such a manner that they have with them no men of any religion or continence, but rather those who are given to laughter, jests, tales (fabulae), feasting, and the other attractions of a lax life, and who daily feed the stomach with feasts more than the soul on the heavenly sacrifice". The proliferation of monasteries was even more sinister since many of their inhabitants were monks only in name, officers of the king having secured chartered endowments from their grateful master, on the pretence that they were going to found monasteries, and then simply settling down as abbots in charge of a motley band of retainers. In addition - "a very ugly and unheard of spectacle" - the very same men were now occupied with wives and the procreation of children, to whom they hoped to pass on their foundation in hereditary right. [91]

Making every allowance for the highly-colored tone of this letter, there is no doubt that Bede's description is substantially accurate. The existence of "secular" monasteries is attested by a canon of the Council of Clovesho, which says that bishops should visit those monasteries - "if it be right to call them that" - which, because of human greed, cannot be forced to change to a Christian way of life, but have been held by presumptuous laymen. Archbishop Egbert's own Dialogue faces the question of how to partition a private monastery among the available heirs of the incumbent abbot. There is also the impressive evidence of extant charters and memoranda from the eighth and ninth centuries, revealing the hereditary principle at work in the houses of God.[92] As for allegedly worldly bishops: the whole career of Bishop Wilfrid, to which I shall return, is prima facie, an illustration of Bede's remarks.

Seventh-and eighth century sources thus seem to bring Alcuin's suspicions into focus. Englishmen in the Church were evidently listening to literature of the Ingeld type, and patronizing the harpists, whose stock in trade such stories were; they were also leading the same kind of splendid life as we find described in Beowulf. They had taken with some enthusiasm to the professions of monk and bishop, but without bothering to abandon traditional patterns of behavior. The prominence of drink is especially notable; more than most societies, the early Germans sought a social lubricant in alchohol.[93] I would suggest that, in these circumstances, the survival of a secular literary tradition is not so hard to understand.

The significance of these developments, and their relevance to the under-standing of Beowulf can be underlined by once again invoking the evidence from the continental church, that was used above to explain the hostility of Alcuin to secular literary tastes. Continental scholars have had more to say than their English counterparts about secular and hereditary monasteries; they have recognized in them an aspect of the regime of the Eigenkirche, or pri-vate church, and whatever the origins of the system, it is clear enough that there very often was a connection between the government of a monastery and the family of its founding abbot. Iona itself, where ten or eleven of the first thirteen abbots were members of St Columba's own branch of the Ui Neill dynasty, is a well-known Irish example. In Gaul, the important abbey of Nivelles was ruled, during the seventh century, by the widow, daughter and grand-daughter of Pippin of Landen, the ancestor of Charlemagne, and there is no reason to believe that this was very unusual.[94] Recent studies by German scholars have also focussed themselves upon the exalted status of early medi-eval bishops, and it is in these terms that Dr Mayr-Harting has explained Wilfrid's own attitude to his bishopric. Two famous cases which scandalized St Boniface in the mid eighth century were Milo, who was bishop both of Trier (in succession to his father) and of Rheims, but who was probably never or-dained, and who met his death at the tusks of a boar; and Gewilib of Mainz, another to inherit his see from his father, who was deposed only when he in-sisted upon personally avenging the latter's death in battle against the Saxons.[95]

The continental evidence also indicates the connection between these fea-tures of church government and the cultivation of secular literature. At St Gall, in the early tenth century, Ekkehard I, whose family was closely linked to the abbacy, wrote a version of the Waltharius (possibly not the one we possess) as a school exercise.[96] Archbishop Fulk of Rheims (881-95), of aristocratic origin and a very active bishop, could refer in the same breath to a letter of Gregory the Great on Frankish kingship, and to "Teutonic books about a cer-tain king Hermenric": the reference must be to the Gothic king of the fourth century, who subsequently acquired a grim reputation in Germanic saga (as it was certainly grim for Fulk), and who appears in Beowulf.[97] The house of Wildeshausen in Saxony was founded, in the mid ninth century, by Count Waldbert, grandson of the Duke Widukind, who had led the original Saxon resistance to Charlemagne's brutal conquest. Waldbert's charter specified that one of his bodily heirs should always be the _rector et gubernator_ of the abbey, and he became abbot himself. In that capacity, he commissioned Rudolf of Fulda to advertize his new foundation's most precious asset, the relics of St Alexander; and Rudolf, whose house of Fulda had, as we have seen, produced a manuscript of the _Hildebrandslied_ two generations earlier, thought it appropriate to preface his account with a long description of the virtues and victories of the pagan ancestors of the Saxons. Thus Wildeshausen had come to represent both family interests in the Christian future, and family traditions from the pagan past.[98] On the Continent as in England, therfore, where we find clerics living in some ways like heroes out of Germanic saga, we also find literature like _Beowulf_ being composed and appreciated.

As well as reinforcing the connection, moreover, continental scholarship offers a rationale for all these developments. An outstanding feature of European research since the war has been the generation of a new interest in the social and cultural history of the aristocracies that dominated barbarian Europe, and can be seen to have influenced the structure and civilization of the Church. The _Eigenkirche_ is now acknowledged to be, among other things, "a manifestation of Germanic _Adelsherrschaft_ in the...Middle Ages".[99] The social prominence of bishops can be understood as arising from their background as noblemen, and their sheer political and military importance in a developing feudal society.[100] The situation as regards the continental Church is summarized in lapidary terms by Professor Karl Schmid: "Adel, Kirche und Königsdienst bildeten die Lebensbereiche dieser Geistlichen". The thought-world of the early medieval clergy was dominated by conceptions of nobility, church, and service to the king, and, Professor Schmid could almost have added, in that order.[101] Naturally the characteristic literature of the early Germanic aristocracy is to be found written in these circles.

A similar trend has yet to establish itself in Anglo-Saxon studies. Much of the canonical and literary evidence from the seventh and eighth centuries that I have been quoting is traditionally taken as indicating the "decline" of the Anglo-Saxon Church, during and after the age of Bede. But it seems likely that British historians might have much to learn from the way in which the character of ecclesiastical life on the Continent has been related by European scholars to aristocratic customs and values, and that the results could have an important bearing on the way in which we understand the emergence and survival of an early English heroic literature. I therefore return to the "abuses" denounced by Bede, Boniface and Alcuin, partly in order to conclude investigations into the probable context of _Beowulf_, but also in the interests of taking a rather less negative view of eighth-century developments in the English church than has often been fashionable.

Probably the most important of these abuses was the family monastery – an institution perhaps better called by its Anglo-Saxon term, _minster_. Bede describes some at least of the recipients of bogus endowments as noblemen, and I think that we should accept that the foundations he so much disliked were essentially expressions of the understandable sense of kindred in the Anglo-Saxon upper classes. To associate the government of a religious house with the members of "Founder's Kin" came naturally to the Anglo-Saxons, as to many other societies, Celtic and Germanic. As the _Beowulf_ poet put it,

'sibb' aefre ne maeg wiht onwendan þam þe wel þenceð'.[102] It would probably
be wrong, moreover, to regard every such <u>minster</u> as a den of vice. No doubt
there were abuses, and "secular encroachment" could, in the long run, be
disastrous, as the tenth-century reformers asserted;[103] but several apparently dubious houses seem to have achieved high standards of Christian culture.
The early ninth-century <u>De Abbatibus</u> of Æthelwulf makes it quite clear that
this otherwise unknown Northumbrian <u>minster</u> was ruled more than once by members of the founder's family, yet the impression given in the poem is of a serious
and sober community. We hear of books illuminated and ornaments made,
while the poet's Latin, if not exactly a model of lucidity, is certainly not
unlearned.[104] It is likely that it was in the form of such foundations that
Christianity reached most parts of the British countryside, and its best monuments may be the surviving early Anglo-Saxon churches. Deerhurst in Gloucestershire is a particularly striking example of a church whose architecture
appears to have benefited in the early ninth century from the patronage of a
noble Mercian family, which treated minsters as part of the family property.[105]

Of particular importance for the student of <u>Beowulf</u>, which has so much to
say of kings and kingship, is the extent to which monasticism and royalty
were intergrated. Northumbria offers the examples of Coldingham, where we
find King Egfrith (671-85) being entertained to dinner by his aunt, the abbess,
and Whitby, a centre distinguished (unlike Coldingham) for its piety, where
three generations of Northumbrian princesses in the seventh century presided
over the burial-places of Edwin and Oswiu.[106] At the other end of the country,
in Kent, Eadberht Praen emerged briefly from holy orders in order to become
king (796-8).[107] But the best evidence comes from Mercia. Repton in Derbyshire was the burial-place of Mercian kings, was ruled by a Mercian princess,
and in the early eighth century was the first choice of retreat for the princely
Mercian would-be hermit, Guthlac, to whom we shall return. It has left us with
one of the most notable early Anglo-Saxon churches.[108] Peterborough in North-
amptonshire was clearly connected with the royal court: King Offa signed a
charter there in 765, and the abbot of Peterborough several times appears as
a witness in grants issued elsewhere during the second half of the eighth century.[109] Both Offa (757-96) and his scarcely less formidable successor,
Cenwulf (797-824) secured papal endorsement for their royal <u>Eigenkirchen</u>.
At Winchcombe, in Gloucestershire, Offa founded a convent (787), to which
Cenwulf added a <u>minster</u>. We know that the Mercian royal family archives
were kept there, and it was there that Cenwulf's son, Kenelm, was buried,
and rapidly developed a highly spurious cult.[110] In short, there was a close
connection between the Mercian dynasty, whose ancestors appear in <u>Beowulf</u>,
and which, incidentally, produced successive kings named Beornwulf and Wiglaf
in the early ninth century, and many of the most important religious foundations
of the time.[111] The association had some controversial results, and led to a
major crisis in relations between the archbishop of Canterbury and the Mercian
kings (816-25), but it is only to be expected that what was already characteristic of the Anglo-Saxon nobility should be practised on a regal scale by kings.[112]

To turn from the corrupt minsters of Bede's letter to its proud bishops
is to encounter immediately the towering figure of St Wilfrid, who was bishop
of various parts of Northumbria at various times between 665-709.[113] It is
certainly not difficult to find echoes of <u>Beowulf</u> in his outwardly worldly career:

the three days of feasting with the king to celebrate the dedication of his
church at Ripon; the heroic struggle on a Sussex beach where his 120 men
(no mean escort) were pitted against Gideon-like odds, and where they swore
to find, "either death with praise or life with triumph"; the famous deathbed
scene where Wilfrid distributed one portion of his extensive treasure to the
abbots of Hexham and Ripon, "so that they might be able to buy the friendship
of kings and bishops", and another to, "those who have labored and suffered
long exile with me, and to whom I have given no lands and estates."   It is not,
somehow, surprising to find Bede referring scornfully to drunkenness in
Wilfrid's household, or that the West Saxon scholar, Aldhelm, in a remarkable
letter, should have compared the obligations of Wilfrid's priestly following
with those of a secular retinue.[114] As in Frankish Gaul, such secularity is
best understood not as backsliding, but as a natural function of the place of
bishops in society. Some bishops, like Egbert himself, were the brothers
and uncles of kings; bishops went to war in England, as in Gaul, and are
found in the casualty lists of the Anglo-Saxon Chronicle. In the laws of
AEthelberht of Kent, from the very earliest years of Anglo-Saxon Christianity,
a bishop's property was more generously assessed for compensation than a
king's.[115] Bishops like this could no more be expected not to cut a splendid
figure for Christ, than can their modern counterparts be expected to avoid
television. Wilfrid himself was actually far from worldly in his personal life;
a tireless missionary as well as a builder, a patron of the poor and of St Peter
(each of whom also received a share of his treasure), he was the greatest,
all things considered, of the early Anglo-Saxon saints. He channelled the
values of the aristocracy from which he came into the service of God, and
God's servants had cause to be grateful. Even lesser figures like Archbishop
Eanbald of York, berated by Alcuin for his extravagant following, may at least be
understood, so long as we remember the prestige which, in a barbarian society,
a bishop automatically possessed.

To concentrate simply upon what Christianity lost by its adoption in the
aristocratic world of the barbarian West is also to ignore some real gains.
The most obvious of these is Anglo-Saxon religious poetry. The Dream of the
Rood is now seen as more than just a reflection of the comitatus ethic, but it
is nonetheless from that ethic that the poem draws so much of its great power.[116]
Andreas is a much less distinguished product of the same tradition, but it seems
to have been influenced by the vocabulary, and even the theme, of Beowulf itself.[117] The point that needs emphasis is that this is more than just a literary
continuity; the miracle of Cædmon and the opinions of Bede notwithstanding,
the idiom of early English Christian poetry is aristocratic, and testifies to
the social ambience of Anglo-Saxon Christianity, as much as it does to the
range of its literary and patristic learning. The usual poetic term for God,
Dryhten, is still used in Beowulf, and in the early Kentish laws, for a secular
lord, and originated in a word for the military leader of a comitatus.[118]

An equal, if less obvious gain is the famous style of manuscript illumination which is to be found in the Lindisfarne Gospels. Traditionally, the origins of
of the style were ascribed to external influences. But brilliant studies by
Dr Bruce Mitford have now demonstrated that the artist, abbot Eadfrith (c.
698), was indebted not only for his artistic motifs, but also for his very techniques, to the elaborate skills and rich repertoire of Celtic and Germanic

metal-workers.[119] Again, there is a link with Beowulf, which is itself such powerful evidence of the aristocratic taste for sophisticated treasures. St Boniface himself made the point clear when he wrote home for, "the letters of St Peter, my lord, written in letters of gold, in order to secure honor and reverence for the Holy Scriptures when they are preached before the eyes of the carnal".[120] What had once distinguished a proud and wealthy warrior was now to glorify Christ.

I would like to make the same sort of point about aspects of Anglo-Saxon hagiography. Professor Whitelock and Dr Mayr-Harting have both noticed the suggestive parallels between Beowulf and the eighth-century Life of the Mercian royal saint, Guthlac (d. 716), by Felix of Crowland.[121] What the overlap seems to amount to is that Guthlac's heroic sanctity is being articulated in terms that would have been familiar to an audience of Beowulf. Felix follows his Mediterranean model, Athanasius' Life of Anthony, (251-356) fairly closely, but there are significant shifts of emphasis. The monstrous is more to the fore. Guthlac's choice of hermitage, on the spot that would later become Crowland abbey, was actually dictated by the terrors that he could anticipate there; Anthony's torments were merely the consequences of the saint's choice. Both saints occupy tombs, but Guthlac's is reminiscent of that which Beowulf's dragon inhabited, and it is situated, like Grendel's abode, in a marshy wilderness. Both saints are haunted by creatures of a relatively "normal" type (though there is no croaking raven in Athanasius), but what had been a preliminary, if painful, whipping in Athanasius, becomes, in Felix, an additional raid by an outlandish menagerie, whose physical characteristics permit Felix to show off his Hesperic vocabulary in all its glory. Anthony had promised that demons could take the form not only of reptiles and giants, but also of troops of soldiers; for Guthlac, a chieftain who had been in exile a-mong the Welsh in his warlike youth, it was appropriate that the demons who tossed him on ghostly spears should have British accents.[122] Rather like the Irish St Brendan, therefore, Guthlac is a saintly hero in something of a tradi-tional secular mould. There is a further point here. St Guthlac, like St Wilfrid, belongs to a class of saint that is now known to German scholars as Adelsheilige (aristocratic saint). We are told about his distinguished family ancestry, and about his lively career in the world before conversion. He is three times brought into contact with his cousin, AEthelbald, the future king of the Mercians and Bretwalda (716-57). These are particular characteris-tics of a new hagiographical fashion in the seventh century, and one which also emphasized, as in Wilfrid's case, if not in Guthlac's, the public splendor of the saint.[123] The fashion seems to arise, not from following any particular model, Mediterranean or Frankish, but simply from writing hagiography in a barbarian environment. This is literature of the taste of a Germanic aristoc-racy, and thus reflecting the social origins not only of Guthlac himself, but also of the communities for whom his deeds were recorded.

One final aspect of early English Christian culture is neither a "gain" nor a "loss", but is worth considering in this context. Most of the Anglo-Saxon royal genealogies trace the various English dynasties back to Woden, whom there is some justification for regarding as the God of the warband. Stenton wrote of, "the aristocratic convention which regarded Woden as the ancestor of most English kings".[124] The genealogies also contain other memorable names of even greater significance for our purposes: Sceaf, Scyld, Beaw,

Heremod, Eormanric, Offa of Angle, Finn and Hwala; the first seven appear in <u>Beowulf</u> (some prominently), and the last four appear in <u>Widsith.</u> As Kenneth Sisam demonstrated, these lists of names are largely fraudulent as real family history, but social anthropologists have taught us that, even when far from reliable as historical fact , genealogies nevertheless express what societies choose to believe, even need to believe, about their past. Seen in this light, the Anglo-Saxon genealogies represent early English society's willingness, and indeed determination, to reach back into the pagan past in order to lend added distinction to the ancestry of its kings. It then becomes especially important that Sisam also demonstrated that most of the genealogies that we have must have been literate products, put together as a body at the end of the eighth century. Their 'educated' character is further underlined by the appearance of Caesar in the East Anglian genealogy, and of the patriachs from Noah back to Adam in the West Saxon.[125] What the Anglo-Saxon royal genealogies thus suggest is that the need for a heroic past was still felt, even in educated, and thus presumably clerical, circles, 150 years after the conversion. Just as the poetic techniques of heroic verse survived, so too did the memory of the heroes themselves and in a context such as to argue their continuing importance. In fact, Alcuin himself, in a remarkable letter to the men of Kent, highlighted the surviving relevance of heroic progenitors: he laments the decline of the ancient English dynasties, urges the Kentings to pick a noble leader, and comments: " The more obscure the origin [of kings] the more they lack valor". [126]

This survey of the character of the early English Church and its culture leads to two conclusions. In the first place, most, if not all, of the features that I have described are perfectly well-known, but they are not usually placed side by side. To me, they all seem to be interrelated. Of course, I do not suggest that Guthlac would have approved of every noble monk, or that Wilfrid could have endorsed all worldly bishops. What I do suggest is that they are all aspects of the same essential truth: the aristocratic environment of early English Christianity. I am not sure that a civilization could have spawned so much that we admire without also giving rise to what we have usually followed Bede in regarding as degenerate. I am sure that very little of the spectacular cultural achievement of the so-called Northumbrian Renaissance would have been possible without the enormous wealth which kings and noblemen brought with them into the Church. If, then, historians are to continue to dismiss developments in the English Church in the eighth century as evidence of decline, they ought perhaps to relect upon what they are throwing out with the bath-water. But in any case talk of decline misses the point, and ignores elementary facts of early medieval life. When the aristocracies of the barbarian West became Christian, they did not, and they could not, lose their awareness of being aristocracies, and this is as true of churchmen as of laymen. If we start from this point, the abuses denounced by the Church Fathers may legitimately be seen as evidence, not of Christianity's failure but of one of its greatest triumphs: it had been successfully assimilated by a warrior nobility, which had no intention of abandoning its culture, or seriously changing its way of life, but which was willing to throw its traditions, customs, tastes and loyalties into the articulation of the new faith, and whose persisting 'secularity' was an important condition of the richness of early English Christian civilization. Quite simply, the Anglo-Saxon Church became part of the Establishment.

Second, though my argument in this paper has taken us a long way from the familiar pastures of Beowulf criticism, it does seem to have yielded something like what we were looking for: a social and cultural context for the composition of heroic literature. It is clear from what the conciliar canons say about secular dress and armed clergy, for example, and it is clear, too, from what can find out about the history of the early Anglo-Saxon minster and about English bishops of the period that the crucial line between clerical and lay, the conventional distinction between ascetic and secular standards, had become blurred at a number of points, and especially, it may be noted, in the area around the king.[127] It is also clear that the Anglo-Saxon Church took over many of the tastes and interests of the secular world, whether for new purposes, as in illumination, hagiography of Christian poetry, or for old, as in genealogies. I can perhaps best put the conclusion in the form of a question. Does the composition by a literate poet, who was probably, therefore, a cleric, of a great secular poem about the pagan kings of the past still seem anomalous in a society where monasteries function partly as the royal court, and partly as royal family property, where bishops go to war, where Gospel-books have begun to look like secular treasures, and where the adventures of saints resemble so closely those of heroes? Is Beowulf an unthinkable product for a monastic scriptorium, when not only Alcuin, but also councils of the Church talk of drunkenness, banquets and the patronage of harpists in clerical environments; when the Mercian royal house, with whom many Beowulf critics have very reasonably felt that the poem may have a connection, was treating its religious foundations as a part of its hereditas? I began this paper by accepting the view that Beowulf was par excellence literature of the aristocracy, and by suggesting that its primary value to the historian was that it opened a window onto the otherwise closed and unknown thought-world of the Anglo-Saxon warrior-classes. We have now seen other evidence that the early English Church was, in a sense, dominated by aristocratic values itself. I conclude that Beowulf is a very intelligible product of such a culture, and that the poem does indeed constitute vital evidence for what was involved in the conversion of the Anglo-Saxon aristocracy.

V

Bede

The argument adopted in this paper leaves me with a final problem. The quest for "alternative perspectives" on the Age of Bede is perhaps characteristic of modern studies. But if one is to argue that Beowulf is in some ways a better symbol of what was involved in the conversion of the Anglo-Saxon aristocracy than Bede, one needs a stronger justification than intellectual fashion. It is necessary to show not only that Beowulf may well have been representative, at least in part, but also that Bede is himself, in some respects, an anomaly. And if Bede is to be regarded as an anomaly, he is, like Beowulf, an anomaly that requires explanation.

Thanks to the modern tendency to see Bede against the background of European historiography in the early Middle Ages, it is in fact possible to suggest that he is a rather isolated figure, and, once again, the argument of this paper can be clarified by giving it a European dimension. Gregory of Tours, the sixth-century historian of the Franks, was certainly known to Bede, and he wrote what is, all in all, a very different book from the Ecclesiastical History. Most of Gregory's ten books were devoted to the period of his own active life as bishop of Tours (573-91), and no small part of them was taken up with vigorous denunciations. As has been observed, this is in marked contrast to Bede's five books, of which only one covers the forty-five years of his own mature life, while the previous ninety are spread over four, and in which Bede veils his dissatisfaction by discreet hints and silences.[128] Another who might be compared with Bede though writing after his day, is the historian of the Lombards, Paul the Deacon, (fl. 774-99). Not only does Paul tell some rousing stories of the secular life (usually without censure); he also says very little at all about his people's religious history, whereas he does say a lot about their pre-Christian past. He even records one story in which the Lombards gained both their name of "Long-beards", and victory over the hated Vandals, under the auspices of Woden, and although he calls the story ridiculous he does report it.[129] Bede, of course, is almost totally silent on the pre-Christian achievements of the Anglo-Saxons, and conversion is the dominant motif of the whole History. Finally, another later historian much more like Paul than Bede was Widukind, the historian of the continental Saxons (c. 968). We hear so much in his early chapters about his people's heathen history, that Professor Karl Hauck has recently been able to reconstruct the pagan iconography of the Wesermund bracteates on the basis of Widukind's account; but the conversion of the Saxons, perhaps too painfully associated with memories of Frankish conquest, is passed over in a short chapter.[130]

I cite these continental parallels, partly to show that Bede might have written quite another sort of book, without even abandoning the genre of early medieval historiography, but also because I have the impression that, if he had, the emergence of Beowulf would have been easier to understand. The two important points are these: first, the continental historians give a clear impression of a Christianity that was recognizably barbarian, and do not encourage illusions about the nature of contemporary society. It was the startling difference in tone between the English historian and his continental counterparts that encouraged R.W. Chambers to contrast the "barbarous" and "sordid" Franks and Lombards, "quarelling over the loot of the Roman Empire, until they lost whatever barbaric virtues they had formerly possessed when they lived in the more austere surroundings of their native forests and swamps", with the early English who had not yet been brought into contaminating contact with the degenerate world of decaying Rome.[131] Second, Paul and Widukind, even Gregory, permit no reader to form the impression that their peoples had forgotten their ancestors.[132] On both counts, it looks as though conversion on the Continent had made comparatively little difference, at least initially. This is scarcely the view that one is encouraged to take by Bede. Apart from the famous passage on the tribal origins of the Angles, Saxons and Jutes, a few shards of Kentish tradition, and a snippet of Northumbrian tribal pride concerning the deeds of King AEthelfrith, conversion for Bede is where the story of the Anglo-Saxons begins and thereafter it is a story of saints, not sinners.[133] We thus miss, in the Ecclesiastical History at least, any extent to which the Anglo-Saxons remained tied, by custom or memory, to their past, and with it we miss the context that I have suggested for Beowulf. So why is Bede so different from continental members of the tradition in which he wrote?

We must recognize, first, that he was a fundamentalist. Bede has inspired the affection of his readers as few other historians have, but there is something in him of the intellectual wolf in sheep's clothing. He was capable of a degree of scholarly ruthlessness which it is not easy to parallel even in his acknowledged disciple, Alcuin. In this context, it is obviously relevant to to remind oneself of Bede's attitude to the two principles which probably explain Alcuin's hostility to songs about Ingeld. Those from whom Bede learned most, Jerome, Augustine and Gregory the Great, never shook off their debt to the Latin grammarian's skills, and thus sought to find a use for the literary legacy of antiquity. Bede, however, produced a grammar, in which nearly all illustrations of stylistic points come from the Bible, and in which none come from secular literature; it has now been seriously doubted whether he had even read Vergil.[134] So far as one can see from his commentaries, moreover, Bede accepted the full implications of the orthodox view that the unbaptized would probably not be saved. Where Augustine, therefore, had publicly debunked the noble pagans of Rome, Bede turned upon the heroes of the English pre-Christian past his unrivalled capacity for withering silence.[135] Bede undoubtedly possessed the great teacher's gift of flexibility, and in this respect his reputation for gentleness is abundantly justified. But he also had the teacher's sense of the irrelevant. The two main keynotes of the prefaces to his commentaries are the desire to teach his "lazy" fellow-countrymen the lessons that he considered urgently necessary, and the determination to stick closely to the vestigia patrum. When Bede came to write his Ecclesiastical History, we may guess from the tone of the last chapter, and we know from the Letter to Egbert, that he had not lost his sense of urgency as he grew old, and his commitment to the salvation of the Anglo-Saxons was as strong as it had been when he wrote about the Bible.[136] In these circumstances, a thinker as loyal to the principles of Latin Christianity as Bede was unlikely to waste time on telling cheerful stories about the pagan past. There are thus no sagas in Bede, as there are in Paul the Deacon and in Widukind, and this is a vital reason why modern historians do not usually recognize the world of saga in Bede's Britain.

There are others. Bede's is, first and foremost, an ecclesiastical history, and, as the example of his grammatical work shows, Bede was outstanding for his capacity to remain faithful to the rules of a genre. Where Paul and Widukind were later exposed to the influence of the "secular" tradition, as mediated above all by classical historiography, Bede is closer to the model established by Eusebius in the early fourth century than any such writer since Eusebius himself, and this certainly helps to explain his overwhelming preoccupation with the process of conversion, and the affairs of the Church.[137] Yet, even by these standards, Bede's work has peculiarities, and chief among these is his reluctance to express criticism. If Bede had followed Gregory of Tours or the mid sixth-century Welsh prophet, Gildas, (whose work he knew well, and who was the only historian other than himself to whom he gave the label historicus), into expressing in public the criticisms that we know him to have voiced in private, we should almost certainly have formed a very different impression of the history of early English Christianity. But Bede believed that it was wrong to criticize priests (he will mention that a bishop bought his see without a word of censure); instead, his method was to highlight the good example, by way of implied contrast, and in a famous passage, he compares the labours of Aidan and his disciples with the segnitia temporis nostri. For all that he wrote in his preface that men learn both by good and by bad example, we hear much more about the former than the latter.[138]

Here too it seems possible that we might find an explanation in Bede's patristic background. The tradition of teaching to which Bede belonged was above all that of Gregory the Great, as laid down in his Dialogues and in his Pastoral Care. One of the main principles of this tradition was that much could be done, especially for the simpler kind of audience, by the force of personal example, or by describing the lives of holy men; it was a specifically monastic inheritance. "The Lives of Saints are often more effective than mere instruction for inspiring us to love heaven as our home", wrote Gregory in the preface to his Dialogues. In the Pastoral Care he taught that a preacher who actually practices what he preaches will make a much bigger impression, than one who merely harangues his congregations, and, on the other hand, no amount of eloquence will undo the bad effects of the failure to set a good example. "There are those who investigate spiritual precepts with cunning care, but what they penetrate in their understanding, they trample upon in their lives... Whence it happens that, when the shepherd walks through steep places, the flock follows to the precipice..."[139] Bede could thus learn from his principal mentor that what a relatively unsophisticated audience needed was the example of lives led by holy men; what they did not need was familiarity with bad men, or even with those good men whose careers had dubious features - for that would be to lead the sheep to the precipice.

I suggest that this is the reason for the otherwise rather surprising balance of the Ecclesiastical History, which Mr Campbell has well described as a "gallery of good examples".[140] Bede was trying to encourage imitation and that was a basic reason why he wrote, but he was afraid that his flock might follow the wrong shepherd. Wilfrid could be praised for his many achievements, but to describe his career in full might run the risk of setting up a flawed model, and it was better to concentrate on the virtues and miracles of those with a more pristine public image, such as Aidan or Cuthbert. Bede, therefore, differed from Gildas not only in accuracy or good sense, but also in his strong sense that history is properly about holy men; and where Gregory of Tours had written copiously about the sins of the present, Bede wrote for preference about the glories of the past. English history, unlike Frankish, began not with another, "melancholy catalogue of the vices and follies of mankind", but with a vision of a new apostolic age. Among the consequences of this gratifying fact is the one that has most concerned me in this paper: we have been half-blind to the real character of the context from which Beowulf probably emerged, and students of the poem have been misled in two opposite directions, concluding either, with Chadwick, that the earliest English epic is largely heathen, despite its strident monotheism, or with Chambers that it is unimpeachably Christian, despite its unconcealed secularity.

If there is much in patristic traditions that will explain the quality of "other-wordliness" in Bede's most famous book, it might also be possible to offer a final explanation along rather different lines. We are nowadays taught to see historians against their social and cultural background, and, in view of the central arguments of this paper, it is perhaps significant that, socially speaking, Bede was without a background. The only thing he ever says about his kindred is that they surrendered him at the age of seven to Benedict Biscop, and thenceforward, as he says in his fine homily on its founder, his kindred was the spiritual family to which he belonged. Bede could have been a nobleman himself, but, if so, he had managed to forget it. There is, perhaps, a suggestive contrast here both with some of the other leading figures of early Anglo-Saxon Christianity, and with the continental historians whom I have mentioned. Wilfrid, for instance, was already thirteen when he went to Lindisfarne, and had spent several years waiting on the guests in his father's aristocratic household. Guthlac spent the nine years before his admission to Repton at the age of twenty-four in a characteristically aristocratic career of rapine. Of Cuthbert's career, we know little, but we do know that he had served in an army.[141] I would be inclinded to see a connection between these environments and what we have seen of Christian culture at Wilfrid's Hexham, Guthlac's Crowland and Cuthbert's Lindisfarne. Similarly, there is no doubting the aristocratic background of Paul the Deacon, and although Widukind's biography is as obscure as Bede's, he never made any secret of his sympathy for the Saxon nobility, and bore a name that was illustrious in Saxon tradition. Gregory of Tours was a Roman nobleman, and not a barbarian, so that rather different considerations apply; nevertheless, his membership of a family of many bishops to some extent committed him to a particular tradition of public service, even if it was not necessarily respnsible for the interest in the Frankish past which he undoubtedly possessed.[142] By contrast, Bede's personal history cut him off from contemporary aristocratic society and its values, and buried him, from boyhood, in a world of books.

Bede, of course, was not the only oblate of the period, but there is the further consideration that, as I have tried to argue elsewhere, Monkwearmouth-Jarrow probably was rather an extraordinary place to be growing up in the later seventh century. To revert to the "norms" that we considered earlier: the lives of Monkwearmouth-Jarrow's abbots share relatively few features of the Adelsheiliger tradition; they say nothing much about family backgrounds, and they are politically "neutral", showing neither a hostile, nor a particularly sympathetic, attitude towards kings.[143] Again, where Wilfrid became a great bishop, and passed his monastic foundations on to his own kinsmen, like so many others in Britain and abroad, Biscop never became a bishop at all, and spent much of his last hours adjuring his monks that on no account was he to be succeeded by a relative; his successor inherited this anxiety.[144] And whereas the Hiberno-Saxon style of illumination is now recognized to be unthinkable without its background in traditional insular metal-work, the greatest of Monkwearmouth-Jarrow's manuscripts, the Codex Amiatinus, which was almost precisely contemporary with the Lindisfarne Gospels, and which was being written while Bede was growing up in the community, seems to strain every nerve in order to escape from its contemporary environment. Its handwriting is a variant of Italian uncial, its text and decoration are distinct, as in the Late Antique tradition, and its art, while betraying indications of insular technique, strives to reproduce the unfamiliar effects of a Mediterranean original: it is a book with its horizons beyond the Alps, and not in barbarian Northumbria.[145] I am not concerned here with how and why Biscop came to set up on Northumbrian soil an island of Mediterranean culture that was lapped, but not at first flooded, by the values of the northern world outside its harbors. What is important is the way that his community seems to anticipate and explain the views of its greatest son. The angry author of the Letter to Egbert is easily recognizable in the pupil of a founder with such strong views on the succession of abbots. Bede's failure, compared to Eddius, to reflect the "thought-world" of the barbarian nobility is intelligible in a member of a community where the court is not known to have feasted for days and nights on end, and where Ceolfrith fought to discipline restless aristocrats.[146] A bible which was for many centuries thought to be an Italian book may help to explain how it was that Bede began with twenty-two chapters on Roman Britain, then utterly ignored the history of his own people in the sixth century before bringing St Augustine to Kent in the footsteps of Julius Caesar. Biscop's library which Professor Laistner did so much to illuminate, was the making of Bede's learning. I would further suggest that though himself a nobleman, Biscop's "ultramontanism" helped to isolate Bede from the aristocratic culture of contemporary Christianity in England, when I have tried to show that the past was remembered in legend as in custom and taste.

Anomaly is much too strong a term for Bede, but it is not, after all, entirely unreasonable to see him as standing apart from the world he wrote about. The Bible was naturally regarded as the most important of all histories in the Middle Ages, and the Old Testament especially offered all early medieval historians the image of a recorder of events who was also their critic in God's name. Alienation is thus, to some extent, a built-in condition of historical writing throughout the period, and its potential is already revealed by the fact that a "zone of silence" between the specifically ecclesiastical, and the pagan or merely secular, traditions existed as early as the fourth century. Even so, Bede was the first major historian to write as a monk, and, in view of the circumstances of his life, it is not surprising that no other historical masterpiece of the Middle Ages so nearly justifies the description, "other-worldly."[147] Again, few early medieval historians were only historians; most had performed in other genres, and regularly imported features of their alternative style into their historical writings. But Bede was the only important barbarian historian who was also a Father of the Church in his own right, and, even by patristic standards, his commitment to the spreading of the Gospel was unusally strong (he never had to face the live problems of running a diocese). Bede's whole training made him a commentator upon, rather than a recorder of, events and his is thus understandably one of the most morally didactic histories of the whole medieval period, if also one of the most gracefully expressed.[148] If Bede is viewed in this sort of perspective, the differences between his Ecclesastical History and its continental counterparts fall into place, and the gulf which separates it from the major vernacular monument of early English literature may be understood.

VI

Conclusions

The conclusions to which the arguments of this paper point can best be grouped under the three main heads of the topics in its title. First, as regards

<u>Beowulf</u>: historicism can debilitate the study of literature when it seeks to dictate to critics in the name of historical reality, and I am not here concerned to limit the range of subjective reaction which is the critic's legitimate, indeed necessary, business.   Nevertheless, nearly all literary criticism depends in part upon historical assumptions, and it cannot be wrong for historians to test the strength of these foundations.   The historical examination of early medieval Christian culture is a better method, in my view, of deciding between alternative interpretations of <u>Beowulf</u> than analogy with the plays of Shakespeare.

I would suggest, therefore, that the right approach to the problem of the Christianity of <u>Beowulf</u> is indicated by two types of historical evidence.   In the first place, Alcuin's letter to Hygebald probably does hold an important clue, in that it teaches us to look not to the <u>principles</u>, but to the social and cultural <u>milieu</u> of early English Christianity, if we are to understand the literate composition of heroic literature among the Anglo-Saxons.   Given their context in early medieval canon law and theology, Alcuin's remarks argue that Chadwick was probably right to feel that a clerical pen had no business with such material as <u>Beowulf</u>, wherever it was plied.   On the other hand, both Alcuin and the conciliar canons indicate that traditional literary tastes did survive in ecclesiastical, even monastic, circles, and the context in this instance indicates that this was because of the domination of the church by the values of the barbarian aristocracy.   There is an analogy here with the older and larger debate about Christianity and the classics.   Few would nowadays make the mistake of divorcing the Church Fathers altogether from the literary legacy of antiquity, but the fact is that their published attitude towards it was seldom sympathetic and often hostile.   If we are to understand the survival of the classical tradition, we need to appreciate the extent to which, in a Christian culture that was more or less created in Latin, traditional literature remained indispensable equipment for an educated man.   Similarly, although the "party-line" of the western Fathers was, if anything, even less sympathetic to secular literature in the vernacular, the heroic style did survive, essentially because the early medieval church was an <u>Adelskirche</u>.   This sort of solution by no means excludes the possibility of Irish influence upon the genesis of <u>Beowulf</u>.   The celebration of their ancestors, real or mythical, must have come naturally to barbarian noblemen, even after their conversion, but the more optimistic Irish attitude to the fate of the unbaptized could have contributed to it, by removing a potential source of discouragement.   Indeed, the Irish sense of the continuing importance of the pre-Christian past may have been one crucial reason for their massive success as missionaries with Germanic aristocracies.[149]

Second, the same sort of point is made by the evidence of manuscript survival.   On the one hand, very little such literature as <u>Beowulf</u>, <u>Waldhere</u> and <u>Finnsburh</u> has survived from early medieval Europe.   Those to whom <u>Beowulf</u> has seemed an unexceptionable product of Christian orthodoxy need to say <u>why</u> only a single copy has survived, in an unpromising manuscript context, and why analogous material is so hard to find.   On the other hand some fragments of Germanic tradition did find their way onto parchment in an age of "restricted literacy", and this must be explained by those to whom <u>Beowulf</u> has seemed to have nothing to do with Christianity.   The suggestion in this paper is that, given the society and culture of the early medieval Church, the survival of a secular tradition is not at all surprising, and it is unnecessary to challenge the many indications that early Anglo-Saxon literacy was effectively a clerical monopoly in order to account for it. But, given also that orthodox opinion should have been unfavorable to the cultivation of this sort of literature, it is not surprising that Beowulf barely survived the English "Carolingian Renaissance" of the mid tenth century, just as the Hildebrandslied barely survived the Frankish; and critics should not be ashamed of their modern conviction that the poem is a masterpiece, merely because of its precarious preservation.

The question, "is Beowulf Christian?" engages too many of the personal convictions of critics ever to evoke agreement upon a wide scale. The ambivalences of the poem are too obvious, and its moral quality too much at variance with what is today understood to be Christianity. But if Alcuin would probably not have thought the English epic Christian, a corollary of my argument is that modern critics have the option of disagreeing, if they wish. The Christian Church in the sixth to ninth centuries directly challenged the old pagan gods, and officially discouraged nostalgia, but it presented less of a threat to the heroic ethos than modern Christians might expect. Much of what barbarians had always chosen to believe and practise could be confirmed out of the Old Testament, if not the New, the Apocrypha if not the Old Testament.[150] Poets, moreover, usually write not about what they merely know, but about what captivates their imagination, and the Beowulf poet was not the only barbarian Christian to be especially interested in a limited, if also quite recherché, portion of Judaeo-Christian revelation. Two of the earliest pieces of Old High German verse, the Wessobrunner Gabet and the Muspilli, concern respectively the creation and the judgement. St Columba, in his Altus Prosator expressed a lively interest in the monsters of Scripture, both giants and dragons, and though he does mention the Trinity, he was scarcely more interested than the Beowulf poet in Christ as Man and Redeemer. It has recently been suggested that Beowulf reads like the work of an Arian, and although there are almost insuperable objections to the theory of Arian influence, the suggestion does remind us that a sizeable proportion of the early Germanic peoples long remained faithful to a doctrinal system in which the role of God the Son was played down by comparison with that of God the Father.[151] In these circumstances, it is probably a misuse of terminology to call the virtues of the heroes of Germanic literature pagan; and it seems a pity to take as evidence of superficial Christianity, or of lack of interest in the Faith, what actually tells us something more interesting, and more moving: the sort of impact that Christian revelation made in its new cultural environment. In Beowulf, the poet's concern was probably not with the inculcation of Christian principles, but we shall massively increase the bulk of 'pagan' English literature if all that we are prepared to call Christian is Paradise Lost or Pilgrim's Progress.

From Beowulf, I turn to the conversion of the Anglo-Saxon aristocracy. European historians of religious change are heirs to a particular tradition of ecclesiastical historiography, which is essentially that of the New Testament, and because Bede's is the greatest of all ecclesiastical histories, English historians have been particularly exposed to it; but the inheritance includes certain critical reflexes which are handicaps to historical understanding of the process. Above all, we have far too concrete a conception of the process of conversion. Dominated by the awe-inspiring assertion that a man may, and

65

indeed must, be born again, historians of conversion think instinctively of the wholesale exchange of one set of values for another; there is an underlying assumption that the set of values abandoned for the Faith were as comprehensive and coherent as is Christianity itself, and these values are given the generic label of 'paganism'. As a result, we describe as survivals of 'paganism' what may not have very much to do with heathen cult at all, and what are often only indications that society had failed to remake itself completely. Historians have, of course, always been aware that all is usually not renewed in the font, but they make the mistake of attributing too much of a religious significance to what survives of the Old Adam. The language of poetry and the process of blood-feud are two aspects of post-conversion life in Britain which have been adduced as evidence of lingering 'paganism', and the criticism of Beowulf has suffered on both counts.

But it is the heroic literature of the Anglo-Saxons that actually enables us to make the necessary distinctions, and this is perhaps the most important implication of the study of Beowulf for the historian of the conversion of the early English nobility. Seen in the wider context of vernacular culture in the early medieval West, Beowulf is really impressive evidence for the totality of the Anglo Saxon conversion. Vast reserves of intellectual energy have been devoted to threshing the poem for gains of authentic pagan belief, but it must be admitted that the harvest has been meagre. The poet may have known that his heroes were pagans, but he did not know much about paganism. Aspects of his vocabulary have numinous associations which owe little to the Mediterranean, but there is a striking contrast between this situation and that revealed by the equivalent literatures of the Irish and Old Norse. Pagan deities do not often figure as dramatis personae in the Irish sagas, but scholars have never had much difficulty in detecting the ample evidence of the old Celtic religion beneath their surface.[152] Even the evidence of the Irish sagas, however, pales into insignificance beside that of the Norse, where we find exactly what we do not find in Beowulf, namely the gods of the Germanic Pantheon on active service. We have been told that Anglo-Saxon poetry is "steeped" in pre-Christian religion, but it is important not to confuse idiom with content or ethics with faith.[153] On the contrary, the unqualified monotheism of Beowulf and Waldhere is of a piece with the Anglo-Saxon evidence as a whole. We know remarkably little about early English heathenism, and although the evidence of conciliar canons, archaeology and even place-names suggest that ancient superstitions lingered in the countryside, the literature is among other indications that, by the eighth century at least, the Anglo-Saxon nobility was suffering from what amounts, by Celtic or Scandinavian standards, to collective religious amnesia.[154] Instead of trying to eke out what scraps of evidence we have with the aid of Scandinavian analogies, historians would do better, I suggest, to ask why the material is so sparse. Why, for instance, is there no English syncretistic tradition? Why are the Anglian stone crosses of the pre-Viking age so unlike the Gosforth cross, with its remarkable blend of Norse creation and Christian crucifixion?

But the disappearance of pagan Germanic gods is not at all the same thing as the disappearance of pagan Germanic heroes, or of the heroic way of life with which they were associated, and though the distinction is blurred by Bede, it is established by Beowulf. The baffling discrepancy in the poem

66

between pagan practice and Christian sentiment is decisive evidence that, although the Anglo-Saxon aristocracy was willing to accept a new God, it was not prepared to jettison the memory or the example of those who had worshipped the old. Aristocracies in these circumstances very rarely are. As anthropological study of societies not dissimilar from the Anglo-Saxons has shown, memories of the past and cultural values are often inseparable. Literature like Beowulf was important to Anglo-Saxon noblemen not because these Scandinavian tales described any part of their real past (so far as we know) but because they encapsulated, and indeed identified, the social and cultural values of the class. We shall fail to understand the persistence of the 'heroic code', unless we can appreciate its real social relevance to a society where courage, loyalty and generosity were fundamental conditions of a nobleman's way of life.[155] Heroic stories were more than just entertainment. To abandon them would have jeopardized the social consciousness of a whole warrior-class.

Like the disappearance of heathenism, the surviving importance of a heroic past is also indicated by other types of evidence. The Anglo-Saxon genealogies, as we have seen, invoke heroes from the continental tradition, as well as Woden (in a "euphemerized" form) in an effort to boost the prestige of kingship.[156] To judge by the manuscript evidence, the West Saxons, like some continental peoples, associated the deeds of their forebears with their ancestral laws.[157] As has always been recognized, the warrior ethic of the late-tenth-century Battle of Maldon is still that of the heroic comitatus, and even though its heroes are "national," not cosmopolitan figures, we are still some way short of the more obviously patriotic and crusading overtones of the Song of Roland.[158]

Now Tolkien saw, more clearly than any before him, that Beowulf is a poem abou about the past, and is most remarkable for the intensity of its feeling about the past. If we can grasp the strength of the social and cultural ties that bind any nobility to its past, we are a long way towards understanding the ambivalence, the mingled pride and sorrow, with which the poet looks back upon his heroes. As a member of the warrior-classes himself, the poet must have admired — perhaps he even imitated — the virtues in which his work glorifies. As a Christian, he knew, and perhaps he lamented, that heroic virtues are not enough. It is not surprising that the ethical quality of Beowulf should have seemed to so many to pull in two different directions at once. To me, the loftiness of tone which transcends the merely secular in the poem is a legacy neither of Christianity nor paganism; it springs from a fundamental tension within the poet's soul.

The long and short of it is that modern historians can afford to distinguish, even if Bede, Boniface and Alcuin could not, between the essentials of pagan belief, and the secular values of pre-Christian society. It is a basic error to confuse a continuity in depth between clerical and secular standards with a linear continuity between paganism and Christianity. The main lesson of the "alternative perspective" furnished by vernacular literature for the student of Bede and his England is that, to some extent, we need to replace the constricted range of vision that is characteristic of ecclesiastical history by an imaginative model of the Anglo-Saxon conversion similar to that supplied by Paul the Deacon for the Lombards or Widukind for the Saxons. The coming of Christianity displaced the old Gods, and diverted traditional values into new pastures, but it did not change those values. The conversion of the

Anglo-Saxon aristocracy was a fact, and a remarkable one, but it was not the sort or miracle that Bede seems to describe. Precisely, perhaps, because Christianity is a religion whose standards are those of another world, it has proved remarkably adaptable in this one, and there have been almost as many "conversions of Christianity" as there have been societies in receipt of the Faith. In Anglo-Saxon England, to adapt the dying words of the Emperor Julian, the Gallilean did not win a bloodless victory; but has he ever?

Finally, I turn to Bede. It is a primary implication of this paper that Bede is a more isolated figure than he has usually been considered. For this, I make no apology, since Bede is indeed extraordinary. Previous generations of historians were ready to welcome him into their own ranks, while making the necessary excuse that his belief in miracles was a legacy of his time; today we must recognize that he is distinguished from his fellow-writers in the early Middle Ages by more than just accuracy, and from us by more than pious superstition. Historians are now readier to admit that his is only one view of what happened in seventh-century Britain, and it is not necessarily the most revealing just because it was the opinion of the cleverest man of the age. Bede's monastic background and patristic commitment put him out of sympathy with much that had happened, and was happening, in the church of his own day; the result is that we have taken some of the evidence that Christianity had been accepted by the early English as indications either that the message had not got through, or that there had been decline from originally high standards and we have, for example, over-simplified the career of St Wilfrid by seeing it as a mere clash between principle and self-interest. [159] Bede's patristically justified refusal to take an interest in the pre-Christian past of his people has greatly confused the interpretation of the only Old English epic, which we might have understood better had it been Lombardic or Old Saxon. In fact, a general feature of the Ecclesiastical History is that it is rarely illuminating on the preoccupations of the Anglo-Saxon aristocracy; and this is one reason why Sir Frank Stenton's book is curiously light on the status and culture of the early English nobility (and has little to say of Beowulf), whereas Hector Munro Chadwick, whose ear was attuned to the rhythms and themes of vernacular poetry, possessed an insight into the political and cultural history of the early Germanic peoples that has never properly been followed up.

But this can only be part of the story. As I have said, the Ecclesiastical History, unlike Beowulf, was one of the great international best-sellers of the early Middle Ages, and in the end Bede came to dominate the historical imaginations of his fellow-countrymen. Such a success can hardly be left unexplained. The truth, I think, is that Bede was representative of his readers in one crucial respect. He crystallized the enthusiasm with which the Anglo-Saxons, like the other early Germanic peoples, threw themselves into the balance of the old Romano-Christian world. The dominant note of the continental Dark Ages, as W. P. Ker clearly recognized, was sounded not by the effort to preserve the past, but (ironically) by the determination of the barbarian peoples to identify with the works of Rome (whether Augustan or Petrine). [160] The commitment of the Anglo-Saxon educated classes to the values of the Mediterranean is just as evident in the evangelist-portraits of the Lindisfarne Gospels as is the insular background in the carpet-pages. After Bede, the most important early Anglo-Saxon scholar was Aldhelm, and his extant works are as uncompromisingly Latin as Bede's, however much, like Plummer, we might have preferred to possess his vernacular poems.[161] Such a commitment indeed explains the effective abandonment of heathenism such as I have argued that Beowulf demonstrates, and ensured that, in the long run, the likes of Alcuin largely had their way about the heroic past also. It is this commitment that is incarnated by Bede. The Ecclesiastical History, a vision of the early English Church transfigured by the New Dispensation, projected an image of a society which, however idealized, was not at all unlike the image of itself which that society wished to see. What is unique about Bede, therefore, is not his interest in the Mediterranean and all that it stood for, but the exclusive character of that interest. The very special relationship which subsequent historians of the Anglo-Saxons have developed with their prototype makes it necessary to dwell occasionally on what he does not reflect: the essentially barbarian context of early Christianity in Britain, where the past was not immediately forgotten; but of course a proper understanding of the Anglo-Saxon church must take full account of Bede as well as Beowulf. Bede represents among the Anglo-Saxons what contemporary history has given the modern historian a good opportunity to appreciate, namely an underdeveloped society's capacity, and indeed determination, to believe in its metamorphosis by "civilization." What I have tried to suggest in this paper is that for the Anglo-Saxons such a determination was not quite unqualified, and that in Beowulf we may recognize neither more nor less than the force of habit which, even in a context of shifting religious allegiances, binds a society to its past.

That this even needs to be said is paradoxically the ultimate measure of Bede's greatness as a historian. Even in conventional terms, his achievement is astonishing. But many historians have told the truth to the best of their ability, and several have succeeded as well as Bede in circumstances that can have been scarcely less trying. Very few historians have ultimately changed a society's whole conception of their past and taught them to see its relevance for the present in a new light, as Bede did. His is great history above all because it is great art.

NOTES

1. One of several earlier (and shorter) drafts of this paper was read at
    Cornell to the Bede centenary class in the spring semester of 1973. I
    have to thank Cornell University for their original invitation, and Profes-
    sor Farrell both for arranging my visit, and for his many helpful criti-
    cisms of my contribution. A multitude of other friends, fully commen-
    surate with the size of this paper, have assisted the final emergence of
    my views, without deserving any blame for my errors of fact or judgment;
    I must, in particular, thank Miss M.E. Griffiths, Dr B. Mitchell, Mr
    J. Campbell and Dr M.T. Clanchy. Two articles which have deeply
    influenced the thought of my paper in general terms are P.R.L. Brown,
    "Aspects of the conversion of the Roman aristocracy," Journal of Roman
    Studies 51 (1961), 1-11; and K. Leyser, "The German aristocracy from
    the ninth to the early twelfth centuries: a social and cultural survey",
    Past and Present 41 (1968), 25-53. For Bede on birthdays, see G.
    Bonner, "Bede and medieval civilization", Anglo-Saxon England 2 (1973),
    74. Laistner's famous essary is entitled "The library of the Venerable
    Bede," Bede, his Life, Times and Writings, ed. A. Hamilton Thompson,
    (Oxford, 1935), 237-66. For a conspectus of other celebratory literature,
    see the other essays in Thompson's volume, and W.F. Bolton, "A Bede
    bibliography," Traditio 18 (1962), 436-45.

2. F.M. Stenton, Anglo-Saxon England 3rd ed. (Oxford, 1970) (henceforth
    ASE), 187; cf. B. Colgrave, "Historical introduction" to Bede's
    Ecclesiastical History of the English People, ed. B. Colgrave and R.A.B.
    Mynors (Oxford, 1969), p.xviii. Citations in this article from Bede's
    Ecclesiastical History (HE), History of the Abbots (HA) and Letter to
    Egbert (ep. Egb), are, unless otherwise stated, by page reference to
    Venerabilis Bedae Opera Historica, ed. C. Plummer (Oxford, 1896).

3. Editions of a good proportion of Bede's theological commentaries on the
    books of Scripture now exist in the series Corpus Christianorum Series
    Latina (henceforth CCSL), mostly edited by D. Hurst. From a Cornell
    stable have come M.L.W. Laistner's edition of the Expositio Actuum
    Apostolorum (Cambridge, Mass., 1939); C.W. Jones's edition of
    Bedae Opera de Temporibus (Cambridge Mass., 1943); and Jones's
    edition of In Principium Genesis, CCSL 118 (1967). Professor Jones has
    now edited the Opera Didascalica in CCSL. G. Musca II Venerabile
    Beda, storico dell' Alto Medioevo (Bari, 1973), now sets Bede's histori-
    cal work in the context of his other writings, and P. Hunter Blair The
    World of Bede (London, 1970), the most modern extant study in English,
    is perhaps the first to describe Bede's literary activity in non-historical
    fields as fully and sympathetically as his historical work. Sister M.T.A.
    Carroll's The Venerable Bede: his Spiritual Teachings (Washington,
    1945) was another post-1935 landmark, inasmuch as it was the first modern
    full-length treatment of Bede's theology. Famulus Christi, Essays in

Commemoration of the Thirteenth Centenary of the Birth of the Venerable Bede, ed. G. Bonne (London, 1976) offers a series of important papers on the non-historical work of Bede, notably by P. Meyvaert " Bede as scholar," and by C.W. Jones "Bede and the medieval schools."

4. R.W. Hanning, The Vision of History in Early Britain (New York, 1966); J.M. Wallace-Hadrill, Early Germanic Kingship in England and on the Continent (Oxford, 1971), 72-97.

5. See R.A. Markus, " The chronology of the Gregorian missions to England," Journal of Ecclesiastical History 14 (1963), 16-30; P. Meyvaert, Bede and Gregory the Great (Jarrow lecture, 1964), 8-13; and Appendix 1 of Dr. Mayr-Harting's book cited in the next note, for effective criticism of the thesis of S. Brechter, Die Quellen zur Angelsachsenmission Gregors des Grossen (Munster, 1941), restated in Settimane di...Spoleto 14 (1967), 191-215. See G. Tessier, " La conversion de Clovis et la christianisation des Francs," ibid., 149-89, for the comparable Frankish problem. Not that Bede's chronology in general has escaped criticism: W. Levison, " The beginning of the year of the incarnation in Bede," England and the Continent in the Eighth Century (Oxford, 1946), 265-79; P. Grosjean, " La date du Colloque de Whitby," Analecta Bollandiana 78 (1960), 235-42; D.P. Kirby, " Bede and Northumbrian chronology," English Historical Review (henceforth EHR), 78, (1963), 514-27; J. Morris, The Age of Arthur (London, 1973), 35-41; K. Harrison, " The beginning of the year in England," Anglo-Saxon England 2 (1973), 55-9.

6. See H. Mayr-Harting, The Coming of Christianity to Anglo-Saxon England (London, 1972), chs. 9,12, and 13; for Bede's treatment of Wilfrid, see J. Campbell, " Bede," Latin Historians, ed. T.A. Dorey (London, 1966), pp.177-9 and nn. 74-6 at pp. 188-9.

7. J. Campbell, " Bede"; Campbell's introduction to Bede, the Ecclesiastical History and other selections (New York, 1968); and " The first century of English Christianity," Ampleforth Journal 76 (1971),12-29.

8. H.M. Chadwick, Origins of the English Nation (Cambridge, 1907); and The Heroic Age (Cambridge, 1912).

9. R. Girvan, Beowulf and the Seventh Century, 2nd ed., with new ch. by R.L.S.Bruce Mitford (London, 1971), esp. 40-8; cf. W.W. Lawrence, Beowulf and the Epic Tradition (New York, 1928), 57-8. References to Beowulf in this paper are by line from the text of F. Klaeber, Beowulf and the Fight at Finnsburg, 3rd ed. (Lexington 1950).

10. HE III.14, pp. 155-6; Beowulf, lines 64-7; Chadwick, Heroic Age, 350-1. For other evidence in Beowulf for this type of warrior, see lines 331-55, 372-89 and 457-78; in Bede: HE III.24, pp. 177-8; ep.Egb., pp. 414-5; in other early English sources: Eddi Stephani Vita Wilfridi, c. lxvi ed. W. Levison, MGH, Script. Rer,Merov., VI 261-2; Felix's Life of Guthlac, cc. xvi-xix, ed. B. Colgrave (Cambridge, 1956) pp. 80-3 references to Felix henceforth from this edition.

11. See Beowulf, lines 67-85, 662-5, 714-26, 767-82, 834-6, and 920-7
for some significant references to Heorot; lines 452-5, 1030-4 and
1192-1214 for treasures, weapons and heirlooms; lines 26-52 and
3137-69 for burial customs. On Sutton Hoo, see R.L.S. Bruce Mitford,
The Sutton Hoo Ship-Burial: a Handbook, 2nd ed. (London, British Museum, 1972), and his supplementary chapter to Girvan, Beowulf, 85-98.
For Yeavering see the progress report of Dr Hope Taylor's excavation
in Medieval Archaeology (henceforth Med. Arch.) 1 (1957), 148-9; and
for their relevance to Beowulf, R. Cramp, "Beowulf and Archaeology",
ibid., 57-77.

12. D. Whitelock, The Audience of Beowulf (Oxford, 1951), 39-53, 71-7
and 79-82.

13. D. Whitelock, "Anglo-Saxon poetry and the historian," Transactions
of the Royal Historical Society 4th series 21 (1949). 78-9; M. Bloch,
Feudal Society, tr. L. A. Manyon (London, 1961), 102.

14. Laws of Aethelbert (Abt) 13, 14, 75; of Hlothere (H1) 1; of Wihtred (Wi)
5; of Ine (In) 30, 34:1, 45, 50, 51, 54, 63, 68, 70, Die Gesetze der
Angelsachsen, ed. F. Liebermann (Halle, 1903-16) (references henceforth to this edition), 1, 4, 7, 9, 12, 102-5, 108-15, 118-9. For further
discussion of the problems of the legal status of the early Anglo-Saxon
aristocracy, see below Appendix A.

15. HE IV 22, p.251

16. Cartularium Saxonicum ed. W. de Gray Birch (henceforth BCS) 154 is a
notable example; cf. Anglo-Saxon Charters : an Annotated List and
Bibliography, ed. P.H. Sawyer (London, 1968) (henceforth SC) 89;
English Historical Documents I, (henceforth, E.H.D.) ed. D. Whitelock
(London, 1955)453-4. See also BCS 157, SC 94; and ep. Egb., pp. 415-6.

17. D. Wilson, The Anglo-Saxons, 2nd ed. (London, 1971), 108-26; full
statistics, perhaps in need of detailed revision, in G. Baldwin Brown,
The Arts in Early England III (London, 1915), 193-6, and 204-8. For
continental comparisons, see F. Stein, Adelsgräber des achten
Jahrhunderts in Deutschland (Berlin, 1967) and F. Irsigler, Untersuchungen zur Geschichte des früfränkischen Adels (Bonn, 1969), 186-220.
For legal evidence bearing on the value of this weaponry, see In 54:1,
pp. 114-5 and the much later Norðleoda Laga 10, pp. 460-1; and, on
the Continent, Lex Ribuaria, xl 11, ed. F. Beyerle and R. Buchner,
MGH Leg: Sect. 1, III, 94-5; Leges Ahistulfi 2, 3, ed. F. Beyerle,
Gesetze der Langobarden (Witzenhausen (Germanenerechte series),
1962), pp. 194-5.

18. See Beowulf, lines 2596-7, and 3169-82 for aristocratic escorts. For
the use of eorls by the poet, see Klaeber's glossary, p. 324; ceorl is
used four times in association with snotor, lines 202, 416, 908 and 1591,
once of the father of the man on the gallows (2444), and once, incongru-
ously, of King Ongentheow, (2972; cf. 2951).

19. Girvan, <u>Beowulf</u>, 41. For weapons in the poem, see <u>Beowulf</u>, lines 333-5 (cf. 321-7), 671-4, 1020-49, 1110-13, 1242-6, 2152-4, 2247-66, 2611-18, 2680, 2811-2, and 2971-88; they are passed down the family as in later Anglo-Saxon wills, <u>Beowulf</u>, lines 452-5 and 2156-62. Cf. also <u>Waldhere</u> lines A 2-5, 28, B 1-24, <u>Runic and Heroic Poems</u>, ed. B. Dickins (Cambridge, 1915), pp. 57-61; <u>Hildebrandslied</u> line 62, <u>ibid.</u>, pp. 84-5; <u>Finnsburh</u>. lines 12, 14-15, 17, 32, 46-7, <u>ibid.</u>, pp. 64-9 (henceforth, references to these poems are to this edition).

20. A. Momigliano, " Pagan and Christian historiography," <u>The Conflict between Paganism and Christianity in the Fourth Century</u>, ed. A. Momigliano (Oxford, 1963), 96; cf. P.R.L. Brown, " Pelagius and his supporters," <u>Journal of Theological Studies</u> n.s.19 (1968), p. 93 - the reference in each case is to the lack of overlap between writers in the pagan and christian traditions; see below, p. 76 and n. 38. R.W. Chambers, <u>Beowulf: an Introduction to the Study of the Poem</u> 3rd ed. (Cambridge 1959), 128 and 329, was impressed by the similarity of tone between history and epic; but cf. J.R. Hulbert, " The Genesis of <u>Beowulf</u>, a caveat," <u>Proceedings of the Modern Language Association of America</u> (henceforth <u>PMLA</u>) 66 (1951), 1170.

21. This is not to say that I would defend the traditional dating of the poem to the " age of Bede," in defiance of the common-sense of Professor Whitelock (cf. above, p. 35, nn. 12 and 13.) For fuller discussion of the implications of the argument here advanced for the date of <u>Beowulf</u>, see below supplementary Appendix C. At this stage, I assume only that <u>Beowulf</u> is likely to belong to the pre-Alfredian phase of Anglo-Saxon culture; it makes no difference to my argument whether the poem comes early or late in that period.

22. J.R.R. Tolkien, "<u>Beowulf</u>, the monsters and the critics," <u>Proceedings of the British Academy</u> 22 (1936), 245-95; also printed in <u>An Anthology of Beowulf Criticism</u>, ed. L.E. Nicholson, (Notre Dame, 1963), 51-103 (from which the article is henceforth quoted). For reservations about Tolkien's thesis, see T.M. Gang, " Approaches to <u>Beowulf</u>," <u>Review of English Studies</u> 53 (1952), 1-12; K. Sisam, <u>The Structure of Beowulf</u> (Oxford, 1965).

23. W.P. Ker, <u>Epic and Romance</u> (repted New York, 1957), 165-7 (and cf. 13-4 for the " Homeric" perspective); W.P. Ker, <u>The Dark Ages</u> (London, 1904), 252-3. For Ker's influence upon his pupil, Chambers, see R.W. Chambers, <u>Widsith</u> (Cambridge, 1912), 180-2; and on Stenton, <u>ASE</u>, 194-5.

24. E.g. Ker, <u>Epic</u>, 157; <u>Dark Ages</u>, pp. 250-1; Lawrence, <u>Epic Tradition</u>, 10-11; Chambers, <u>Introduction</u>, 121-8; Girvan, <u>Beowulf</u>, 12-13; Klaeber, pp. cxvii-cxxii i; but cf Chambers's <u>Introduction</u>, 109; Chadwick, <u>Heroic Age</u>, 73-6; Sisam, <u>Structure</u>, 63-7. When speaking of " literate composition," I am fully aware that medieval writers often dictated their material to a scribe, but such a process is significantly different from oral composition, or even from the procedure of Caedmon, <u>HE</u> IV. 24, pp. 260-1, because the author can instantly read what he has

dictated; the techniques of an oral poet are conditioned by the fact that he cannot read any more than he can write.

25.   For examples of critics who have sought to integrate Beowulf with the scholarship of Latin Christianity, see Nicholson's Anthology, paene passim.   Two writers in particular, in that volume who share Tolkien's caution about a more allegorical approach, are M.P. Hamilton, "The religious principle in Beowulf," and R.E. Kaske, "Sapientia et Fortitudo as the controlling theme of Beowulf," ibid., 105-35, and 269-310. Cf. also, M.W. Bloomfield, "Patristics and Old English literature," ibid., 367-72. For distinguished reassessments of the "anomalies" of Beowulf, following Tolkien's example, A. Brodeur, The Art of Beowulf (Berkeley, 1959); A. Bonjour, The Digressions in Beowulf (London, 1960).

26.   A.B. Lord, The Singer of Tales, (Harvard, 1960); F. P. Magoun, "The oral-formulaic character of Anglo-Saxon verse," Speculum 28 (1953) (also in Nicholson's Anthology, 189-221); R.P. Creed, "The making of an Anglo-Saxon poem," Journal of English Literary History 26 (1959), 445-54. For the critique, Brodeur, Art of Beowulf, chs. 1 and 2; L.D. Benson, "The literary character of Anglo-Saxon formulaic poetry," PMLA 8 (1966), 334-41; S.B. Greenfield, The Interpretation of Old English Poems (London, 1972)., 31-59 and 122-30. On the general character of oral verse, G.S. Kirk, "Formula, language and oral quality," Yale Classical Studies 20 (1966), 174; W. Whallon, Formula, Language and Context (Cambridge, Mass., 1969), 116; also, J. Vansina, Oral Tradition, trans. H.M. Wright, (London, 1965), 55-62. On Beowulf's resemblance to literate, rather than oral, verse, A. Campbell, "The use in Beowulf of earlier heroic verse," England before the Conquest: Studies in Primary Sources presented to Dorothy Whitelock, ed. P. Clemoes and K. Hughes (henceforth, Whitelock Studies)(Cambridge, 1971 (283-92).

27.   Klaeber, p. cxlx, concluded from the poet's literacy that he was probably a cleric, as did Professor Whitelock (Audience, 19-20). It is significant that those modern scholars most inclined to emphasize the relative "paganism" of the Beowulf poet have been those most influenced by the oral-formulaic school: see Whallon, Formula, 118, together with his, "The Christianity of Beowulf," Modern Philology (henceforth MP), 60 (1962), pp. 81-94, and "The Idea of God in Beowulf," PMLA 80 (1965), pp. 19-23; R.D. Stevick, "Christian elements and the genesis of Beowulf," MP 61 (1963), pp. 79-89; M.D. Cherniss, Ingeld and Christ (Mouton, 1972), 16-29 and 120-50.

28.   J.W. Thompson, The Literacy of the Laity in the Middle Ages (repted New York, 1963), 116-20, and J.W. Adamson, The Illiterate Anglo-Saxon and other Essays (Cambridge, 1946), 11-20, argue the opposite, but neither is a satisfactory basis for further discussion. By far the most important survey of the problem in early medieval Europe as a whole is that of H. Grundmann, "Litteratus-illiteratus," Archiv für Kulturgeschichte 40 (1958), 1-65, and see also P. Riché, "L'Enseignement et la culture des laïcs dans l'Occident pre-Carolingien," Settimana Spoleto,[19] (1972), 231-53. For further debate upon the problem, see

my, "The Uses of Literacy in Anglo-Saxon England and its neighbours"
T.R.H.S. 5th series 27(1977), 95-114. In suggesting that literate composition
implies monastic authorship, I am differing both from Professor Whitelock,
Audience, pp. 19-20, and from Professor Wallace-Hadrill, Early Germanic
Kingship, p. 212; and this is a prospect no scholar can relish. Nevertheless,
I cannot see the force of the argument that Beowulf is too massive an irrele-
vance for a monastic scriptorium, given that monks were prepared to be
entertained by such literature (see pp.43 , and nn. 51,89,90), and given that
at least one community, and arguably several, were prepared to "waste"
valuable parchment on preserving Beowulf for posterity.

29. For Aldfrith, HE IV.26, p. 268 and V. 15, p. 317; HA xv, p. 380;
Eddius xliv, p. 238. Cf. Plummer's note, II, 263-4, and, for Aldfrith's
identity with Aldhelm's Acircius, Aldhelmi Opera, ed. R. Ehwald. MGH,
Auct. Antiq., XV, 61, n.1. For lay nobles and their education, HE IV. 13,
pp. 312-13; Eddius xxi, p. 216; and also, P. Riché, Education et
cultrue dans l'occident barbare (Paris, 1962), 369-70 and 445-6.

30. Asser's Life of King Alfred, ed. W.H. Stevenson,, 2nd ed. (Oxford, 1959),
chs. xxxii-xxv, pp. 19-22; lxxvii, pp. 58-63; lxxxvii-lxxxix, pp. 73-5
and cvi, pp. 94-5.

31. D.A. Binchy, "The background of early Irish literature," Studia
Hibernica i. (1969), 10-11; D. O'Corrain, Ireland Before the Normans,
(Dublin, 1972), 74-9.

32. Compare, e.g., J. Fleckenstein, Die Hofkapelle der deutschen Könige I
(Stuttgart, 1959), esp. pp. 74-95 with P. Chaplais, "The origins and authenticity
of the Anglo-Saxon royal diploma," Journal of the Society of Archivists 3 (1965-
9), 48-61 (and cf ibid., 160-6); and compare B. Bischoff, "Die Hofbib-
liothek Karls des Grossen," Karl der Grosse, ed. W. Braunfels II
(Dusseldorf, 1965), 42-62, with N.R. Ker, Catalogue of Manuscripts
Containing Anglo-Saxon, (Oxford, 1957), nos 39 and 42; F. Wormald,
The Benedictional of Aethelwold (London, 1959), 10; and F. Wormald,
"The Winchester School before St. Aethelwold. " Whitelock Studies,
305-13.

33. J. Goody, "Restricted literacy in Northern Ghana," Literacy in Traditional Societies, ed. J. Goody (Cambridge, 1968), 199-264. For early
medieval methods of education, Riché, Education et Culturc, 499-520.

34. Ker, Dark Ages, 250-2; Ker, Epic, 79-93 and 116-22; A. Campbell,
"The Old English epic style, "English and Medieval Studies for J.R.R.
Tolkein, ed. N. Davis and C.L. Wrenn (London, 1962); cf also M.L.W.
Laistner, Thought and Letters in W. Europe, 500-900 (London, 1955),
370, whose view is especially significant in that it was founded on the
author's profound knowledge of early medieval culture as a whole.

35. Tolkien, "Beowulf," 69.

36. Beowulf, lines 175-83, 1107-24, 2124-30, 2802-8 and 3092-182. Cf,
e.g., Codex Theodosianus XVI x 12, ed. T. Mommsen (Hannover, 1905),
pp. 900-1; Childeberti regis Praeceptum, Capitularia regum Francorum,
ed. A. Boretius, MGH, Leg., Sect.II, I, 2; Charlemagne's Capitulare
de partibus Saxoniae, vii, ix, ibid., p. 69; Indiculum Superstitionum,
ibid., p. 223. Cf also an anonymous sermon of Charlemagne's time,
printed, along with other relevant material, by W. Lange, Texte zur
germanischen Bekehrungsgeschichte (Darmstadt, 1962), 168-72.

37. *Beowulf*, lines 685-7 and 700-2. Cf also 1700-84 for Hrothgar's speech to Beowulf, the most concentrated passage of "Christian" wisdom in the poem; and F. Klaeber, "Die christlichen Elemente in *Beowulf*," I *Anglia* 35 (1911-12), 112-27. A similar style of deity appears in *Waldhere*, A 23, B 25-9, pp. 58-9, 62-3; and *Hildebrandslied*, 30, 49, pp. 80-3.

38. Professor Whallon has argued that the poet's words for God are no more Christian than is similar terminology when used by Plato or Vergil, and that they are cognate with similar terminology in the Norse Elder Edda. But Germanic paganism, which was the only serious available alternative to Judaeo-Christian revelation for the *Beowulf* poet, was undoubtedly basically polytheistic, as is established by the names for the days of the week, and by the Old Saxon baptismal formula (*Capitularia* I, 222). When Scandinavians gravitated towards monotheism, this was either out of loyalty to one God among several, or under Christian influence, already marked in Iceland by c. 900. See J. de Vries, *Altgermanische Religionsgeschichte*, 2nd edn. (Berlin, 1956-7), I, 4, 356-8; K.D. Schmidt, *Die Bekehrung der Germanen zum Christentum*, (Göttingen, 1939), pp. 158-60; H. Kuhn, "Das Fortleben des germanischen Heidentums nach der Christianisierung," *Settimana Spoleto*, 14, (1967), 743-57. It must be Christian influence that is responsible for the way in which Snorri attributes to Othinn some of the qualities of the Christian God, and, generally speaking, Othinn is neither Creator nor Judge: See G. Turville Petre, *Myth and Religion of the North*, (London, 1964), pp. 35, 55-6; K. Helm, *Altgermanische Religionsgeschichte*, (Heidelberg, 1953), II, 262-3; de Vries, II, 84-7. We know that Caedmon and the authors of *Genesis* and *Exodus* applied the same terminology to their Christian God as did the *Beowulf* poet to his; it seems perverse to suggest that such language is nevertheless essentially pagan on the basis of Scandinavian evidence that can hardly be purely pagan itself.

39. *Beowulf*, lines 90-101 and 175-88. Brodeur, *Art of Beowulf*, 187-208, successfully rebuts the suggestions in Tolkien's Appendix 91-103 and argues that the poet's attitude to pagans was not unsympathetic.

40. *Beowulf*, lines 106, 1572 and 1600; Whitelock, *Audience*, 5-6.

41. *Beowulf*, lines 198, 1663, 2140, 2280 and 3051; G.V. Smithers, "Destiny and the heroic warrior in *Beowulf*", *Philological Essays in honour of H.D. Meritt*, ed. J.L. Rosier (Mouton, 1970), 71-3.

42. *Beowulf*, lines 477-9, 572 (cf 2291-3), 697 and 2814-6; but also 1056-8 and 1657-64. Among critical authorities, contrast B.J. Timmer, "*Wyrd* in Anglo-Saxon prose and poetry," *Neophilologus* 26 (1940-1), 24-33 and 213-28; and E.G. Stanley, "The quest for Anglo-Saxon paganism," *Notes and Queries* ii (1965), 285-93 and 322-7 reprinted as a book under the same title (London, 1975); with A. Roper, "Boethius and the three fates of *Beowulf*," *Philological Quarterly* 61:1 (1962), 386-400; and Smithers, "Destiny," 66-75. For the background in Germanic paganism, K. Helm, *Altgermanische Religionsgeschichte* II (Heidelberg, 1963), 280-5; J. de Vries, *Altgermanische Religionsgeschichte*, 2nd ed. (Berlin, 1956-7) I, 267-74.

43. *Beowulf*, lines 90-8, 106-14, 1258-78 and 1687-93; for judgement, 588-9, 850-2, 977-9 and 2820, and for other possible echoes of the after

life, 1201, 1759-60 and 2468-9. Among critics, contrast J. Halverson, "Beowulf and the pitfalls of piety," Toronto University Quarterly 55 (1965-6), 268 and E. John, "Beowulf and the margins of literacy, "Bulletin of the John Rylands Library," (henceforth, BJRL) 56, (1973/4), pp. 888-922. Whitelock, Audience, 5.

44. J. Clark Hall, Beowulf and the Fight at Finnsburg: a Translation into modern English Prose (London, 1901), p. xxviii.

45. Beowulf, lines 491-8, 611-31, 1159-62 and 1232, for wine, women and song; 1020-49 and 2752-87 for treasures. Cf Sisam, Structure, 11-13.

46. Beowulf, lines 1383-9. Cf C. Moorman, "The essential paganism of Beowulf," Modern Language Quarterly 28 (1967), 4-6; E.G. Stanley, "Haethenra Hyht in Beowulf," Studies in Old English in Honour of A. G. Brodeur, ed. S.B. Greenfield (Oregon, 1963), 136-61.

47. Beowulf, lines 3174-82. Cf Klaeber's edition, pp. xlix-li, and "Christliche Elemente," IV, Anglia 36 (1912), 175-9; Chambers, Introduction, 102 and 324-6; Hulbert, "Genesis of Beowulf", p. 1170 but cf Smithers, "Destiny," 76 and 80.

48. Nicholson's Anthology contains several examples of this approach. E.g. D.W. Robertson, "The doctrine of charity in medieval literary gardens," A. Cabaniss, "Beowulf and liturgy," M.B. Macnamee, "Beowulf: an allegory of salvation?" and M.E. Goldsmith, "The Christian perspective in Beowulf." Cf also Nicholson's own essay, "The literal meaning and symbolic structure of Beowulf," Classica et Medievalia 25 (1964) and J. Gardner, "Fulgentius...and the plan of Beowulf," Papers on Language and Literature 6 (1970), 227-62. The most striking monument to the approach is now M.E. Goldsmith's, The Mode and Meaning of Beowulf (London, 1970); cf her contribution to the debate between herself, Professor Whallon, and Professor C. Donahue, "Allegorical, typological or neither?" Anglo-Saxon England 2 (1973), 289-90. For some effective objections, see Greenfield, Interpretation, 140-54; A. Bonjour, "Beowulf et le démon de l'analogie," Twelve Beowulf Papers (Neufchâtel, 1962), 183-9; Donahue's contribution to the debate in Anglo-Saxon England 2 (1973), 293-6; and P. Rollinson, "The influence of christian doctrine and exegesis upon Old English poetry," ibid., 271-84. See further, Appendix B.

49. Chambers, Introduction, 102 and 324-6; Tolkien, "Beowulf," 71; Chadwick, Heroic Age, 73; Whitelock, Audience, 5-12 and 19-22; Sisam, Structure 72-9.

50. H.I. Marrou, Saint Augustin et la fin de la culture antique (Paris, 1938), plus Retractatio, (1949), 50; Marrou, History of Education in Antiquity, tr. G. Lamb, (London, 1956), 318-24; M.L.W. Laitner, Christianity and Pagan Culture in the Later Roman Empire (Cornell, 1951); Laistner, Thought and Letters, 44-54 and 108-10; H. Chadwick, Early Christian Thought and the Classical Tradition (Oxford, 1966). The only similar work on Germanic literature known to me is H. Kuhn, "Heldensage und Christentum," K. Hauck, Zur germanischdeutschen Heldensage (Darmstadt, 1965), 416-26, which, like most of this scholar's valuable work, consistently overestimates the mutual compatibility of Germanic and Mediterranean traditions. Cherniss, Ingeld and Christ, and R.

Levine "Ingeld and Christ, a medieval problem," Viator 2 (1971), pp. 105-28, discuss the problem from an almost exclusively literary angle.

51. Alcuini Epistolae, 124, ed. E. Dümmler, MGH, Ep. Sel. Karolini Aevi, II, p. 183 (future references to Alc. Ep. by page reference from this edition.)

52. Beowulf, 2020-69; Widsith, 45-9, ed. R.W. Chambers (Cambridge, 1912), and cf the introduction, pp. 79-84 (future references to Widsith are from this edition). Chambers, Introduction, 20-5; Klaeber's edition, pp. xxxiv-xxxvi and 202-3.

53. Thus Kuhn, "Heldensage," 416-7; also Chambers, Introduction, 123 and 332; Brodeur, Art of Beowulf, 216; Goldsmith, Mode, 11, 53 and 178.

54. Regula cuiusdam patris ad Virgines, ix, Patrologia Latina (henceforth PL) 88, cols. 1061-2. On the origins of this Rule, see L. Gougaud, "Inventaire des règles monastiques irlandaises," Revue Benedictine (henceforth Rev. Ben) 25 (1908), 328-31. For other comparable monastic legislation, cf Regula Caesarii ad Virgines, xvii, ed. G. Morin, Sancti Caesarii Opera II, (Maretioli, 1942), 105: Regula Ferreoli, xxiv PL 66, cols, 967-8; Regula Benedicti xliii 18, ed. A. de Vogue, La Règle de Saint Benôit, Sources Chretiennes II (Paris), pp. 588-9, 602-3 and notes; Regula Leandri, v, vii, PL 72, cols. 883-4; Regula Isidori, vi, ix, PL 103, cols. 561 and 563; Regula Donati, xx, PL 87, cols. 281-2.

55. Conc. Tol. III (589), vii, Concilios Visigoticos e Hispano-Romanos, ed. J. Vives (Madrid, 1963), p. 127; Wulfstan's Canons of Edgar, lix, ed. R. Fowler, Early English Text Society, (London, 1972), pp. 14-15 and 38-9. Cf also, e.g., Admonitio Generalis (789), lxxi, Capitularia I, 59; Episcoporum relatio ad Hludovicum regem (829), liv, ibid., II pp. 45-6.

56. Conc. Clovesho (746/7), xii, Councils and Ecclesiastical Documents Relating to Great Britain and Ireland, ed. A.W. Haddan and W. Stubbs (Oxford, 1871) (henceforth H&S) III, p. 366.

57. Epistola de obitu Bedae, ed. Plummer, Opera Historica I clxi; HE IV. 24, pp. 258-61; IV. 25, p. 265 and IV. 22, p. 250. Cf Bede's prose life of St. Cuthbert, c. xxvii, Two Lives of St Cuthbert, ed. B. Colgrave (Cambridge, 1940), p. 246; Bede, In Sam. II xiii 20, xiv 27, ed. D. Hurst, CCSL 119, pp. 112 and 114. See Hunter Blair, World of Bede 286-8.

58. William of Malmesbury Gesta Pontificum, ed. N.E.S.A. Hamilton, Rolls Series, 52 p. 336.

59. Tertullian, De Praescriptione Haereticorum, vii 9, ed. E. Dekkers, CCSL 1, p. 193; cf Apologeticum, xlvi 18, ibid., p. 162; Jerome, Epistolae, xxii 29-30, ed. I. Hilberg, Corpus Scriptorum Ecclesiasticorum Latinorum (henceforth CSEL) 54, pp. 188-91; Gregorii Magni Epistolae, XI 34, ed. P. Ewald and L.M. Hartmann, MGH, Ep.Sel. II, 303. Cf the literature referred to above p. 42 no.50 and Hunter Blair, World of Bede, 282-3.

60. The early medieval West developed a distinctive literature of barbarian kingship from the seventh century at the latest. See J.M. Wallace-Hadrill, "The Via Regia of the Carolingian Age," Trends in Medieval Political Thought, ed. B. Smalley (Oxford, 1964), 22-41; and his Early Germanic Kingship, passim; H.H. Anton, Fürstenspiegel und Herrscher-ethos in der Karolingerzeit, (Bonn, 1968) esp. 357-446; W. Ullmann, The Carolingian Renaissance and the Idea of Kingship (London, 1969). But in the last resort the most striking feature of this ideology is its unitary perspective: kings, bishops, priests and laymen are all to take their model from the same divine hierarchy of values, as revealed in the Bible, and enunciated by the church. Dual standards appear only under Aristotelian influence in the thirteenth century: cf. G. Kurth, Principles of Government and Politics in the Middle Ages, 2nd ed. (London, 1966), 231-79.

61. Greg. Ep. XI 34 (cf above, p.44, n.59; Jonas, De Instituione laicali, I xi, xiii, PL 106, cols 143-4 and 147. Cf Bede, Homily I 22, Opera Homiletica, ed. D. Hurst, CCSL 122, p. 160, and also the remarks of the Council of Paris, Concilia, ed. A. Werminghoff, MGH, Leg. Sect., III II, 657-8. which was here under Jonas's influence: Anton, Fürstenspiegel, 204-18.

62. Einhard, Vita Caroli, xxix, ed. O. Holder-Egger, MGH, in us. Schol., p. 33; Thegan, Vita Hludovici Imperatoris, xix, PL 106, cols. 413-4. Attempts have been made to evade the implications of this passage by denying that Thegan can be referring to vernacular verse: Cf G. Kurth, Histoire poetique des Merovingiens (Paris, 1893), 55-6; but cf Grundmann (See p. 38 and n. 28 above), p. 41 who rightly challenges Kurth, and links Louis's behaviour to the expressed principles of Alcuin.

63. Romans I. 18-23, II. 6-7 and 13-15. Cf A.D. Horgan, "Religious attitudes in Beowulf," Essays and poems presented to Lord David Cecil ed. W.W. Robson (London, 1970), 9-12; Hamilton, "Religious principle," 110-13; Goldsmith, Mode, 149-57 and 180-1.

64. P. Brown, Augustine of Hippo (London, 1967) 307-8, quoting Augustine's letter to Bishop Evodius, Epistolae 164, CSEL 44, pp. 521-41. Gregory did say that "infideles" should not be prayed for: Moralia in Job XXXIV xix, PL 76 col. 739.

65. C.N.L. Brooke, The Twelfth-Century Renaissance (London, 1969) 155-62. This point is missed by Kuhn, who also ignores the face that, although many of the Gothic heroes, like Theodoric, were Christian, they were Arian, and, as such, doubly damned.

66. Bede, In Cantica Canticorum, Praef. PL 91, cols. 1075-6. Miss Hamilton herself pointed out that Anglo-Saxon Christian poets were obsessed by the difference between the chosen and the damned, ("Religious principle," 111-12) and this is precisely the issue that Beowulf avoids: E.G. Stanley "Haethenra Hyht," 137-43. On all of this, see the excellent remarks of C. Donahue in the articles referred to below, pp. 49 and n. 83.

67. Annales Xantenses, s.a. 718, ed. G.H. Pertz, MGH, Scriptores in fol., II, p. 221.

68. Boniface Epistolae, 46, 73, ed. M. Tangl, Die Briefe des Heiligen Bonifatius und Lullus, MGH in us. schol, Ep. Sel., I (reference to Bon. Ep. henceforth by page from this edition), pp. 74-5, 150; cf EHD, I, pp. 753-4. For a rather different interpretation of this correspondence, see the essay by L.D. Benson, referred to below, pp. 000, and n. 86.

69. HE I. 27, pp. 51-2 and I-30, pp. 65-6.

70. Penitential of Theodore, II i 4, 5, H&S III, pp. 190-1.

71. Nicholas, Epistolae, xcix, Qu. 47, 59, 88, ed. E. Perels, MGH Ep. Sel. Kar Aev., IV pp. 585-6, 588 and 596. Bede's interpretation of the passage from St John was, however, more liberal: PL 93, cols. 117-8.

72. H.M. and N.K. Chadwick, The Growth of Literature (Cambridge, 1940) I, pp. 556-7.

73. Alc. Ep. 136, p. 209; 178, p. 294; 309, p. 475. Cf his Carmen lxxviii, ed. E. Dümmler, MGH Poet. Lat. I, p. 299; Vita Alcuini, ii, xvi, ed. W. Arndt, MGH, Scriptores in fol. XV, 185 and 193. For the arti-ficiality of much of the hostility thus traditionally expressed, see the works cited above p. 42 n.50 plus J. Leclercq, L'Amour des lettres et le desir de Dieu (Paris, 1957), 40-52 and 108-41; H. de Lubac, Exegèse Medievale (Paris, 1959-64) I, 67-73 and 290-6, II.1, 53-77; P. Meyvaert, Bede and Gregory the Great, 14.

74. Augustine, De Doctrina Christiana II 40-2, CCSL 32, pp. 73-7; cf Marrou, Saint Augustin 387-413; Hraban Maur, De clericorum insti-tutione, III 18 PL 107 col 396. Cf de Lubac, Exegèse Medievale I 290-6 and II.ii, 182-97; Theodulf, "De libris quos legere solebam...," ed. E. Dümmler, MGH, Poet. Lat. I, pp. 543-4.

75. Hraban, De cler, inst. III 18, as above.

76. Asser, lxxv, p. 59.

77. Cassiodori Institutiones, I i 8, ed. R.A.B. Mynors, (Oxford, 1937), p.14; Cf Jerome Ep. cvii 12, CSEL. 55, p. 303. As Professor Donahue points out in his contribution to the "Allegorical..." debate, (Anglo-Saxon England 2 (1973), 292-3), Augustine believed that teachers should not imitate the "salubrious obscurity" of Holy Writ; "their first and special aim should be that they understood": De Doct. Christ. IV 8, CCSL 32, pp. 131-2.

78. Otfrids Evangelienbuch, praef., ed. O. Erdmann (Halle, 1882), p. 4. The other works are the translation of Tatian, still in a Fulda manu-script, and the Heliand itself, which is based, in part, on Hraban's commentary on St. Matthew, and on Tatian. Cf Laistner, Thought and Letters, 375-6.

79. For the Hildebrandslied, see the edition and translation by Dickins, cited above, p. 36 n. 19; Waltharius, ed. K. Strecker, MGH, Poet Lat. VI.1 pp. 1-85.

80. Ker, Catalogue, no. 215. Cf. K. Malone, The Nowell Codex, Early
     English Manuscripts in Facsimile 12 (Copenhagen, 1963), and K.
     Sisam, "The compilation of the Beowulf Manuscript," Studies in the
     History of Old English Literature, (Oxford, 1953), 65-96. The manu-
     script fragments of Finnsburh and Maldon are now lost; for Wald-
     here, Ker, Catalogue, no. 101. Widsith and Deor are respectively
     ff. 84v-87 and 100-100v of the Exeter Book: cf. Ker, Catalogue,
     no. 116, and R.W. Chambers, M. Forster and R. Flower, The
     Exeter Book of Old English Poetry (London, 1933).

81. Greg. Moralia, Praef. iii contains a side-swipe at secular literature,
     PL 75, col. 513.

82. Bede, In Princ. Gen., ed. C. W. Jones, CCSL 118 A, p. 1. But Acca
     himself was a noted book-collector, HE V.20, p. 331, and quoted
     Jerome and Augustine in the letter that called forth Bede's In Luc., ed.
     D. Hurst, CCSL 120, pp. 5-6. Cf. J. D. A. Ogilvy, Books Known to
     the English, 597-1066 (Cambridge Mass., 1967) (it is important to use
     this second edition, in that it incorporates most of the research of
     E. A. Lowe, Codices Latini Antiquiores (Oxford, 1935-71)); I doubt
     whether the palaeographical evidence will support Professor Ogilvy's
     much-quoted assertion (p. 14) that, in general, it would be safer to
     assume that the early English knew any given work of Augustine's than
     they did not.

83. C. Donahue, "Beowulf, Ireland and the Natural Good," Traditio 7
     (1949-51), 263-77; "Beowulf and the Christian Tradition: a recon-
     struction from a Celtic standpoint," ibid., 21 (1965), 55-116; Can.
     Hib. III 8, The Irish Penitentials, ed. L. Bieler (Dublin, 1963), pp.
     168-9; R. Flower, The Irish Tradition (Oxford, 1947), 8. Cf. K.
     Hughes, "Sanctity and secularity in the early Irish Church," Studies
     in Church History, 10, (Oxford, 1973), 28; Bon. Ep. 59, pp. 110- 12.

84. The Tain, trans. T. Kinsella, (Oxford, 1970), p. 1; F.J. Byrne,
     "The Ireland of St Columba," Irish Historical Studies, V, ed. J.L.
     McCracken (Dublin, 1965), 39; "Seventh-century documents,"
     Proceedings of the Irish Catholic Historical Committee (1965-7), 8.
     But Collectio Canonum Hibernesis LX 3, ed. J. Wasserschleben, 2nd en
     edn. Leipzig, 1885, p. 226, is a typical canon against lax standards
     of entertainment in clerical contexts.

85. Donahue, "Beowulf, Ireland," 273-4; J. Carney, "The Irish elements
     in Beowulf," Studies in Irish Literature and History, (Dublin, 1955), esp.
     97-8, 102-12 and 114-22. For the Scandinavian analogues G. V.
     Smithers, The Making of Beowulf (Durham, 1961), is the culmination of
     a tradition that began with Lawrence, Beowulf and the Epic Tradition,
     161-203. On Lindisfarne in the later seventh century, see Mayr-Harting,
     Coming of Christianity, 225-6. Mrs. Goldsmith, Mode, pp. 22-39,
     cannot be considered to have answered Professor Donahue's case; the
     Irish church may have been as orthodox doctrinally, and even as cos-
     mopolitan culturally, as most others, but there remains overwhelming
     evidence for distinct idiosyncracies in the Christian civilization of early
     Ireland. See, e.g. B. Bischoff, "Wendepunkte in der Geschichte der

lateinischen Exegese im Frümittelalter," <u>Sacris Erudiri</u>, 6 (1954) 196-220; K. Hughes, <u>The Church in Early Irish Society</u> (London, 1966); and F. J. Byrne, <u>Irish Kings and High-Kings</u> (London, 1973). Mrs. Goldsmith ignores the actual evidence for a cult of the pagan hero in early Ireland.

86.   L. D. Benson, "The pagan coloring in <u>Beowulf</u>," <u>Old English Poetry</u>: <u>Fifteen Essays</u>, ed. R. P. Creed (Providence, R.I., 1967), 193-213. For the manuscript of the <u>Hildebrandslied</u>, see B. Bischoff, "Paläographische Fragen deutscher Denkmäler der Karolingerzeit," <u>Früh-mittelalterliche Studien</u> 5 (1971), 112-3.

87.   D. A. Binchy, "The linguistic and historical value of the Irish law-tracts," <u>PBA</u> 29 (1943), 195-227; and "Background of early Irish literature" (see above, p.75 , n.31); Byrne, <u>Irish Kings</u>, pp. 12-15. I am also indebted here to an unpublished paper by Dr. T. M. Charles-Edwards on, "The conversion of the Irish learned professions."

88.   <u>Alc. Ep.</u> 124, pp. 182-3; 20, pp. 57-8; 67, p. 211; and 233, p. 378. Cf. Abbot Cuthbert of Monkwearmouth's letter to Lull, <u>Bon. Ep.</u> 116, pp. 251-2.

89.   <u>Conc. Clovesho</u> (746), i, viii, ix, xii, xvi, xix, xx, xxviii, xxix, H&S, pp. 363-76; <u>Bon. Ep.</u> 78, pp. 170-1 (and, for the connection, Levison, <u>England and the Continent</u>, 86, n. 1). Cf. also the <u>Legatine Council</u> (786), xix, <u>Alc. Ep.</u> 3, p. 27.

90.   Roman Council: H&S, p. 133 (and cf. W. Levison, "Die Akten der römischen Synode von 679," <u>Aus rheinischer und fränkischer Frühzeit</u>, (Dusseldorf, 1948), 267-94, esp. 284) <u>Penit. Theod,</u> I i, H&S, pp. 177-8.

91.   <u>Ep. Egb.</u>, pp. 407-18; translation from <u>EHD</u>, pp. 737-42.

92.   <u>Conc. Clovesho</u> (746), v, H&S, p. 364; <u>Dial. Egb.</u>, xi, ibid., p. 408; <u>BCS</u> 154, 220, 241, 247-8, 378; <u>SC</u>89, 1411, 1257, 123, 125, 1434; cf. <u>Conc. Chelsea</u> (816), viii, H&S, pp. 582-3; and, generally, H. Böhmer, "Das Eigenkirchentum in England," <u>Festgabe für F.Liebermann</u> ed. M. Förster et al. (Halle, 1921), 334-45.

93.   For the relevant passages in <u>Beowulf</u>, see above p. 77, n.45. There is no comparable reference in the poem to the consumption of food; cf. Tacitus, <u>Germania</u>, xxi, xxiii, ed. M. Hutton (Harvard, Loeb series,) pp. 294-7.

94.   U. Stutz, "The proprietary church," trans. G. Barraclough, <u>Medieval Germany: Essays by German Historians</u> (Oxford, 1938), 35-70. For some interesting archaeological evidence, see Irsigler, <u>Untersuchungen</u>, (see above, p.72 , n.17), 207-8 and 212-3. For the Irish evidence, Hughes, <u>Church</u>, 160-4; Byrne, <u>Irish Kings</u>, 258. Cf. also I. B. Cowan, "The post-Columban Church in Scotland," <u>Proceedings of the Church History Society of Scotland</u> (1974), 245-60. For the Frankish evidence, F. Prinz, <u>Frühes Mönchtum im Frankenreich</u> (Munich, 1965), 185-7, 190, 278-9 and 502-3.

95. E. Ewig, "Milo et eiusmodi similes," Sankt Bonifatius Gedenkgabe (Fulda, 1954), 412-40. F. Prinz, Klerus und Krieg im früheren Mittelalter; (Stuttgart, 1971), e.g. 104-13; cf. Mayr-Harting, Coming of Christianity, 130-9; J. M. Wallace-Hadrill, "Rome and the early English church: some problems of transmission," Settimane Spoleto 7 (1960), 540-1; and "A background to St. Boniface," Whitelock Studies, 40-2.

96. Ekkehard, Casus Sancti Galli ix, ed. G. H. Pertz, MGH, Script in fol., II 117-8. On the Waltharius, see Strecker's introduction to his MGH edition (above p.80 , n.79) and Laistner, Thought and Letters, 357-9. On all of this, see Leyser, art. cit above, p.70 , n. 1 . esp. 30-1.

97. Flodoard, Historia Remensis Ecclesiae, IV.5, ed. J. Heller and G. Waitz, MGH, Script in fol., XIII, p. 564; for Eormanric, cf. Beowulf, lines 1197-1201; Widsith, pp. 15-36 (where Chambers does not cite the reference from Flodoard).

98. Rudolf of Fulda, Translatio sancti Alexandri, ed. G. H. Pertz, MGH, Script in fol, II, pp. 673-7; K. Schmid, "Die Nachfaren Widukinds," Deutsches Archiv 20 (1964), 1-47; and "Religiöses und sippen-gebundenes Gemeinschaftsbewusstsein in Frühmittelalterlichn Gedenkenbucheinträgen," ibid. 21 (1965), 63-4. H. Grundmann, "Die Frauen und die Literatur im Mittelalter," Archiv für Kulturgeschichte 26 (1936), 219-61, cites Charlemagne's Duplex Edictum (789), xix, Capitularia, I, p. 63 against the writing and sending of winileodas (apparently love-songs) by nuns, and suggests a connection between communities of female religious and the composition of vernacular literature; for some reason, he does not support his case with the example of Whitby, where Bede believed Anglo-Saxon religious poetry to have originated.

99. K. Bosl, "Die germanische Kontinuität im deutschen Mittelalter," Frühformen der Gesellschaft im mittelalterlichen Europa, (Munich, 1964), 93.

100. Ewig, "Milo," 430-40; Prinz, Klerus, 11-12, 73-104 and passim.

101. Schmid, "Religiöses," 69.

102. Beowulf, lines 2600-1. For the Minster, M. Deanesley, The Pre-conquest Church in England, 2nd ed. (London, 1963), pp. 191-220. and C. A. Ralegh Radford, "Pre-Conquest Minster Churches," Archaeological Journal 130 (1973), 126-40. For the interpretation of Bede's letter to Edgbert adopted in the text, see E. John, Land Tenure in Early England (Leicester, 1960), 44-9; "Folkland reconsidered," Orbis Britanniae and Other Studies (Leicester, 1966), 83-91; and "Saecularium Prioratus and the Rule of St Benedict," Rev. Ben. 75 (1965), 223-7. It is unnecessary to go into the vexed question of whether Anglo-Saxon kindreds insisted upon hereditary tenure before the coming of the church, since all scholars agree that bookland was at least open to the claims of heirs afterwards; but I share some of the reservations about Mr John's important thesis expressed by D. A. Bullough, "Anglo-Saxon institutions and the structure of Old English Society," Annali della fondazione italiana per la storia amministrativa 2 (1965), 652.

103. E. John, "The king and the monks in the tenth-century reformation," Orbis Britanniae, 154-80.

104. AEthelwulf, De Abbatibus, ed. A. Campbell (Oxford, 1967), p. xxii. Compare Alcuini Vita Willibrordi, i-ii, ed. W. Levison, MGH, Script. rer. Merov. VII, pp. 116-7, and EHD, pp. 713-4, and cf. p. 77.

105. For Deerhurst and its enlargement in the pre-Viking period, see H. M. and J. Taylor, Anglo-Saxon Architecture I (Cambridge, 1965), 193-209. For the transactions of its patrons, see BCS 274, 313 and 379, SC 139, 1187 and 1433, and the valuable comments of Professor Whitelock, EHD, pp. 471-3 and 476-7. The even more celebrated church at Brixworth, Taylor and Taylor, Anglo-Saxon Architecture, I, 108-14, was connected by Sir Frank Stenton, "Medehamstede and its colonies," Preparatory to Anglo-Saxon England, ed. D. M. Stenton (Oxford, 1969), pp. 183-5, to the mother-house at Peterborough, as was the artistically important early foundation at Breedon-on-the-Hill; and the initiative at Breedon was taken by a princeps of very considerable wealth, although there is no evidence that subsequent abbots were connected with his family. I do not of course maintain that every major Anglo-Saxon church was dominated by its founding family.

106. Eddius c. xxxiv, pp. 231-2; HE III.24, p. 179; IV, 23, p. 254 and IV.26, pp. 267-8; The Earliest Life of Gregory the Great, ed. B. Colgrave,(Kansas, 1968), pp. 35 & 39.

107. Alc. Ep. 127, p. 188; Anglo-Saxon Chronicle, s.a. 796, 798, Two of the Saxon Chronicles Parallel, ed. C. Plummer (Oxford, 1892), pp. 56-7; (future references to this edition), Symeon of Durham, Historia Regum, ed. T. Arnold, (Rolls Series) 75, II, 59; EHD, pp. 167-8, and 249.

108. Felix, c. xx, pp. 84-5; D. P. Kirby, "Bede's native sources for the Historia Ecclesiastica," BJRL, 48 (1965-6), 370; Taylor and Taylor, Anglo-Saxon Architecture II, 510-16; H. M. Taylor, "Repton reconsidered," Whitelock Studies, 351-89 (with especial emphasis on the importance of royal burials for the architecture of the church).

109. BCS, 196, SC 34; Stenton "Medehamstede," 191.

110. Levison, England and the Continent, 27-33 and 249-59.

111. Sisam, Structure, 50; Whitelock, Audience, 58-64. For other illustrations of Mercian treatment of royal minsters, see, e.g., BCS 234, 236 and 241; (SC 116, 117 and 1257).

112. BCS 384 (SC 1436). This charter, and the conflict underlying it, has been illuminated as never before by Dr N. P. Brooks, in his forthcoming study, The Early History of Christ Church, Canterbury, which he was kind enough to show me.

113. For Wilfrid's career, HE V.19, pp. 322-30, and II, pp. 315-29.

114. Eddius, xiii, pp. 207-8; xvii, pp. 211-12; and lxii, pp. 257-8; Bede, "Ep. ad Pleguinam," Bedae Opera de Temporibus, ed. Jones, P. 315; Gesta Pontificum (see above, p. 78, n. 58), pp. 338-9, and Whitelock,

"Anglo-Saxon poetry," pp. 89-90. On the interpretation of Wilfrid's career, see Mayr-Harting, Coming of Christianity, ch. 9; and E. John, "The social and political problems of the early English Church," Land, Church and People: Essays presented to H. P. R. Finberg, ed. J. Thirsk, (Reading, 1970), 39-63.

115. For Egbert, ep. ad Egb., p. 412, and II, p. 378; cf. Alcuin, Carmen de pontificibus et sanctis Ecclesiae Eborancensis, lines 1250-2 and 1273-5, Historians of the Church of York and its Archbishops, ed. J. Raine, Rolls Series 71, 386; Symeon of Durham, Historia Ecclesiae Dunelmensis, ed. Arnold, I, 49. For episcopal casualties, Anglo-Saxon Chronicle, 871, pp. 72-3; for episcopal compensation, Abt. 1, p. 3, and cf. Dial. Egb., xii, H&S, pp. 408-9.

116. R. Woolf, "Doctrinal influences on the Dream of the Rood," Medium Aevum 27 (1958), 137-53; J.V. Fleming, "The Dream of the Rood; and Anglo-Saxon monasticism," Traditio 22 (1966), 43-72.

117. K. R. Brooks, Andreas and the Fates of the Apostles (Oxford, 1961), pp. xxii-xxvi.

118. C. L. Wrenn, "The poetry of Caedmon," PBA 32 (1946), 284-8; D. H. Green, The Carolingian Lord (Cambridge, 1965), 270-401.

119. R. L. S. Bruce Mitford, "The decoration," T. Kendrick, T. J. Brown and R. L. S. Bruce Mitford, Evangeliorum Quattuor Codex Lindisfarnensis (Lausanne, 1956-60), II, 110-259, esp. 250ff; cf. Bruce Mitford's "Reception by the Anglo-Saxons of Mediterranean Art," Settimane Spoleto 14 (1967), 797-825. And see David Wilson's essay in this volume, above, pp.1-22.

120. Bon. Ep. 35, p. 60.

121. See above. cf. Whitelock, Audience, 80-2; Mayr-Harting, Coming of Christianity 230-9.

122. Felix, cc. xxiv and xxv, pp. 86-9; c. xxxi, pp. 100-7; c. xxiv, pp. 108-11; and c. xxxvi, pp. 114-7; cf. Athanasius's Life of Anthony, vii-x, trans. R. J. Deferrari, Early Christian Biographies, Fathers of of the Church 15 (Washington, 1952), pp. 142-5.

123. Felix, c. xxxv, pp. 110-13; c. xl, pp. 124-7; c. xlix, pp. 148-51; and c. li-lii, pp. 160-7. For the Adelsheiliger, see Prinz, Frühes Mönchtum, 496-503; Klerus, 58-62; and his. "Heiligenkult und Adelsherrschaft im Spiegel merovingischer Hagiographie," Historische Zeitschrift 204 (1967), 529-44; K. Bosl, "Der Adelsheiliger," Speculum Historiale: Festschrift J. Spörl (Munich, 1965), 167-87. For a rather different approach, F. Graus, Volk, Herrscher und Heiliger im Reich der Merovinger (Prague, 1965).

124. de Vries (see above, p. 76, n. 38) II, 99-100, 105 and 153; F. M. Stenton, Anglo-Saxon heathenism, Preparatory to ASE, 295.

125. The Oldest English Texts, ed. H. Sweet Early English Text Society 83 (London, 1885; reptd 1966), pp. 169-71; Nennius, Historia

Brittonum, ed. T. Mommsen, MGH Auct. Antiq. XIII, 202-5; Beowulf, lines 4, 18, 53, 901, 1068ff., 1201, 1709, 1949, 1960-2; Widsith, 14, 18, 88, 27, 35-44. K. Sisam, "Anglo-Saxon royal genealogies," PBA 39 (1953), 287-346; Goody and Watt, "The consequences of literacy," (see above, p.75, n.33), 31-4; Vansina, Oral Tradition (see above, p.74, n.26), 153. For the East Anglian genealogy in full, see Bruce Mitford, Sutton Hoo, 62, (and cf. B. Green in Antiquaries' Journal 51 (1971), 321-3); for the West Saxon, Anglo-Saxon Chronicle, s.a. 855, p. 66. For a revised date and provenance of the genealogy collection, see now D.N. Dumville, "The Anglian collection of royal genealogies and regnal lists," Anglo-Saxon England, 5 (1976), 23-50.

126. Alc. Ep. 129, p. 192; on all of this, cf. M. C. W. Hunter, "Germanic and Roman antiquity and the sense of the past in Anglo-Saxon England," Anglo-Saxon England 3 (1974), 29-51, which the author kindly showed me before publication, when my own paper was still germinating.

127. Stanley, "Haethenra Hyht," 136. In his "Beowulf," Continuations and Beginnings, ed. E. G. Stanley, (London, 1966), 139-40, Professor Stanley comes close to the view adopted in this paper.

128. Gregorii Turonensis Historia Francorum, ed. B. Krusch and W. Levison, MGH, Script. Rer. Merov., I, 2nd edn. (1951). For discussion of Gregory, see J. M. Wallace-Hadrill, "The work of Gregory of Tours in the light of modern research," The Long-Haired Kings (London, 1962), 49-70; and, "Gregory of Tours and Bede," Frühmittelalterliche Studien 2 (1968), 31-44; for further discussion of the contrast with Bede, Campbell, "Bede," 172 and 176-9; and Bede, p. xv (full references above, p. 71, nn. 6, 7). See also R.A. Markus Bede and theTradition of Ecclesiastical History (Jarrow Lecture, 1975).

129. Pauli Diaconi Historia Langobardorum, I 7-9 ed. G. Waitz, MGH, Script. Rer. Langobard., pp. 52-3; cf. Origo Gentis Langobardorum in the same edition, pp. 2-3. There is no major modern study of Paul, but see E. Sestan, "La Storiografia dell'Italia longobarda," Settimane Spoleto 17 (1970), 357-86.

130. Widukindi Res Gestae Saxonicae, I iii-xv, ed. G. Waitz, P. Hirsch and P. Lohmann, MGH, in us. schol., pp. 4-25; cf. K. Hauck, Goldbrakteaten aus Sievern (Munich, 1970), esp. 43-112. On Widukind see, above all, H. Beumann, Widukind von Korvei (Weimar, 1950), and Beumann's "Historiographische Konzeption und politische Ziele Widukinds von Korvei," Settimane Spoleto 17 (1970), 857-94.

131. Chambers, "Bede," PBA, 22 (1936), 132 and 137-8.

132. Attention should also be drawn here to the sea-beast saga with which Fredegar amplifies Gregory's account of the pagan past of the Franks, Fredegarii Chronicon III, 9, ed. B. Krusch, MGH Script. Rer. Merov. II, 95, and cf. J. M. Wallace-Hadrill, "Fredegar and the history of France," Long-Haired Kings, p. 84. It should be emphasized that both the Franks and the Saxons envisaged an originally Mediterranean origin for their peoples (Trojan and Macedonian respectively). Like the East Anglians, their past had to do with more than primeval German forests; cf. Leyser (above, p. 70, n.1), pp. 29-30.

133. HE I. 15, pp. 30-3; and I. 34, pp. 71-2.

134. Bede, De Schematibus et Tropis, ed. G. H. Tanenhaus, Quarterly Journal of Speech 48 (1962), pp. 237-53; cf. E. R. Curtius, European Literature and the Latin Middle Ages, trans. W. R. Trask (New York, (1953), 46-7; Hunter Blair, World of Bede, 282-97, and his, "From Bede to Akuin," Famulus Christi, 239-60.

135. Bede, Expos. in Act. xvii 23, ed. Laistner (see above, p. 71 , n. 3), p. 66, observes that God was known in Judaea and rejected, and unknown in Achaea though sought. He coments that he who does not know God is himself ignored, and he who is obstinate is punished, that neither is immune from blame, but that those who never received the Faith are excusabiliores than those who laid hands on the Christ they did know. For Augustine's treatment of the noble pagans of Rome, see Brown, Augustine, 299-312.

136. Bede Explanatio Apocalypsis, Praef., PL, 93 col. 134; Expos. in Act. Praef. ep. ad Accam, p. 3; HE v. 23, pp. 349-51 (note especially the two comets, the advance of the Arabs, the chaos of Ceolwulf's reign and the proliferation of monasticism, for which cf. ep. Egb. as above, p. 82 , n. 91); Mayr-Harting, Coming of Christianity, pp. 217-9, has brilliantly captured the urgent note in Bede's life's work. For a rather different view, see Bonner's article (cited above, p. 70 , n. 1), p. 84.

137. Campbell, Bede, pp. xiv-xvi. For classical influences upon Paul and Widukind, see Sestan, pp. 359-62, 384; and Beumann, Widukind, pp. 18-21 and "Historiographische Konzeption," pp. 872-3.

138. For Bede on Gildas, HE I. 22, p. 42 (cf. III. 17, p. 161); for his use of Gildas, Hanning, Vision of History, 44-90, and Wallace-Hadrill, Early Germanic Kingship, 74-6. For the uncensured bishop, HE III. 7, p. 141, and for the principle of not criticizing priests, Bede, In Sam. xv, 30-1, p. 135, xxvi, pp. 244-5; cf. Carroll, Bede's Spiritual Teachings, 150-2, and Campbell, "Bede," 177. For Aidan, HE III.5, p. 136; and for the use of example, HE Praef., p. 5.

139. Gregory, Dialogues, ed. U. Moricca, (Rome, 1924), p. 16 (trans. O. J. Zimmermann, Fathers of the Church 39 (Washington, 1959), p. 6); Liber Regulae Pastoralis, I 2, PL 77 cols. 15-16; (trans. J. Barmby, Select Library of the Nicene and post-Nicene Fathers 12 ii, p. 2); cf. also II 3, III 6, PL 77, cols. 28-30 and 56-7, and A. de Vogue, "Sub regula vel abbate," Collectanea Cisterciana 33 (1971), 209-41.

140. Campbell, "Bede," 182.

141. HE V. 24, p. 357; Bede, Homily I 13, p. 93; cf. Eddius c. ii, pp. 194-5; Felix cc. xviii-xix, pp. 80-3; Anon. Vita Cuthberti I vii (for edition, see p. 78 , n.57), p. 73.

142. For Paul, HL IV.37, pp. 131-2, cf. II.9, pp. 77-8, and Waitz's intro-duction, p. 15; cf. also Sestan, 360-1, 374-5; for Widukind, Beumann,

Widukind, 2-3, 22-4, and "Historiographische Konzeption," 870-2; for Gregory, HF, p. x.

143. C. P. Wormald, "Bede and Benedict Biscop," Famulus Christi, 141-69, esp. p. 151 and n. 80 (p. 166). Cf. above p.85 n.123, and Prinz, Frühes Mönchtum, p. 457-64. It should be noted that the independent Vita Ceolfridi (VC), edited by Plummer in the Opera Historica, pp. 388-404, shares the same tone as Bede's HA, which confirms that this tone is a function of community traditions, and not an idiosyncracy of Bede's. Bede's life of Cuthbert is very different, but here Bede was following an earlier life, and the additions that he makes have nothing to do with Adelsheiliger norms: cf. C. G. Loomis, "The miracle tradition of the Venerable Bede," Speculum 21 (1946), 404-18.

144. HA xi, pp. 375-6 and xvii, p. 381; VC xvi, pp. 393-4 and xxv, p. 396; cf. Eddius cc. lxii-lxiii, pp. 258-9; and HE IV.16, p. 237.

145. E. A. Lowe, English Uncial (Oxford, 1961); R. L. S. Bruce Mitford, "The art of the Codex Amiatinus," Journal of the British Archaeological Association 32 (1969), 1-25; C. Nordenfalk, "Before the Book of Durrow," Acta Archaeologica 18 (1947), pp. 159-66; cf. p. 85 and n.119 above; also R. W. Southern, "Bede," Medieval Humanism and other Studies (London, 1970), p. 2.

146. VC viii, pp. 390-1.

147. See p. 73 and n.20 above. This is not to deny that Bede does, on occasion, reflect the values of Germanic society; HE I.34, pp. 71-2; II.9, p. 99; III.14, p. 155; IV.15, p. 236; and IV.21, p. 249; what remains surprising nevertheless, especially by comparison with continental writers, is not the existence of evidence that Bede was a seventh-century Barbarian, but its paucity.

148. Wallace-Hadrill, "Work of Gregory of Tours," 54-5, emphasizes the hagiographical training from which Gregory proceeded to history. Cassiodorus became one of the most important minor fathers after his (lost) history of the Goths was written, and apparently it was almost entirely secular and politic in motivation. Cf. A. Momigliano, "Cassiodorus and the Italian culture of his time," Studies in Historiography (1966), 181-210; so also Isidore of Seville's Historia Gothorum, ed. T. Mommsen, MGH Auct. Antiq. XI; cf. J. Messmer, Hispania-idee und Gotenmythos (Zurich, 1960), 85-137 and J. N. Hillgarth, "Historiography in Visigothic Spain," Settimane Spoleto 17 (1970), 295-9.

149. Campbell, "First Century," (see above, p.71, n. 7), pp. 20-9.

150. For the blood-feud, see Whitelock, Audience, 13-19; and the important article by J. M. Wallace-Hadrill, "The blood-feud of the Franks," Long-Haired Kings, 121-47. For the popularity of the Apocrypha, see R.E. Kaske, "Beowulf and the Book of Enoch," Speculum, 46 (1971), 421-31, and Ogilvy, Books Known to the English, 66-74.

151. For the Wessobrunner Gebet and the Muspilli, see Die kleineren althoch-
      deutschen Sprachdenkmäller, ed. E. von Steinmayer (Berlin, 1916), pp.
      16-19 and 66-81, and cf. Ker, Dark Ages, 240-1. For the Altus Prosator,
      The Irish Liber Hymnorum, ed. J. H. Bernard and R. Atkinson, Henry
      Bradshaw Society (London, 1898) I 62-83, and II, 146; Mrs Goldsmith,
      Mode, pp. 42-7 intelligently draws attention to the imaginative overlap
      between this poem and Beowulf. For Beowulf and the Arians, J. Halver-
      son, "Pitfalls of piety," (see above, p. 76 , n. 43), p. 275; but the dif-
      ference between the Gothic and insular terminology of Godhead is a
      crucial argument against Arian influence: Green, Carolingian Lord,
      233-321, and W. Baetke, Das Heilige im Germanischen (Tübingen, 1942),
      213-6 and 220-6. For the appeal of Arianism, see E. A. Thompson,
      The Visigoths in the Time of Ulfila (Oxford, 1966), 107-10.

152. K. Hughes, Early Christian Ireland; an Introduction to the Sources
      (London, 1972), 170-1.

153. W. A. Chaney, "Paganism to Christianity in Anglo-Saxon England,"
      Harvard Theological Review 53 (1960), 200; but cf. H. Kuhn, "Das
      Fortleben," Spoleto (1967), (see above, p. 76 , n. 38), 743; "besonders
      irreführend ist es das Ethische in den Begriff der Religionen aufzunehmen."
      E. G. Stanley, "The quest" see above, (p. 76 , n. 42) is an entertaining
      critique of the paganizers of early English literature.

154. Conc Clovesho (746) iii, H&S, pp. 303-4; cf. Stenton, "Anglo-Saxon
      Heathenism," 281-97; Mayr-Harting, Coming of Christianity 22-30.

155. Vansina, Oral Tradition, 96. For the curiously similar determination
      of the later Roman aristocracy not to accept the Augustinian dismissal
      of the legends of the Republic, or to abandon Vergil and Livy, though
      willing to accept baptism and patronize Prudentius, cf. Momigliano,
      "Cassiodorus" (see above, p.88 , n.148), 185-6; and Brown, "The
      conversion" (see above, p.70 , n. 1), 10.

156. For the euhemerization of Woden, see the letter of Bishop Daniel to
      Boniface, Bon.Ep. 23, pp. 39-41; and the Chronicle of AEthelweard,
      ed. A. Campbell, (London, 1962), pp. 7 and 9. For the genealogies,
      see above.

157. K. Hauck, "Lebensnormen und Kultmythen in germanischen Stammes
      - und Herrschergenealogien," Saeculum, 6 (1955), 204-5, Professor
      Hauck misses the case of the West Saxons, but cf. Ker, Catalogue, nos.
      39 and 180. I hope to consider the significance of this point in a study
      provisionally entitled The English Legislative Tradition and its Analogues:
      Alfred to Wulfstan. Note also the association between the codification
      of the poetry and the laws in Einhard's Life of Charlemagne, xxix, (see
      above,p. 79, n. 62.

158. W. G. Ker, Epic and Romance, 54-7; Chadwick, Heroic Age, 30-40
      and 329-32.

159. John, "Social and political problems," (see p. 84 and n.114 above) is
      good on the limitations of this view.

160. Ker, _Epic and Romance_, 45-7.

161. Bruce Mitford _Codex Lindisfarnensis_ II, 126-73; Plummer, II, p. 309; cf. Mayr-Harting, _Coming of Christianity_, 192-204.

APPENDICES

A: THE EARLY ENGLISH ARISTOCRACY AND ITS STATUS

For the legal evidence bearing upon the existence of an aristocracy in seventh century England, see above, p.72 , n. 14. Between the laws of Hlothere (685-6) and those of Wihtred (695), the word for nobleman changes from eorl to gesith, and it is gesith that is the term in the laws of Ine (also c. 693-4). But from the start, the word gesith has the suffix -cund: see, e.g. Wi 5, In 34:1, 45. As Professor Whitelock points out, EHD, p. 362. this establishes that, whatever the etymological significance of the word gesith, the status it conferred passed by birth. The much later evidence of Norðleoda Laga 9-12, pp. 460-1 associates the maintenance of noble status with the inheritance of a property qualification over two generations: see Liebermann, Vol. II, Sachglossar, s.v. Adel, sections 1, 3, 4, 11, pp. 268-70. On a matter such as this, one is unwilling to differ from Sir Frank Stenton, but it is difficult, in the light of the above, to agree with ASE, pp. 303-4, that the old hereditary nobility of the Anglo-Saxons had failed to survive the invasions; especially since one can adduce the contrary opinion of H. M. Chadwick, Studies on Anglo-Saxon Institutions, (Cambridge, 1905; New York reissue, 1963), pp. 378-83. For a modern compromise, see H. R. Loyn, "Gesiths and Thegns in England from the seventh to the tenth centuries," EHR, 70 (1955), pp. 529-40; and, Anglo-Saxon England and the Norman Conquest (London, 1963), pp. 200-9.

Stenton's view was presumably influenced by the orthodoxy then prevailing with regard to Frankish history. See, e.g. H. Brunner, Deutsche Rechtsgeschichte, 2nd ed. (Leipzig, 1906) I, pp. 135-40 and 349-51. It must obviously affect a British historian's view that few continental scholars would now accept this opinion of the early Germanic peoples without reservation, despite the absence of an aristocratic wergild from most of the continental codes. See H. Dannenbauer, "Adel, Burg and Herrschaft bei den Germanen," Grundlagen der mittelalterlichen Welt (Stuttgart, 1958), pp. 121-78; G. Duby, "La noblesse dans la Francie medievale: une enquête a poursuivre," Revue Historique, 226 (1961), pp. 1-22; L. Genicot, "La Noblesse au Moyen Age dans l'ancienne Francie," Annales 17 (1962), pp. 1-22 (cf Comparative Studies in Society and History 5 (1962-3), pp. 52-9); K. F. Werner, "Bedeutende Adelsfamilien im Reich Karls des Grossen," Karl der Grosse, ed. W. Braunfels et al. Vol. I (Dusseldorf, 1965), 83-142; and F. Irsigler, Untersuchungen, (see p.72 ,n. 17), who begins with a useful bibliographical survey, and whose arguments have been of special value to me. But D. A. Bullough, "Europae Pater: Charlemagne and his achievement," EHR, 85 (1970), pp. 73-82, sounds an important warning note against the exaggerations of this school; and, for the older view, cf R. Sprandel, "Struktur and Geschichte des merovingischen Adels," Historische Zeitschrift 193 (1961), pp. 33-71.

This is no place to enter further into what should be a major topic of research in its own right, but two points that are worth emphasizing provisionally are these. First, noble families might easily fail to maintain their line beyond two or three generations in early medieval circumstances, and this might make even a hereditary nobility difficult to trace for long: see Duby, "La noblesse," pp. 20-1, and cf K. B. Macfarlane, The Nobility of Later Medieval England (Oxford, 1973), pp. 132-76. Second, even where title and property were inherited, renewed royal patronage might remain very important; it could help to establish novi homines, as indicated in the tract, Geþyncðo, 2, 3, pp. 456-7; cf Bullough, "Europae Pater", Macfarlane, Nobility, pp. 158-67, and Stenton's "Thriving of the Anglo-Saxon ceorl," Preparatory to Anglo-Saxon England , pp. 383-93. It could also supply additional endowment sufficient to cope with the difficulties of partible, or disputed, inheritance: Cf in general terms, T. M. Charles-Edwards, "Kinship, status and the origins of the hide," PP 56 (1972), pp. 1-33; and J. Holt, Politics and property in early medieval England", ibid. 58, pp. 3-52. A Geburtsadel might then need to be a Dienstadel also, which would accou for the connotations of service in such words as Gesith and Thegn, and for the evidence of ep. Egb. that Northumbrian nobles needed to be continually seeking hereditary endowments from the king in return for service at his court. Thus, neither the "fragility" of an early medieval aristocracy, nor its close relationship to royal power weigh against the positive legal evidence that there was an Anglo-Saxon nobility, which was, in some sense, hereditary.

B: BEOWULF AS ALLEGORY

See above, pp.77 , n.48 for examples of the allegorical approach and for the most effective objections to it. The allegorical approach fails to make sense of the poem, because it is so difficult to be sure that Beowulf has any one coherent message of an edifying type; few scholars have thought so until recently. It can perhaps be suggested that Beowulf himself is criticized by secular standards for his pursuit of the dragon, and this case is made by J. Leyerle, "Beowulf, the hero and the king," Medium Aevum 34 (1965), pp. 89-102; but cf. S. B. Greenfield, "Beowulf and epic tragedy," Comparative Literature, (1962), pp. 91-105; B. Mitchell, "Until the dragon comes...," Neophilologus, (1963), pp. 131, 137 n. 30; Smithers, "Destiny and the heroic warrior in Beowulf," pp. 80-1; Donahue pp. 293-6. Mrs Goldsmith's case that the hero is criticized from the standpoint of Christian morality is open to more serious objections. It is difficult to agree that "the secular material" in the poem is, "concentrated within one small sphere of interest" (Mode., p. 8). On the contrary, Mrs Goldsmith's interpretation depends heavily upon a single passage in the poem, Hrothgar's long admonition to Beowulf (lines 1700-84), and it is not clear that even this passage conveys an unambiguously Christian case against secular values, as compared, for example, with the continental Waltharius, lines 857-75, in which one of the heroes launches into an eloquent discourse against greed as such. As I read it, the speech is a warning, not only against oferhygd (which is not necessarily the same thing as superbia), but also against complacency, cruelty to retainers and above all parsimony (not cupidity). Parsimony, as the anthropologists teach us, is a major solecism in primitive societies and widely condemned, quite apart from Christian teaching: see M. Mauss, The Gift, tr. J. Cunnison, revised edn. (London, 1969); and M. Gluckmann, Politics, Law, and Ritual in Tribal Society (Oxford, 1965), pp. 45-80. This aspect of the speech is also argued powerfully by J. Golden, in his unpublished Cornell Ph.D. thesis, "Societal bonds in Old English Heroic poetry," 1970, ch. 2; and cf. M. Cherniss, Ingeld and Christ, pp. 79-101. Germanic poetry was congenitally gnomic and sententious; there is nothing very distinctive about the Beowulf poet's attitude to the "changes and chances of this fleeting world," and we find the same keynote struck by King Gelimer of the Vandals, trapped on a Mauretanian mountainside with the Byzantine army beneath (Procopius, De Bello Vandalico, IV.vi 31-3, ed. H. B. Dewing (Harvard, Loeb series, 1963), pp. 262-3).

More generally, though Beowulf has its structural problems, these will not, in themselves, suffice as signposts to hidden allegory (cf. J. E. Cross, Latin themes in Old English poetry (Lund, 1962), p. 10); and I am not convinced that the unusual conclusion to the Dragon fight would immediately have reminded an Anglo-Saxon audience of Job, rather than Sigurd. But argument on this sort of point is scarcely likely to lead to proof, and, where so much depends upon subjective reaction, it would be ungenerous not to acknowledge that I am much indebted to Mrs Goldsmith for the stimulus of her ideas.

Beowulf as allegory is, however, objectionable on principle also. The very secular medium whereby the poet sought to transmit his message (if he had one) argues that he was addressing an audience of relative "beginners," one that would respond the better for being taught in the terms that were familiar to it. In the early Middle Ages, however, it was generally agreed that the allegorical approach was for specialists. Gregory the Great was following a tradition that went back to Origen, when he declared in the preface to his Moralia in Job that, "just as the divine word exercises the prudent by its mysteries, so it generally nourishes the simple by its surface. It holds in public what feeds the little ones; it keeps in secret what suspends in admiration the minds of the more advanced": Moralia, Praef iv, PL 75, col. 515; cf. Augustine De catechizandis rudibus, ix, ed. J. P. Christopher (Washington, 1926), p. 42; de Lubac (see above, n. 73   ) I, 199, 410, 522-3; II.ii, 170-1; Brown, Augustine, pp. 259-62. The Moralia has often been invoked by defenders of an allegorical Beowulf, but it is worth noting that Gregory himself was furious that what he had published as the private discourses of intellectuals in Constantinople were being publicly expounded by the bishop of Ravenna: Ep. XII 6, p. 352. Here then is a painful tension between two premisses in the argument that Beowulf is allegory: the nature of the poem that is being used to teach is pulling in one direction, indicating an unsophisticated audience; the method of teaching that is being used, arguing a readership of intellectuals, is pulling in the other.

There is no doubt that medieval allegory had a future, and it is probable that some Anglo-Saxon poetry is allegorical: e.g. J. E. Cross, "The conception of the Old English Phoenix," Creed, Essays (cf. n. 86), pp. 219-52; cf. de Lubac, II.ii, pp. 197-233. But it would be easier to believe in an allegorical Beowulf if its defenders could point to anything remotely similar being written for this purpose at anything like so early a date.

C: THE DATE OF BEOWULF

See above, p.73, n.21. For the purposes of this paper, I have left the question of the date of Beowulf open, although I have usually assumed that it is likely to belong to the first pre-Alfredian phase of Anglo-Saxon history. The evidence presented in this paper overall bears in two ways upon the dating of Beowulf. First, it perhaps reinforces the unlikelihood of a tenth-century date. In excluding the post-Viking period, it is less relevant that the poet is proud of Scandinavians, than that he is celebrating apparent heathens. At least in Wessex and southern Mercia, King Alfred and his successors were trying to create a "crusading" atmosphere, and I should be surprised if anyone who had been effectively exposed to this movement would have wished to compose a work in which the heroes occasionally practised pagan rites, and (except in lines 175-88) without censure; they might, on the other hand, have been willing to listen to such works: R. L. Reynolds, "An echo of Beowulf in King Aethelstan's charters?" Medium Aevum, 24 (1955), pp. 101-3. Later in the tenth century, we are not only reaching the terminus ante quem for the necessary prototypes of our manuscript, but also the period in which the Carolingian currents that obliterated much of the continental material (see above, pp.78 and 79, nn. 55, 61-2) were at their strongest in England. See, further, Chadwick, Heroic Age, pp. 30-40, on the different style of tenth-century hero. Second, these arguments would certainly tend to justify Professor Whitelock's extension of the possible dating limits for the poem up to the end of the pre-Viking period, Audience, pp. 22-30, 57-64, 99-105). The "aristocratic" climate of early English Christianity is, if anything, more apparent in the Age of Offa than in the Age of Bede, and if Offa's court was capable of compiling royal genealogies out of tales of Scandinavian heroes, there is no reason why they should not also have written up the tales themselves.

Two other considerations that weigh with me are these: Aspects of the poem's "archaeology" (for which cf. Cramp, as above, p.72, n. 11) point towards an earlier rather than a post-Viking date. Secondly, Chadwick, Heroic Age, pp. 64-6, made the quite exceptionally interesting point, to which I have seen no subsequent reference, that until about 800, Anglo-Saxon families were continuing to give their sons and daughters "heroic" names, but that the habit died away during the ninth and tenth centuries. Chadwick's statistics would need revision in the light of Dr Sisam's work on the genealogies, but this would not alter the validity of a change after 800 (see also, C. E. Wright, The Cultivation of Saga in Anglo-Saxon England, London, 1939, pp. 19-20). Assuming that linguistic scholars, whose arguments I cannot claim to judge, are unable to reach agreement on the dating of the poem's language, I would defend dating limits of 675-875, but would wish to make no further commitment on historical grounds.

IV. THE ARCHER AND ASSOCIATED FIGURES
ON THE RUTHWELL CROSS — A RECONSIDERATION

R. T. Farrell

Since a number of widely variant opinions are current regarding the significance of the archer on Ruthwell and other English crosses, it seems necessary to examine the Ruthwell figure yet again, as Ruthwell is early in the series of English stone crosses, and is thus of central importance for all discussions.[1] The cross-head, in its present condition,[2] appears as follows. (As will be noted below, the reconstruction is incorrect. The description given here is provisional in some minor respects, pending further examination and photography.)

North Face (plate VIII): Top. Full-length frontal figure of a bird of prey, with head in profile. It clutches a piece of foliage in its left claw, and holds its right leg close up to its body. There are traces of a runic inscription in the borders, but these are no help in identification since only odd letters can be made out at present. The transom is a modern insertion. Bottom. Two figures, shown about half-length; though the panel is very worn, it appears that the left figure is winged, and that the right figure holds a book in draped hands and is half turned with inclined head towards the left figure.

South Face (plate IX): Top. The figure of a man, possibly seated, is on the right. His head is inclined towards a large bird on his right. The bird has its beak turned towards the human figure. One of its claws is on his wrist; the other leg is extended and the large claw is partially masked by the drapery folds of the human figure. There are traces of a Latin inscription visible. IN .... UM, generally expanded to IN PRINCIPIO ERAT VERBUM, the first words of St John's gospel. The transom is a modern insertion. Bottom. An archer, shown in profile and half length, in the act of drawing his bow; the arrow's head is clearly visible in the upper right hand corner of the panel, and a quiver can be seen on the lower part of the figure.

The only hint at identification for any of these figures is the reconstructed inscription around the top of the present south face, which leads me to identify the bird and human figure with John the Evangelist and his symbol, the eagle. It appears that the top arm of the cross was restored back to front. The reasons for supposing this come from the congruity of the two evangelist panels, John and his eagle (on the top arm of the present south face) and that of the man with book and winged figure, which can be interpreted as Matthew and his angel, (on the bottom of the present north face.[2a] A reversal would bring the archer and the bird onto the same side of the cross, though the relationship between the two is by no means as clear as that between the evangelist

Plate VIII   Ruthwell cross head, north face.
Copyright David Wilson.

Plate IX   Ruthwell cross head, south face.   Crown copyright.

figures on the opposite face. It must be stressed that the reason for assuming the cross-head to be the wrong way round has nothing to do with the conjunction of the bird and archer; they are associated because an evangelist series on the opposite face seems a very likely possibility.

We can now turn to interpretations of the archer made in the past forty years. Baldwin Brown saw the archer and eagle as linked, perhaps as a representation of a secular theme of hunting, with the bird as "nothing but a noble quarry, that the archer will presently transfix with his shaft".[3] Professor Schapiro supported a predominantly secular interpretation of these figures, and was firm in the belief that the archer and the eagle were both images of force, with a poetic and emotional significance. He cited scenes of violence elsewhere in medieval art, such as the Meigle stones in Scotland, on one of which Daniel with the lions is surrounded by "hunters, hounds, a centaur with two axes, a man with a club, and a dragon fighting a horned beast."[4]

No fewer than four different religious meanings for the archer have been put forward. Dr Saxl held that the archer was a representation of "the enemies by which the Roman church was surrounded, pagans and heretics alike."[5] Professor Kantorowitz identified the archer as Ishmael, the figura of the good man in the desert protected by God, and cited St John Chrysostom in support of his interpretation.[6] His argument was vigorously refuted by Schapiro, who re-stated his conception of the secular nature of the archer and the eagle, with further documentation and analogues.[7] The rediscovery in 1965 of an eleventh- or twelfth-century walrus ivory reliquary cross, now in the Victoria and Albert Museum, led to further discussion of the archer on English sculpture.[8] This reliquary, which may have served also as a pectoral, has as principal decoration of one of its faces the figure of an archer, half length, drawing his bow, and pointing directly at a bird (almost certainly not an eagle, by pose and shape) on the upper part of the shaft.[9] Beckwith identified the archer on the pectoral as Ishmael, and saw him as a type of the Old Testament, citing Augustine for this interpretation.[10] He linked the archer on this cross to Ruthwell:

> The representation of Ishmael the archer on one side of a cross had been current in England for a long time. He appears in almost the same position on the back of the Ruthwell cross, Dumfriesshire, about the middle of the eighth century, and again on the cross at St Andrew, Auckland, Co. Durham, towards the end of the eighth century.[11]

Most recently, Dr Raw, in studying the pectoral once again, and its scheme in relation to other ivory and monumental crosses, saw the archer and his arrow on the pectoral (and on Ruthwell as well) as symbols of God's word and of the preacher, respectively.[12]

There are several reasons for questioning direct relations drawn between the Ruthwell archer and the archer on the walrus ivory pectoral. The wide difference in date and background can be overlooked, in fact must be overlooked, if the two closely parallel one another, and if no other comparable objects can be found. However, there are significant differences between the presentation of the archer and the eagle on the two. Ruthwell has an eagle on the top of its cross-head; below, separated by the central field of the transom, is an archer. The pectoral has an eagle, but it is on the terminal of one of the arms, not above the archer, (pl. Xa). There is indeed a bird above the archer on the pectoral, but it is not an eagle, and it is no noble bird, with its long neck twisted about, and its scrawny body. It is also significant that both the archer and the bird on this face of the pectoral are enmeshed in vine-scroll, while neither figure on the Ruthwell cross is so treated. The Ruthwell bird grasps a bit of stylized foliage, the archer is free-standing.

With these differences between the pectoral and the Ruthwell cross in mind, the relations of the Ruthwell archer with archers on other sculpture can be considered, and the spectrum of recent opinion reviewed. A solution of this problematic figure is not easily found, since we have no inscription on the cross itself to identify the archer. Professor Schapiro's concept of secular representations of force is attractive, though his analogues for the most part come from a much later period,[13] or from traditions in carving and iconography far removed from Ruthwell. Those he cites in the English series of crosses are significantly different. The Ruthwell archer is not in a vine-scroll; he stands fully independently, among the figure-sculpture, on a different face from the vine-scroll. Schapiro cites sculpture at Hexham, Halton, Sheffield, Bishop Auckland and elsewhere as having "the same conception of a a bowman and a bird" as at Ruthwell.[14] Let us take each of these in turn. The Hexham piece is not a parallel for Ruthwell, for it is clearly derived from the classic Ara Pacis style.[15] At Halton an archer aims at a bird, hovering above him; the bird does not look like an eagle, and is enmeshed in vine-scroll, as is the archer. The St Andrew Auckland cross (pl. XI) has an archer at the base, but he is standing on the vine-scroll and aiming up at a dog-like creature in an inhabited vine-scroll; there is a bird above. The Sheffield cross has an archer in secular dress pointing up into a vine-scroll. There are two further parallels not cited by Shapiro. A fragment from Bradbourne has an archer in a position similar to the Sheffield Figure (pl. XII) pointing up into a vine-scroll, and a cross at Bakewell provides yet another similar example. It is clear that none of these instances are parallels for the Ruthwell eagle and archer. As far as I know, no early English sculpture parallels the Ruthwell treatment of the archer and the eagle.

Provisionally excluding Shapiro's secular interpretation of the archer and the bird, the various religious interpretations of the archer can be examined. Roughly speaking, these can be divided into two groups. The archer has been interpreted as a benign figure standing for either (1) the good man in the desert, or (2) the teachings and teachers of the church. With negative significance, the archer has been seen as Ishmael-heretic, or, in Saxl's words cited above, "all the enemies by which the Roman church was surrounded, pagans and heretics alike." Both positive interpretations are based on evidence far removed from Ruthwell in time, place and theme. Though St John Chrysostom identified Ishmael as a good man in the desert, protected by God, the climate of opinion by Bede's time, as reflected in his historical and exegetical writings, was of another order entirely, as will be pointed out below. Dr Raw's citations from the Fathers, especially those which identify arrows as figures of God's word, are commentaries on Psalm 119, Psalm 77, 2

Plate X   Walrus ivory pectoral from Victoria and Albert Museum,
London. Crown copyright.
Above: Eagle on terminal
Below: Archer in vine scroll

Plate XI   Cross shaft from St Andrew Auckland, Co. Durham.
(Photo T. Middlemass)

Plate XII   Bradbourne, Derbyshire, Bottom of west face.
(Photo T. Middlemass)

Kings I.25, and other passages not associated with Ruthwell. An identification of archer as preacher is made by Hrabanus, but only in a series of glosses, [16] and only in the context of Job XLI.19: "Sagittarius est quidlibet praedicator, ut in Job: 'Non fugabit eum vir sagittarius', quod per sine adjutorio Dei a mente hominis diabolum ejicere non potest praedictor." Hrabanus assigns sagitta the meaning sermo Dei in the context of 2 Kings I.25, but manifesta persecutio in the context of Psalm 90.6.[17] While Dr Raw's citations may apply to the ivory reliquary which is her main object of interest, it will be shown below that the Ruthwell iconography is more closely associated with Psalm 90 and interpretation of that psalm.

When one turns to early English sources for discussions of archers, the field of reference is indeed dark. As Schapiro has pointed out, Bede saw Ishmael-archer as the ancestor of the Saracens, wicked, wandering, destructive heathens.[18] His commentary on Genesis XVI.11-12 makes quite clear his negative view of Ishmael:

> Ecce, ait, concepisti et paries filium, et vocabis nomen eius Ismahel. Ismahel interpretatus "exauditio Dei", causaque nominis exponitur cum protinus subinfertur, Eo quod audierit Dominus adflictionem tuam. Notandum autem quia hic primus antequam nasceretur secundus Isaac a Domino nomen accepit, certi utique gratia mysterii, quia et ueteris testamenti, quod significatur in Ismahel, et noui, quod in Isaac, haeredes ante secula fuerunt in diuina electione praecogniti. Hic erit ferus homo, manus eius contra omnes, et manus omnium contra cum, et e regione uniuersorum fratrum suorum figet tabernacula. Significat semen eius habitaturum in eremo, id est Saracenos uagos, incertisque sedibus. Qui uniuersas gentes quibus desertum ex latere iungitur incursant, et expugnantur ab omnibus. Sed haec antiquitus. Nunc autem in tantum manus eius contra omnes, et manus sunt omnia contra eum, ut Africam totam in longitudine sua ditione premant, sed et Asiae maximam partem, et Europae nonnullam omnibus exosi et contrarii teneant. Quod autem dicit, Figet tabernacula, morem gentis antiquum ostendit, quae in tabernaculis semper, non in domibus, habitare solebant.[19]

Thus, if the archer is to be identified as Ishmael-archer, the view expressed in Bede is hardly favourable. The identification of Ishmael as the father of the Saracens has its basis in the Bible, for it was promised in Genesis XVII. 20 that Ishmael would be father to twelve princes, and beget a great nation:

> Super Ishmael quoque exaudivi te; ecce, benedicam ei, et augebo et multiplicabo eum valde; duodecim duces generabit, et faciam illam in gentem magnam.

This is the text that underlies St John Chrysostom's view of Ishmael as a good man in the desert, protected by God; but the Ishmaelites, through references in the Old Testament, seem more often to be seen as the reverse image of the chosen people. Instead of having a settled place of abode, they are wanderers — in fact, all sorts of wandering tribes were called Ishmaelites in the Old Testament, without regard to true race or origin.[20] Thus, the connection of Ishmaelite-Saracen is a natural one, especially in connection with the description of Ishmael himself, a man hostile to all men, with all against him.[21] Thus, if the archer is to be seen as Ishmael, a negative interpretation is almost certainly to be expected in eighth-century England.

A more general interpretation of the archer and his arrow as a force for evil seems likely, in view of the conjunction of a number of sources of evidence. The Ruthwell carver was careful to show the arrow clearly, and its very large head is seen in the upper right-hand corner of the panel. In addition, a quiver has a prominent part in the composition. The interpretation I wish to propose here takes the archer and his arrow, the eagle, and the portrait of Christ on the beasts as linked; the basis of this conjunction is found in Psalm 90,[22] and commentaries on that psalm. It is no new suggestion to link the Ruthwell cross with Psalm 90; both Saxl and Schapiro have attempted to do so. Saxl saw a possible relation between the illustration of Psalm 90 in the Utrecht Psalter and the Ruthwell archer, but felt the evidence to be inconclusive:

> We are reminded of the "arrow that flieth by day" (Psalm 90.6) which in the Utrecht Psalter is represented by Christ standing over the Beasts, but the inscription around the archer is unfortunately effaced, and there is no external evidence to support the comparison.[23]

Schapiro saw Christ standing on the beasts as related to "the familiar type of Christ treading on the lion"[24] (i.e., an illustration of Psalm 90), though the inscription around the panel (Judex aequitatis: bestiae et dracones cognoverunt in deserto salvatorem mundi) as related to Mark 1.13 ("et erat in deserto quadraginta diebus et quadriginta noctibus, et angeli ministrabant illi").

Psalm 90 is interesting in form, as it is a very strong statement of God's protection of the just man; it is particularly remarkable in its dialogue form. The just man speaks of how he is preserved, the Lord promises protection.[25] The verses that are significant for the student of the Ruthwell cross are the following;

1   Qui habitat in adiutorio Altissimi
       in protectione Dei caeli commorabitur

2   Dicet Domino; Susceptor meus es tu
       et refugium meum, deus meus; sperabo in eum

3   Quoniam ipse liberavit me de laqueo
       venantium et a verbo aspero

4   Scapulis suis obumbrabit tibi
       et sub pennis ejus sperabis.

5   Scuto circumdabit te veritas ejus;
       non timebis a timore nocturno.

6   a sagitta volante in die,
a negotio perambulante in tenebris,
ab incursu et daemonio meridiano...

11   Quoniam angelis suis mandavit
de te ut custodiant te in omnibus viis tuis

12   In manibus portabunt te ne forte
offendas ad lapidem pedum tuum

13   Super aspidem et basiliscum ambulabis,
et conculcabis leonem et draconem,

14   Quoniam in me speravit liberabo eum;
protegam eum quoniam cognovit nomen meum

15   Clamabit ad me, et ego exaudiam eum;
cum ipso sum in tribulatione,
eripiam eum et glorificabo eum.

16   Longitudine dierum replebo eum,
et ostendam illi salutare meum.

It is clear that the Divine is here portrayed as a winged creature, that the archer is a force for evil, and that the theme of the psalm is protection, salutare in Domino. The just man speaks to God, and is answered, or projects an answer. On Ruthwell, we have a bird, Christ on the beasts, and an archer. Can these three be linked? The commentaries of the Fathers on Psalm 90 tend towards such a conclusion, and the use of Psalm 90 and associated texts in liturgy also supports such an interpretation.

From this point, evidence must be found to show that Psalm 90 would have been well known in the eighth-century church and secondly, that commentaries on this psalm which support the identification of the eagle as Christ, and the archer as some force of evil, were also available to the early Anglo-Saxon church. In this investigation, I am making an assumption, that the Ruthwell cross is associated with Bede's milieu, and that the cross and its decoration, particularly its rich iconography, are to be associated with the joint monastery of Wearmouth-Jarrow, though the cross itself need not have been erected, and indeed probably was not erected, until after Bede's death. Professor Cramp has elsewhere made a case for such a localization.[26]

The psalms were of course of major importance in Christian worship, both public and private from the earliest times. One of Bishop Wilfrid's earliest accomplishments was his committing of the entire psalter to memory.[27] This, to the modern scholar, was no mean accomplishment; but in view of the use of the psalms in the primitive Church, not as remarkable as one might suppose. In eastern monasticism, the entire psalter was repeated daily, a practice also followed by the early Fathers. In the older Roman rite and the Benedictio office, the psalter was gone through once a week, in the various offices.[28] The further question arises, can an independent use of Psalm 90 be attested? An answer is not easy to find. Psalm 90 (11, 12) is fo course quoted by the devil in the accounts of the Temptation in Matthew (IV.6) and Luke (IV.10,11). As has been pointed out above, it is a commonplace in patristic commentary to mark Christ's victory by citing the next verse of the psalm, in which Christ tramples on the monsters and wild beasts that symbolize the devil.

In the later Roman rite, Paslm 90 is central to the liturgy of the first Sunday in Lent — where the various parts of the psalm are used as Introit, Gradual, Offertory, and Communion, while the Gospel is Matthew IV.1-11, the account of the Temptation, in which the devil quotes Psalm 90 and is confuted. The Epistle in this service is Paul to the Corinthians 2, VI.1-10. While we cannot be sure that the rite practiced in eighth-century England had exactly the same lectiones, we do know that the Epistle and Gospel were the same as the latter Roman use in many of the liturgies which are taken to be closest to those practiced in England.[29] We also know that Bede made an interpretation of Luke which linked the Temptation to Psalm 90 in the traditional manner:

> Scriptum est enim quod angelis suis mandauit de te ut conseruent
> te et quia in manibus tollent te ne forte offendas ad lapidem pedem
> tuum. Hoc in nonagesimo psalmo legimus, uerum ibi non de
> Christo sed de uiro sancto prophetia est. Male ergo interpretatur
> scripturas diabolus. Certe si uere de saluatore scriptum nouerat,
> debuerat et illud dicere quod in eodem psalmo contra se sequitur:
> Super aspidem et basiliscum ambulabis et conculcabis leonem et
> draconem. De angelorum auxilio quasi ad infirmum loquitur de
> sui conculcatione quasi tergiuersator tacet.[30]

Thus, the linking of Psalm 90 to the Temptation was already accomplished, and the use of Psalm 90 in the Mass for Quadragesima Sunday (Dominica Prima in Quadregesima) is a natural consequent step. Though I cannot prove that it had already taken place in liturgy in Bede's day, it is highly probable that this was the case. The readings throughout the Mass depend heavily on the psalms; in the modern (Tridentine) Roman liturgy, all the Introits are verses from the psalter. Though this was not always the case in the Middle Ages, the Introit would usually serve to announce the theme of the day.[31] The appropriateness of Psalm 90 for Quadragesima cannot be doubted, especially in view of the common link between Christ's Temptation and the psalm made by the Fathers.

In addition to the possible use of this psalm in the liturgy for Quadragesima, we do know that there were commentaries on Psalm 90 available to Bede which made interpretations which are in keeping with the relationship of eagle, archer, and Christ standing on the beasts on the Ruthwell cross. Bede also had available to him commentaries on the psalms by Augustine, Jerome, Cassiodorus, and Arnobius the Younger. He actually uses Augustine's, Jerome's and Arnobius's commentaries,[32] and since other products of Cassiodorus's Vivarium were well known in Bede's monastery, and Durham Cathedral Library has a copy of Cassiodorus's massive work on the psalms which is of Northumbrian provenance and dates to the mid eighth century (See CLA II, 152), it is highly probable that the work was known to Bede as well.

In all four of these Fathers, the archer and his arrow are seen as forces for evil. Augustine has two commentaries on the psalm; in the first, he develops the idea that those who yield knowingly to temptation are struck by the arrow volans per diem.[33] He expresses his view more succinctly in the second commentary: "Tentationes ignorantiae, timor nocturnus; peccata scientiae, sagitta volens per diem; in nocte enim ignorantia intelligitur, in die manifestatio."[34] Cassiodorus saw sagitta volans per diem as manifesto persecutio tyrannorum, an interpretation later echoed by Hrabanus.[35]

Arnobius's interpretation of the psalm is very brief, and the pertinent lines are as follows: "Libidinosae silicet voluptatis, cujus sagitta volat per diem. Quod enim in aspectu luminis concupiscitur, hujus negotium in tenebris perpetratur, aut in ruina, aut in daemonia meridano perficitur."[36] Interesting as these comments are, it is almost certainly Jerome's two commentaries on Psalm 90 that are most important for our present purpose, especially since both are in agreement on central points of interpretation.[37] His explications of verses 5 and 6 are most relevant:

> In scapulis suis ombumbrabit tibi. Quis obumbrabit?
> Utique Deus caeli, sicut gallina pullos suos, et
> quasi aquila nidum suum. Unde et in cantico Deuteronomii
> dicitur, quod populum Israhel in humeris portaverit,
> et quasi aquila protexerit. [Deuteronomy XXXII, 32:11] Potest et
> de Salvatore intellegi, quod in cruce sua nos suis alis
> protexerit. Et sub pennis ejus sperabis. "Tota
> die expandi manus meas ad populum non credentem et
> contradicentem mihi". [Romans 10.21] Manus Domini ad
> caelum levate, non auxilium postulabant, sed nos
> miseros protegebant. Scuto circumdabit te veritas
> ejus: hoc est, in girum circumdaberis veritate.
> Et quid sequitur? Non timebis a timore nocturno.
> Justus non habet nocturnum timorem, sed diei.
> "Venite, filii, audite me, timorem Domini docebo
> vos". [Psalm 33.12] Qui filii sunt prophetarum,
> timorem non habent nocturnum, neque tenebrarum,
> sed lucis et diei. "Ut sagittent in abscondito
> rectos corde". [Psalm 10-3] Diabolus sagittas suas in
> die non mittet, ne videatur. Omne enim quod in
> luce fit, manifestatur a luce. Sed dicat aliquis:
> Si diabolus non sagittat in die, quomodo ergo
> sequenti versiculo psalmista dicit, A sagitta volante
> per diem? Quae est ista sagitta, quae per diem volat?
> Doctrina haereticorum est: quae quasi per diem, hoc est,
> legem Dei huc illucque volitat, dum adversus nos sollicite
> inquisita congerunt testimonia, quae interpretationibus
> suis a veritate depravant.[38]

Here we have a relation drawn between Christ and the eagle protecting his young, with specific reference to his posture on the cross as an indication and type of this protection. The eagle, as Christ, is linked by Jerome to Moses' last song in Deuteronomy, and is thus related to protection in the desert:

Quando dividebat Altissimus gentes,
quando separabat filios Adam,
constituit terminos populorum juxta numerum
filiorum Israel; pars autem Domini, populus ejus,
Jacob funiculus hereditatis ejus.
Invenit eum in terra deserta, in loco horroris,
et vastae solitudinis;
Circumduxit eum, et docuit;
et custodivit quasi pullum oculum suum
quasi aquila provocans ad volandum pullos suos,
et super eos volitans,
expandit alas suas, et assumpsit eum,
atque portavit in humeris suis. (Deuteronomy xxxii.8-11)

In his second commentary on the same psalm, Jerome specifically links the eagle as Christ with our protection in deserto istius saeculi. The archer is also identified in the same way as in the first commentary:

In scapulis suis obumbrabit tibi. Exaltabitur in cruce, extendet manus, et proteget nos. Et sub pennis ejus sperabis. Aspicies, inquit, manus ejus crucifixas, et si te serpens momorderit, sanaberis. Licet ambules in deserto istius saeculi: si te percusserit scorpio, si regulus, si aspis, si cetera venenata animalia, securus esto de sanitate: serpens in eremo suspensus est.
A sagitta volante in die. Huic sensui quasi videtur esse contrarium, a sagitta volante in die. Sagitta volans diaboli videtur mihi sermo esse haereticorum, et philosophorum. Et isti enim lucem scientiae promittunt, et dicunt se habere diem; et non possunt decipere, nisi lucem promiserint. Verum lux ista, quam promittunt, de ardentibus sagittis est.[39]

The song of Moses in Deuteronomy in which the representation of God's protective power as an eagle was made is present in all the complete psalters, Roman and Gallician, which have come down to us.[40] Benedict himself stipulated further that this canticle was to be used regularly in Lauds on Saturdays: "Sabbatorum autem centisimum quadragesimum secundum et canticum deuteronium, qui dividatur in duas glorias."[41]

Thus, the association would have been bringing together texts that were very well known in liturgical uses in eighth-century England.[42] There are further sources which suggest that the interpretation of the archer and his arrow as figures of evil had achieved a wider currency in early Anglo-Saxon England. A most striking example of this image in Anglo-Saxon secular literature is found in Beowulf.[43] Just before the hero's departure from Denmark, after he had destroyed the unholy monsters which had for so long ravaged the kingdom, Beowulf is given good advice by the old king Hrothgar.

The speech is one of the most important and revealing statements of Christian ethics in the poem:

> Wundor is to secganne,
> hu mihtig God   manna cynne
> þurh sidne sefan   synttru bryttað
> eard ond eorlscipe;   he ah ealra geweald.
> Hwilum he on lufan   læteð hworfan
> monnes mod-geþonc   mæran cynnes,
> seleð him on eþle   eorþan wynne
> to healdanne,   hleo-burh wera;
> gedeð him swa gewealdene   worolde dælas,
> side rice,   þæt he his selfa ne mæg
> for his unsnyttrum   ende geþencean.
> Wunað he in wiste,   no hine wiht dweleð
> adl ne yldo,   ne him inwit-sorh
> on sefan sweorceð,   ne gesacu ohwær
> ecg-hete eoweð,   ac him eal worold
> wendeð on willan.   He þæt wyrse ne con,
> oð þæt him on innan   ofer-hygda dæl
> weaxeð,   þonne se weard swefeð,
> sawele hyrde;   bið se slæp to fæst,
> bisgum gebunden;   bona swiðe neah,
> se þe of flan-bogan   fyrenum sceote.
> þonne bið on hreþre   under helm drepen
> biteran stræle — him bebeorgan ne con —
> wom wundor-bedodum   wergan gastes.
> þinceð him to lytel   þæt he to lange heold;
> gytsað grom-hydig   nallas on gylp seleð
> fætte beagas; one he þa forð-gesceaft
> forgyteð ond forgymeð,   þæs þe him ær God sealde,
> wuldres Waldend, weorð-mynda dæl.[44]

(It is a wondrous thing to say how mighty God deals out to mankind wisdom, lands and rank, by His vast spirit. He has control of all. Sometimes He allows the spirit of man of famous stock to wander in delight: gives him in his native land enjoyment of this world, a fenced fortress of men to hold; makes regions of the world, a spacious empire, subject to him in such wise that in his folly he himself thinks it will never end. He lives in plenty; nothing — sickness nor old age — stands in his way. No trouble caused by malice clouds his thoughts, nor does strife bring about deadly warfare anywhere, but all the world moves to his will. He knows no worse estate [XXV] until a measure of overbearing pride waxes and grows in him, when the warder, the soul's guardian, sleeps. That sleep is too sound, hedged in with cares: the slayer is very close, who from the winged bow shoots with evil intent. Then he is struck at the heart, under his armour, by the piercing arrow, — the crooked mysterious promptings of the accursed sprite. He cannot defend himself. What he had held for a long time seems to him too little. He covets, hostile in mind; never gives, in proud rejoicing, circlets overlaid with gold. No thought has he about the world to come, and he disdains the share of honours God, the Lord of Glory, gave him in time past.)[45]

110

S. J. Crawford saw a parallel to the Beowulf passage in a letter of Boniface, in which he warned Athelbald, king of Mercia, to repent.[46] The parallel is not exact, for Boniface's letter calls to mind dangers mentioned in Psalm 90, but not in Beowulf. It is therefore more probable that the Boniface letter, and the Beowulf image, each derive from Psalm 90, and the commentaries on it.

> fili carissime, cares tibi foveam, in quam
> vidiste coram te alios eecidisse. Cave tibi
> jacula antiqui hostis ... adtende tibi a laqueo
> insidiatoris, in quo votos et commilitones tuos
> strangulatos et praesentem vitam et futuram pendere.[47]

In the commentary on Luke by Bede cited above, the arrows in the psalm it identified in the very next lines:

> Et respondens Jesus, ait illi: Dictum est: Non
> tentabis Dominum Deum tuum. Falsas de Scripturis
> diaboli sagittas, veris Scripturarum frangit
> clypeis.[48]

Finally, it is important to note that the image of the arrows of sin appears frequently in other contexts in the literature of the Anglo-Saxon period in poetry and prose, in both Latin and the vernacular. Paul ends his letter to the Ephesians with an injunction that could well be an echo of the tradition of Psalm 90, in which he encourages them to be comforted in the power and arms of the Lord, and to take up "sacertum fidei in quo pessitis omnia tela nequissimi ignea extinguere..." (vi.16).[49]

CONCLUSIONS

There are, therefore, a number of considerations which make it highly probable that the iconography of the eagle, the archer, and Christ over the beasts are to be related to Psalm 90 and texts associated with it in the liturgy. It is no new suggestion to link the lone eagle with Christ;[50] it is something of a change to link the Ruthwell bird with Christ as protector, but the points of concord between liturgy and patristic commentary known to Bede are such that this interpretation is at least a very strong possibility. The psalter was an integral part of worship in the church from the earliest times, and it was recited right through in the course of every week in the normal course of monastic worship.

In addition to this regular use of the psalms in series, both Psalm 90 and the associated Canticle of Moses in Deuteronomy are singled out for especial uses, as recorded above. Finally, the testimony of the Fathers adds further links. Jerome's identification of the protective wings in Psalm 90 as Christ on the cross, and his linking of Christ with the eagle in Dueteronomy is particularly attractive, because of the eremetical associations which are in accord both the iconography of the South face of the Ruthwell cross, and the tradition of monasticism with which the cross is associated.[51] Christ, on the cross, protects us as an eagle, the eagle who protected the chosen people

in terra deserta, in loco horroris et vastae solitudinis (Deuteronomy xxxii.
10). This protection will not fail for the just man in any age. "Licet ambules
in deserto istius saeculi; si te percusserit scorpio, si regulus, si aspis, si
cetera venenata animalia, securus esto de sanitate: serpens in eremo
suspensus est." [52] I am fully aware that the arguments presented here are
not conclusive, and I do not wish to make more of the evidence than can be
made. The Ruthwell archer is a problematical figure; Professor Schapiro's
case for the secular interpretation cannot be dismissed lightly, even though
his parallels for the Ruthwell archer are not exact. However, it does appear
that any interpretation which gives a benign religious significance to the figure
is dubious. Insofar as we are able to know the climate of opinion about
archers, and Ishmael as archer in eighth-century England, it does not tend
towards a benign interpretation. It therefore seems to me highly probable
that the archer is best interpreted as an inimical figure, whose religious significance can best be seen in relation to the other essential figures on the cross,
the eagle on the head, and the whole series on the south face.

NOTES

1. The dating of the Ruthwell and Bewcastle crosses has been a source of
controversy for many years. For a number of reasons, stylistic,
linguistic and historical, I date Ruthwell to the early part of the eighth
century. Professor Rosemary Cramp has elsewhere expressed reasons
for this dating; see her Early Northumbrian Sculpture (Jarrow Lecture,
1965). For a survey of other views see E. Mercer, "The Ruthwell and
Bewcastle crosses," Antiquity 38 (1964), 268-76. Dr. R. I. Page
Introduction to English Runes (London, 1973), p. 148) dates Ruthwell
650-750.

2. In 1642 the cross was knocked to pieced under an "Act annent Idolatrous
monuments of Ruthwall," and lay in fragments until 1802, when it was
re-erected in the garden of the manse by Dr Henry Duncan. In 1823,
a transom was added, the decoration being entirely spurious and out of
keeping with the rest of the monument. In 1827, the cross was moved
into a specially-constructed apse in the church. See Dr H Duncan,
"An account of a remarkable monument...," Archaeologia Scotica 4,
(1833), 313-25.

2a. For a discussion of the evangelist series, see below,

3. Baldwin-Brown, The Arts in Early England V (1921), 125.

4. M. Schapiro, "The bowman and the bird on the Ruthwell cross," Art
Bulletin 45 (1963), 351-5, quotation, 351.

5. F. Saxl, "The Ruthwell cross," Journal of the Warburg and Courtauld
Institutes, 6 (1943), 1-19, quotation, 6. This suggestion was made on
the basis of Saxl's own reconstruction of the cross-head, in which the
eagle represents the Ascension, and stands over the central panel on
the head, which Saxl reconstructs on analogy with two eleventh-century
cross-heads from Durham. See below, p. 118, n. 50.

6. R. H. Kantorowicz, "The archer on the Ruthwell cross," <u>Art Bulletin</u> 27 (1960) 57-9.

7. Schapiro, "The bowman and the bird on the Ruthwell cross," pp. 351-5.

8. J. Beckwith "A rediscovered English reliquary cross," <u>Victoria and Albert Museum Bulletin</u> 2 (1966), 122, holds for a date "towards the end of the eleventh or in the beginning of the twelfth century."

9. Beckwith (<u>ibid</u>., p. 118), argues that the archer is on the front of the pectoral, since the other side "is more rubbed than the lid." This wear is most evident, says Beckwith, on the St Luke figure at the bottom. The opposite face has the Agnus Dei with cross-staff in the centre, and evangelist symbols at the terminals. The intervening space is filled with a vine-scroll, containing symmetrically arranged animals. If the archer face is taken as the front, the right side has inhabited vine-scroll all over, with intertwined leafy scrolls carved on the end of the arm, while the left side has vine-scroll, with a magnificent eagle, frontal, wings spread, head in profile, occupying the end of the left arm.

10. Augustine, <u>Enarrationes in Psalmis</u>, <u>PL</u>, 37, col. 1603. Beckwith's interpretation of the scheme of the pectoral is hard to accept, unless one posits a very debased understanding of typology on the part of the carver or designer of the work. Ishmael is more usually paired with Isaac as types of the Old and New Testaments, respectively. According to Beckwith, "on the pectoral cross, however, the artist has substituted for Isaac the Agnus Dei and the symbols of the Evangelists," "A rediscovered English reliquary cross," p. 120.

11. <u>Ibid</u>., p. 118.

12. B. Raw, "The archer, the eagle and the lamb," <u>Journal of the Warburg and Courtauld Institutes</u> 30 (1967), 391-4.

13. His bases seem to be in Romanesque art of the twelfth and thirteenth centuries; the concept of art as pure decoration is readily attested by commentators of that period, as Schapiro has shown in another essay, "The aesthetic attitude in romanesque art," <u>Art and Thought: Essays in Honour of A. K. Coomaraswamy</u> (1948), p. 133ff. Schapiro's citation of Daniel in the lion's den on one of the Meigle stones is not to the point, for it is clear that the various traditions of free-standing crosses differ widely, though they seem to have some parallel developments. The Meigle cross Schapiro cites (No. 2 according to Steward Cruden's enumeration, <u>The Early Christian and Pictish Monuments of Scotland</u>, 2nd ed. (1964), pp. 18-19, and pl. 26-7) can hardly be viewed as any sort of parallel for Ruthwell. Mr Cruden says of the decoration: "The subject-matter is a notable combination of native-and-foreign and pagan-and-Christian ideas. The realistic and spirited horsemen are characteristically 'Pictish', the centaur and Daniel are faithfully reproduced from foreign sources: the centaur is a pagan motif, Daniel is Christian" (<u>ibid</u>., p. 19). Similar mixed decoration is found on Irish high crosses in the early Christian period, but Dr Henry has made a convincing case for the Christian interpretation of apparently pagan scenes on these

monuments. See her Irish Art in the Early Christian Period (London, 1965), esp. pp. 147-58.

14. Schapiro, "The bowman and the bird on the Ruthwell cross," p. 352.

15. W. G. Collingwood (Northumbrian Crosses of the Pre-Norman Age (London, 1927), p. 22) states flatly: "This stone never served as a model for any Anglian design."

16. Hrabanus, Allegoriae in Sacrum Scripturam, PL 112, cols. 850-1088, 1043-4.

17. These are not the only meanings; different glosses are given for the various contexts in which sagitta, sagittarius, and arcus appear in various contexts in the Bible. See Hrabanus, Allegoriae, passim. Throughout this paper, the Vulgate numbering of both psalms and verses is followed.

18. Schapiro, "The bowman and the bird on the Ruthwell cross," p. 353. See also Bede, HE V.23 (ed. Plummer I, 349, and also II, 338-9). As Dr J. M. Wallace-Hadrill has pointed out, Bede's antipathy to the Saracens seems to have become strong after their intervention in Spain in 711. See his Bede's Europe (Jarrow Lecture, 1962), esp. pp. 5-7.

19. In Genesim IV, CCSL 118A, pp. 200-201, Significant sermon ... ab omnibus is from Jerome, HQG xvi, 12. Ishmael is identified as an archer in a commentary on the Pentateuch (PL 91, ccl. 24) which has been attributed to Bede, but which is apparently spurious: "Ismael sagittarius dicitur, non incongrue popula Judaico convenit, hoc est jugulando hostias Regis ...".

20. See Genesis xxxvii.25, and 27-28; xxxix.1; Judges viii.24, Psalm 82. 7, etc.

21. As Schapiro points out "The bowman and the bird on the Ruthwell cross," p. 354), "already before Islam the Bedouins were described by St Jerome as Saracens and Ishmaelites who attack a caravan of Christians and enslave them." See Jerome's Vita Malchi Monachi (PL 23, col. 57), "a Saracenis praedonibus et Ishmaelites grassatoribus obvia quaque vastantibus." The relation made in Jerome almost certainly stems from the Bible tradition as well.

22. The wording of the psalm is something of a problem. Of the three versions of the psalms extant we know that the text of the Codex Amiatinus, a product of Bede's monastery, was juxta Hebraeos, but the other versions were certainly current, and some of the best texts of the Roman psalter from early English contexts. See R. Weber, Le Psautier Romain et les autres anciens Psautiers Latins (Rome, 1953).

23. Saxl, "The Ruthwell cross," p. 6. The Utrecht Psalter (fol. 163) has Christ standing on two beasts as its central figure, and two archers point their shafts at him. The same iconography is followed in Trinity College, Cambridge, R.17.1 (The Canterbury Psalter), fol. 163.r.

24. M. Schapiro, "The religious meaning of the Ruthwell cross" Art Bulletin 26 (1944), 231-45, quotation, 233. He saw the link between the two events as due to patristic commentary: "The motif of Christ in the desert belongs to the Temptation, which already in the Gospels is connected with Psalm 90. In the accounts of the episode in Matthew (IV.6) and Luke (IV.10, 11), the devil, in urging Christ to cast himself down from the pinnacle of the temple, quotes Psalm 90, 11 and 12 ... Jesus will not tempt the Lord, and the commentaries celebrate his victory over the devil by quoting the next verse of Psalm 90, in which the feet of Christ trample on the monsters and wild beasts that symbolise the demon. The passage is implicit for the commentators in the Gospel story and completes the episode of the Temptation; it reveals the deceit of the devil, who, in quoting scripture leaves out, like the heretics, the essential concluding line that betrays him" (p. 233).

25. As a highly speculative suggestion, it might be pointed out that such a form is not unlike that of the Dream of the Rood, with the cross promising protection to the dreamer. Such a relationship is of extreme interest because the runic inscriptions on Ruthwell are either exerpted from an earlier version of the tenth-century Dream of the Rood, or at very least strongly connected to the same vernacular textual tradition that led to the tenth-century poem. Cassiodorus outlines the structure of the psalm as follows: "In prima parte Psalmista profitetur omnem fidelissimum divina protectione vallari. Secunda laudem decantat Domino Salvatori. Tertia verba sunt Patris ad omnem fidelem, quem in se devotissime sperare cognoscit, et in mundum isto defensionem, et in futuro illi (recte ille) praemia compromittens," PL 70, col. 650.

26. See Early Northumbrian Sculpture.

27. He had been sent off as a young boy to help one Cudda, who had taken up the monastic life on Lindisfarne, when, stricken with paralysis:

Jam enim ille secundum praeceptum reginae, accepta diligenti ministratione, domino suo et omnibus senioribus in monasterio quasi filius et coetaneis quasi frater statim in amore factus est, pro eo quod omnem regularem vitam cum intimo cordis amore in humilitate et obedentia adimplere nitebatur et omnem psalmorum seriem memoraliter et aliquandos libros didicit. Eddius Stephanus, Life of Bishop Wilfrid, ed. and trans. B. Colgrave (Cambridge, 1927), p. 6.

For further discussion on the use and popularity of the psalter in Anglo-Saxon contexts, see Peter Hunter Blair, The World of Bede (London, 1970) pp. 254-8.

28. See A. Baumstark, Comparative Liturgy, rev. Bernard Botte, and trans. F. L. Cross, (London, 1958), p. 114.

29. It is very difficult to establish the form of the proper of the Mass for Quadragesima Sunday in eighth-century England. The pericope of the Lindisfarne Gospels gives Matthew IV.1-11 (the account of the

Temptation) as the reading for Quadragesima, a practice which reflects some early Spanish uses, and, apparently that of Pope Gregory the Great. See S. Beissel, "Entstehung der Perikopen des Romischen Messbuches Zur Geschichte der Evangelienbuche in der ersten halfte des Mittelalters," Stimmung aus Mara-Laach, Erganzungs-Band 24, Erganzungsheft 96 (Freiburg in Breslau, 1906-8), pp. 401-620. On Lindisfarne, see pp. 509-19; the Spanish rite is cited on p. 479, and Gregory's use on pp. 460-4.

30. In Lucae Evangelium Expositio, CCSL 120, p. 97. Once again, Bede's source is Jerome, In Matt. (PL 26, cols. 32-4).

31. See S. J. R. van Dijk, O.F.M., "The Bible in liturgical use," The Cambridge History of the Bible II, ed. G. W. H. Lampe (Cambridge, 1969), pp. 220-51.

32. See M. L. W. Laistner, "The library of the Venerable Bede," Intellectual Heritage of the Middle Ages (Ithaca, 1957), pp. 117-49. (First printed in Bede: His Life, Times and Writings, ed. A. H. Thompson (Oxford, 1935), pp. 237-66. See also J. D. A. Ogilvy, Books Known to the English, 597-1066 (Cambridge, Mass., 1967).

33. Augustine, Enarratio in Psalmo xc, Sermo I, PL 37, cols. 1149-58, Sermo II, cols. 1158-70.

34. Ibid., col. 1161.

35. Cassiodorus, PL 70, col. 652. On Hrabanus's gloss, see above,

36. Arnobius junioris, Commentarii in Psalmos, PL 53, col. 458.

37. See Dom Germanus Morin, Anecdota Maresolana III, pt. 2 (Maredsous, 1897), 113-19; pt. 3 (Maredsous, 1903), 67-72.

38. Ibid., pt. 3, 68-9.

39. Ibid., pt. 2, 114-5.

40. See James Mearns, The Canticles of the Christian Church, Eastern and Western in Early Medieval Times (Cambridge, 1914), esp. pp. 52-88.

41. H. Logeman, The Rule of St. Benet, Early English Text Society original series 90 (Oxford, 1888) pp. 43-4. The text is that of British Library. Cotton Tiberius A.3.

42. It may further be pointed out that Moses in Deuteronomy plays an important role in the Bangor antiphonary. This perplexing document begins with Moses in Deuteronomy, and uses as its bases two other canticles, Moses in Exodus, and the Song of the Three Children from Daniel. See also the edition by H. E. Warren, Henry Bradshaw Society 4 (London, 1893).

43. The dating and milieu of Beowulf are two of the most difficult problems associated with the poem. I do not cite the poem as necessarily directly associated with Bede's milieu, but rather as an example of the currency of the image of the archer as a force for evil. It is a strong personal conviction of mine that Beowulf and the cultural rise of Northumbria are associated phenomena.

44. *Beowulf*, ed. C. L. Wrenn, 2nd ed., (London, 1958).

45. *Beowulf*, trans. J. R. Clark-Hall, rev. C. L. Wrenn (London, 1949).

46. "Beowulfiana," *Review of English Studies* o.s. 7, 448-9. The letter dates from *c*. 744-7.

47. Crawford, *ibid*., p. 449. A further parallel for the archer as devil has been cited from the Vercelli Homilies, number 10 in M. Forster's edition (*Die Vercelli-Homilien*, Bibliothek der Angelsächsischen Prosa 12 (Hamburg, 1932), p. 103). When the condemned are sent to hell, the devil attacks them with a bow: "*se boga bið geworht of ofermettum* ... [The arrows are] *swa swa manigra cynna, swa swa mannes synna bioð* "

48. See above, p. 104, and n. 30.

49. I am indebted to my colleague Professor Thomas Hill both for information on this point, and for his careful reading of this paper in draft. The contexts in which the arrows of the enemy are seen are numerous, including *Juliana* (especially 382-109a), *Vainglory* (36b-39), Aldhelm (*De Laudibus Virginitatis* XII 12.5), and others. See further James Doubleday, "The allegory of the soul as fortress in Old English Poetry, *Anglia* 88 (1970), 503-8, and Fr. Klaeber, "Die christlichen Elemente im *Beowulf* I," *Anglia* 35 (1922), especially 129-30.

50. See Saxl, "The Ruthwell cross," p. 6: "The eagle at the summit must undoubtedly be interpreted as a symbol of the Ascension."

51. The desert interest was stressed by Schapiro "The religious meaning of the Ruthwell cross," and again, linked with the *Dream of the Rood*, by J. Fleming, *The Dream of the Rood* and Anglo-Saxon monasticism," *Traditio*, 22 (1966), pp. 43-72.

52. Jerome, *op.cit*., III 2, p. 115.

V. THE EVANGELIST SYMBOLS AND THEIR PARALLELS
IN ANGLO-SAXON SCULPTURE.

Rosemary Cramp

Among the great stone crosses which survive from the pre-Viking period
in Northumbria, Ruthwell stands supreme in the complex iconographic relation-
ships of its figural panels. It is true that the fragments from Rothbury[1] hint
at an equal complexity had the monument been complete, but, as I have stressed
elsewhere, Rothbury appears to develop from the same school as Ruthwell.[2]
The formula for the ornament of the cross is very similar: figural scenes
from the life and miracles of Christ on the broad faces of the shaft, and an inhabited scroll on one narrow face; figural scenes on the cross-head; even the
heavy figure style and tubular folds in the drapery are similar. Nevertheless
the iconography of the Rothbury cross is more advanced and clearly linked with
developments also found in Carolingian art.[3] Ruthwell with its association of
picture and elaborate inscriptions, deriving both from the Latin liturgy and
vernacular poetry is unique among Anglo-Saxon crosses. In all its details, as
Robert Farrell shows in his contribution to this volume, one is conscious of
a deeply absorbed theology behind the planning of the iconography. It seems
moreover to have established a tradition which one can see surviving in Northumbria for 150 years.

In attempting to reconstruct the only part of the cross now lost, the centre
piece and cross arms of the head, I shall consider its surviving affiliations in
Anglo-Saxon sculpture. The figures surviving on the head are as Robert Farrell
has described them more fully above. On the north face in the top arm, is the
full length figure of a bird of prey grasping a piece of foliage, and in the lower
arm, two figures, the left one of which is winged, the right one of which holds
a book in its draped hands (pl. VIII). On the upper arm of the south face is
a human figure on the right, and a bird of prey on the left. On the lower arm
is an archer (pl. IX). I accept Farrell's hypothesis that the upper arm should
be turned to bring the two pairs of figures onto one face, and that we should
see them as portraits and symbols of the Evangelists John and Matthew. One
could add to this one other fragment which can be fitted into the Ruthwell head.
In the church at Ruthwell, now set in a metal frame beside the cross, is a mutilated fragment of the remains of two human figures carved in the same style
as the rest of the head. This could be part of the centre of the cross but in
scale it is better seen as part of an arm. On one face (pl. XIII), only the head
of the figure survives, slightly turned and inclined to the left in the manner of
the evangelist portraits of St Matthew and St John. If the figure is an evangelist,
it would stand by analogy with the others on the right of its symbol and so would
be part of the western arm of the cross. On the other face (pl. XIV), is a
figure in profile: the head, shoulders, and what appear to be folds of a sleeve
are shown. But the figure seems to be enmeshed in strands which pass over

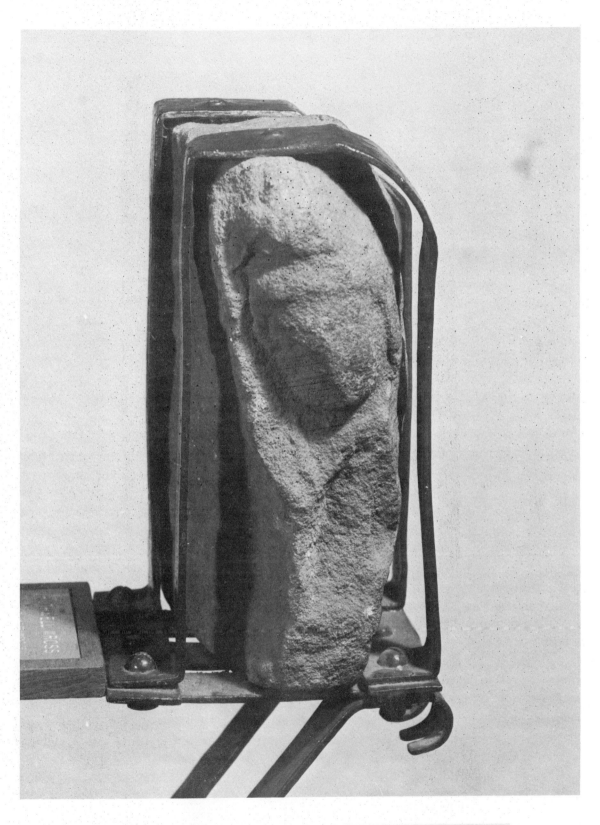

Plate XIII   Fragment with inclined figure, Ruthwell church.
Copyright R. Cramp.

Plate XIV   Fragment with ?fowler, Ruthwell church.
Copyright R. Cramp.

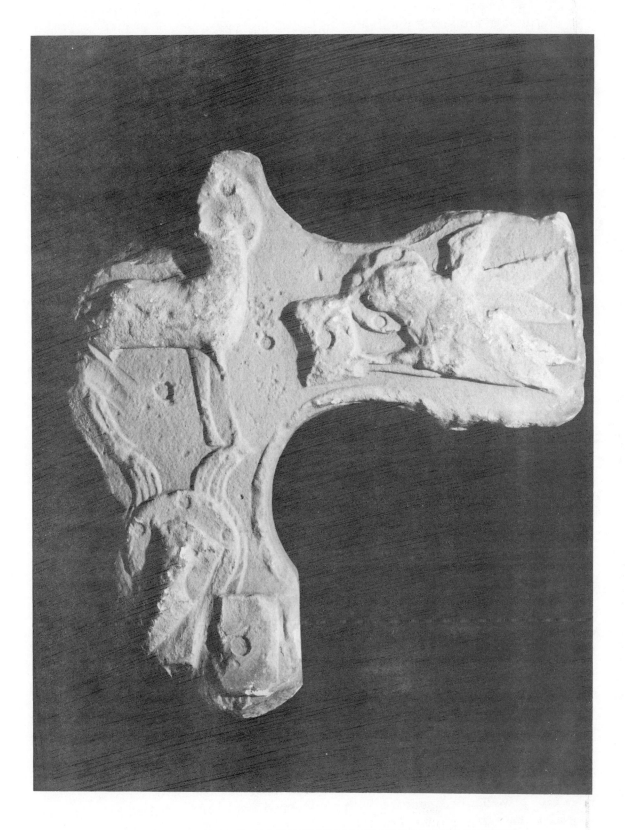

Plate XV   Hart cross-head.
            Copyright R. Cramp.   (Photo T. Middlemass)

his shoulders and neck and are held either by his arm or another strand. The profile figure, if part of a cross arm, would stand therefore on the left of the archer facing in the same direction. Could it be that this is a depiction of the fowler and his snare mentioned in Psalm 90, verse 3? It is just possible that we are to see the figure as the victim in the snare, but without the full scheme on the cross-head, one can only guess. If one accepts this as a further support for Farrell's hypothesis of the importance of Psalm 90 on this face, one figure only remains unknown on the eastern arm: the target of the archer's arrow and the hunter's snare.

My main preoccupation here, however, is with the north side of the cross. If the evangelist portraits and symbols were on that face, the desert face, they would stand above the symbol of St John and the Agnus Dei, and Christ, judge and Savior. In this position their apocalyptic nature would be emphasized.

However, let us first examine their relationship with other cross-heads. The Ruthwell head is unique in that portraits and symbols occur together.[5] The symbol of the eagle is full length but the angel is, as often elsewhere, half length.[4] The symbols are winged, but are without haloes, and the books denoting the evangelist are held by the portraits. Only three other crosses have full length symbols and all are clearly stressing the apocalyptic origin of the creatures.

At Hart in Co. Durham is a recently discovered cross-head.[6] It is so far unpublished, and in view of its iconographic importance it deserves detailed description. The lower arm, centrepiece and one transverse arm survive (pl. XV). The head shape is the same as that of Ruthwell, but this is a type which remains popular in Durham and Northumberland up to the eleventh century. The fragment is 68cm high and 71cm wide, the height of each arm is 20cm. The cross-head would seem to have had originally a span of about 90cm. The edge is surrounded with a single roll moulding and the carving appears only on the two broad faces.

Face I   In the centre is a lamb facing right but with head turned back. It is motionless and there is no sign of a cross behind it. Its head, which is mutilated, was framed with a halo on which there are two sunken roundels. Two similar roundels are found in front of the lamb and between its legs. Below its feet, with upraised wings touching its hooves, is a frontal facing figure. It appears to have horns, has a nimbus with sunken roundels, and holds a book in which a single roundel is centrally placed. On the right-hand arm is a full length figure with a similar nimbus, and book clasped between its tow front paws. It is winged, with apparently two pairs raised and one pair lowered on to its back. It appears to have a blunt rounded head. The lack of detail on the figures and the sunken roundels which presumably represent jewels imply that the sculpture could have been painted. Because of the imprecision of the beasts it is impossible to be certain about the lower animal but it appears to be the symbol of St Luke and the right-hand figure that of St Mark. This scheme can be paralleled in an eighth-century manuscript painting of a cross, in the centre of which is Agnus Dei with backturned head, and jewelled halo, and evangelist busts in the arms.[7]

<u>Face II</u>   The centrepiece has been chipped away but could hardly have contained other than a small motif (pl. XVI).   The arms are covered with a thin plant-scroll in which the leaves and berries are very worn and lack helpful diagnostic details.   The flowing spreading plant-scroll covering one face of a cross-head is a feature of Yorkshire crosses, for example, Lastingham, Otley, Masham, all of which date from the late eighth - early ninth - centuries. One might date this Hart cross to the ninth century.

The other depictions of full length symbols also surround a lamb - on the cross-heads discovered in the foundations of the Norman Chapter House at Durham.   These cannot be earlier than the early eleventh century when the Community of St Cuthbert settled on the peninsula.   However the Community, originally from Lindisfarne and later occupying Chester-le-Street and then Durham, were extraordinarily conservative in their sculpture[8] and could have been using earlier models.   In fact the Durham workshop in the early eleventh century seems to have had four motifs which could be arbitrarily combined. The heads are numbered according to Greenwell's <u>Catalogue</u>.[9]

(a)   The apocalyptic scene of a lamb holding a book with a cross on a pedestal behind.   There is also what could have been a vestige of the chalice such as appears on the Gauzelin Gospels.[10]   This creature faces to the spectator's left and is on cross XX surrounded by crude renderings of the apocalyptic symbols.[11]   The lamb occurs again on No. XXIII without attendant symbols.

(b)   A baptism or annointing scene which Saxl[12] has interpreted as the giving of the keys to Peter.   This scene with accompanying figures of apostles or ecclesiastics occurs three times, twice with what appears to be a bird above.

(c)   A crucifixion scene.   This occurs in different form three times.   Once on No. XXII with a man and bird below.

Motifs (b) and (c) combine twice, (a) and (b) once, and (a) and (c) once. Such variations seem of little use for deciding on the iconography of the Ruthwell head.   There is no evidence that the Durham cross is anything more than a late and garbled edition of the historiated heads such as are found at Rothbury or Dewsbury.

The second type of evangelist symbol found on Northumbrian cross-heads is the bust of a creature with wings and halo holding a book.   This type derives from the early western apocalyptic depictions where the symbols emerge from clouds.[13]   The one surviving arm of a cross from Otley, Yorkshire[14] shows the symbol of St Luke.   The back of the head was carved into a plant-scroll as at Hart.   One arm also survives from the head of a famous cross from St Andrew's Auckland, Co Durham (pl. XVII).   The carving is very worn and indistinct, and the identity of the symbol is not clear, but it has wings, a book, and possibly a halo.   Both Otley and St Andrew Auckland could date from the late eighth early ninth century.

The lamb appears as a centrepiece on a cross from Hoddom, Dumfriesshire, a site very near to Ruthwell and producing sculpture which has some affiliations with the Ruthwell cross.[15]   However one cannot say whether or not the lamb on the Hoddom cross was surrounded by evangelist symbols.   It is possibly significant that wherever the symbols can be restored on the cross-head and

Plate XVI   Hart cross-head.
Copyright R. Cramp.   (Photo T. Middlemass)

Plate XVII Part of surviving cross arm from St Andrew Auckland,
Co. Durham.

linked with a shaft they are part of an elaborately conceived cross with figural panels. By the time Rothbury was carved the fashion had died out.

At Halton, Ilkley and Sandbach human busts with animal heads are found on the cross-shaft. At Halton they are half length with frontal or half turned figures. They have wings, haloes and books. John and ?Luke, are on the broad faces, Matthew and Mark on the narrower. At Ilkley (mid ninth century) there are half length busts, wingless, but with haloes and books. The heads of Mark, Luke and John are turned. St Matthew is at the bottom of the shaft and they read upward in the order of the Gospels.[16] At Sandbach, the symbols are half length with wings and books, but only the symbol of St Matthew has a halo. Matthew is shown frontal, the others in three-quarter view. They are disposed around a crucifixion and read: Matthew top left, Mark top right, Luke bottom left, John bottom right.[17] The placing of evangelist symbols on the shafts of crosses may have a different theological significance from placing them on the head.

Several different traditions are reflected clearly in these English schemes. It is difficult to compare the disposition of the symbols on cross-heads with series as set out in manuscript Canon tables or when they are paired on either side of some central figure such as a cross or a Majestas. Often Matthew and John are paired above Mark and Luke as in St Radegunde's reading desk, the MacDurnan Gospels, the Amiens Gospels or the Codex Amiatinus. However scarcely less frequent is the pairing of Matthew and Mark above Luke and John as on Cuthbert's coffin or the Lichfield Gospels.[18]

The order of the Ruthwell evangelists with John at the top and Matthew at the bottom is found in Carolingian art where the lion is on the spectator's left and the bull on his right. In the Gospel of Saint Gauzelin they surround an Agnus Dei, in the Moutier Grandval bible, a Majestas. This could also be the order of the Otley head, but the Hart cross has origins in a different scheme as I have shown.[19] The Irish High crosses do not provide any close parallels for Ruthwell, and indeed the apocalyptic vision is not frequently found. As Francoise Henry says: "It remains however very striking that the only explicit Irish representation of the Vision is at Kells on the Tower Cross. There Christ is carved in the centre of the west side of the cross, and he is standing in the same attitude, as in the Irish carvings of the Last Judgement".[20] Christ is in the centre; to his right is the lion and to his left the bull. Both are winged and hold books but have no halo above. The symbol of St Matthew holds up a lamb in glory. Below is an eagle with a book. The reversed position of the eagle and angel brings the eagle into juxtaposition with the crucifixion scene below.

Otherwise in Irish tradition the evangelist symbols rarely appear on these crosses. The eagle and the ox, winged and holding books but without haloes, are on the Duleek cross,[21] and the symbols of St Matthew and St John appear over the head of an evangelist portrait on the scripture cross at Clonmacnoise.[22] This is their position on many manuscript paintings, but on the tall cross at Monasterboice, Francoise Henry has interpreted the two winged creatures held by human seated figures as evangelist symbols. If this attribution is correct these are the only sculptural parallels for the intimate depiction of portrait and symbol from Ruthwell. The Monasterboice figures are not unambiguously evangelist portraits with symbols. It therefore seems that the closest parallel for the Ruthwell scheme is to be found on the <u>Majestas</u> page of the Codex Amiatinus (fol. 796v). Certainly here we have portrait figures which are elongated and inclined in the Ruthwell manner.

Can we, however, use related schemes on sculpture to put forward suggestions as to what would have occupied the centre of the Ruthwell cross-head? Saxl[23] suggests that on the face with the evangelist symbols, the centrepiece should be the lamb, and, on analogy with Durham XX, that the other side would have a scene of Christ and St Peter holding the keys. There is plenty of support in Christian art from the third century to the eleventh, for the <u>Agnus Dei</u> as a possible centrepiece, and as we have seen the lamb in its motionless form, if found at Hart with the surrounding symbols.

No other Anglo-Saxon carver seems to have used all the available space on a cross for such a complete didactic scheme as on the Ruthwell cross. For example Hart 5 and Otley 1 which do show evangelist symbols on one face covered the other side of the head with plant-scrolls in the Yorkshire manner. However there are examples of seated figures or busts of Christ occupying the centre of a cross, as at Easby where one face survives, and Hoddom where there was a complete <u>Majestas</u> figure on one side with an attendant angel in the surviving arm, and on the other a bust of Christ holding a book with paired figures on the arms.[24] The two sides of the Ruthwell head should be complementary, but it is impossible to be dogmatic.

We have seen how very often the <u>Majestas</u> figure is an alternative to the lamb centrepiece, and it seems probable that the Saviour should be seated under the eagle, symbol of his salvation, on one side of the head. He, like the evangelist portraits on that face could, in the manner of one of the Hoddom figures, be holding a book. On the other face Christ in his role as judge could have been surrounded by the evangelist figures and their symbols as on the Codex Amiatinus.[25]

The Codex is a product of the Wearmouth-Jarrow Scriptorium, and in discussing Ruthwell - its inhabited plant-scrolls, its figure style and its iconography - one constantly returns to that centre. It is the centre where Bede wrote his scriptural commentaries and indeed advice on dogma for the Pictish church.[26] Placed within the ancient Christian territory of the Britons which in 731 was ruled for the first time by an English bishop at Whithorn, it is fitting that the cross should be so richly provided with material for doctrinal and devotional meditation. More richly provided in fact than one would think necessary for the generality of the surrounding population.

Evidence in all forms for the artistic and intellectual contribution of the various monastic centres of early Christian England, is very sparsely distributed. It is therefore easy to see too wide an influence deriving from a few well known works. Obviously one cannot claim unambiguously that the programme for the Ruthwell cross-head best fits what we know of the art and theology of Wearmouth-Jarrow. This would be especially difficult since no major crosses have emerged from the wealth of architectural carvings on these sites. However we do know the type of cross favored at Hexham/Ripon which seems to be based on a metalwork prototype,[27] with an almost iconoclastic lack of figural scenes and different head shapes. Lindisfarne favors

the insular tradition of ornament and also has no tradition of good figure
drawing, although the double curved head shape is known there.[28] The Whitby
and Carlisle crosses have plain heads with inscriptions across the transom
as by early tradition had the Bewcastle head.[29]

The Ruthwell monument, like The Dream of the Rood, stresses that aspect
of the cross which symbolizes protection and salvation both during the individual
human life and at the final judgement. Christ's crucifixion exists as a separate
scene at the bottom of the shaft, perhaps carved as a secondary feature. This
placing of the crucifixion scene on the shaft before the cross itself is conceived
as a stone crucifixion is also found at Hexham and St Andrew Auckland.[30]
It seems then to be a period feature to stress the apocalyptic significance of
Christ in Majesty rather than Christ suffering. The popularity of the Ruthwell
programme is, as we have seen, confined by its later occurrences, all of
which are on crosses which have elaborately planned figural themes.

NOTES

1.   W.G. Collingwood, Northumbrian Crosses of the Pre-Norman Age
      (London, 1927), pp. 76-8, 84, 106 and figs. 94 and 95. C.C. Hodges,
      "The ancient cross of Rothbury," Archaeologia Aeliana, 4th ser. 1 (1925),
      pp. 159-68. A detailed discussion of the cross is included in a forth-
      coming publication by R.J. Cramp and R. Miket, Catalogue of Anglo-
      Saxon Antiquities in the University Museum, Newcastle upon Tyne.

2.   See R.J. Cramp, Early Northumbrian Sculpture (Jarrow Lecture, 1965),
      Jarrow upon Tyne.

3.   See Cramp and Miket, Newcastle Museum Catalogue. The point is also
      discussed by Miss E. Coatsworth in her Durham University thesis which
      is in course of preparation, The Crucifixion in Anglo-Saxon Sculpture.

4.   E. Kitzinger, "The coffin reliquary," in The Relics of St. Cuthbert, ed.
      C.F. Battiscombe, (Oxford, 1956), pp. 202-304, esp. p.239.

5.   Since writing this, I have noted that there is at Aycliffe, Co. Durham,
      one arm of a later cross head with on one side a bird and on the opposite
      face a pair of haloed figures possibly holding books.

6.   This was ploughed up at the east end of the village in 1967 in a field
      called Old Kirk Field. It is now in the western end of the nave in the
      parish church. The head is carved from a very soft limestone which
      has been finely dressed. The carving would always have been shallow
      but details of the relief have been badly eroded away.

7.   Laon 137, Orosius fol. 1b. E.H. Zimmerman, Vorkarolingishche Min-
      iaturen II, Tafel 144, dated c.740.

8.   See R.J. Cramp, "A cross from St Oswald's church, Durham, and its
      stylistic relationships," Durham University Journal 58 (1965-6), 119-24;
      and G. Adcock, A Study of the Types of Interlace on Northumbrian
      Sculpture, unpublished M. Phil. dissertation (Durham, 1974), chap. 5,
      esp. pp. 209-15.

9.   F.J. Haverfield and W. Greenwell, A Catalogue of the Inscribed and
      Sculptured Stones in the Cathedral Library, Durham (Durham, 1899),
      pp. 79-87.

10.   Now in Nancy Cathedral. J. Hubert, J. Porcher, and W.F. Volbach, l'Empire Carolingien (Paris, 1968), p. 132.

11.   A grave-cover with a decorated cross, also from Durham, has what could be apocalyptic symbols with an angel at the base of the cross-head and two anonymous wingless animals on the side arms. The centre of the cross is filled with another cross, see Haverfield and Greenwell, Catalogue pp. 88-9. Recently Michael Dolley ("The nummular brooch from Sulgrave, " England Before the Conquest, ed. P. Clemoes and K. Hughes, (Cambridge, 1971, p. 343), has denied the apocalyptic association of this figure, but to me it is clearly present.

12.   F. Saxl, "The Ruthwell cross, " Journal of the Warburg and Courtauld Institutes 6 (1943), 1-19, esp. 6 and n. 8.

13.   See the symbols from St Vitale, Ravenna, and Kitzinger, "The coffin reliquary."

14.   R.J. Cramp, "The position of the Otley crosses in English sculpture of the eighth to ninth centuries, " Kolloquium über Spätantike und Frühmittelalterliche Skulptur II (1971), pl. 45, (4) and p. 62, note 29.

15.   C.A. Ralegh Radford, "Hoddom, " Transactions of the Dumfriesshire and Galloway Natural History and Antiquarian Society, 3rd ser. (1952-3), 174-97 and pl. IV.

16.   Halton: Cramp, "Otley crosses, " pl. 48 (2) and p. 62. Ilkley: W.G. Collingwood, Northumbrian crosses, fig. 63.

17.   T.D. Kendrick, Anglo-Saxon Art to A.D. 900 (London, 1938), pl. XCIV.

18.   The development and insular types of the evangelist symbols have been fully discussed by Kitzinger, "Coffin reliquary." See also R. Crozet, "Les quatre evangelistes et leur symbols, " in Les Cahiers Techniques de l'Art (Strasbourg, 1962), pp. 5-26; A.M. Friend, "The portraiture of the evangelists in Greek and Latin manuscripts, " Art Studies 7 (1930), 3-29; and Martin Werner, "The four evangelist symbols page in the Book of Durrow, " Gesta 8 (1969), 3f.

19.   Above pp.

20.   F. Henry, Irish Art During the Viking Invasions: 800 - 1020, (London, 1967), p. 164 and pl. 74.

21.   Ibid., pl. 73

22.   Ibid., pls. 91 and 95.

23.   "The Ruthwell cross, " p. 6.

24.   C.A. Ralegh Radford, "Hoddom, " pls. II and III.

25.   Florence, Biblioteca Laurenziana, Amiatinus I.

26.   Bede was especially interested in the Apocalypse of St John. See G.I. Bonner, Saint Bede in the Tradition of Western Apocalyptic Commentary (Jarrow Lecture, 1966).

27. R. Cramp, "Early Northumbrian sculpture at Hexham," Saint Wilfrid at Hexham, ed. D. P. Kirby, (Newcastle upon Tyne, 1974), pp. 115-40, esp. p. 120.

28. C. R. Peers, "The inscribed and sculptured stones at Lindisfarne," Archaeologia 74 (1925), 255-70, esp. 269 and Plate LIV (5).

29. A. S. Cook, Some Accounts of the Bewcastle Cross, Yale Studies in English 50 (New York, 1914), pp. 128-33.

30. E. Coatsworth, "Two examples of the crucifixion at Hexham," (Appendix III), Saint Wilfrid at Hexham, ed. Kirby, pp. 180-4.

VI. LITURGICAL INNOVATIONS ASSOCIATED WITH POPE SERGIUS AND THE ICONOGRAPHY OF THE RUTHWELL AND BEWCASTLE CROSSES

Éamonn Ó Carragáin

In their papers in the present volume, Professors Cramp and Farrell have attempted to explicate the iconography of the Ruthwell cross-head by reference to evidence from art history, liturgy and patristic writings. In this paper, I shall argue that part of the sequence of panels on the shaft of the Ruthwell cross, and also the three figural panels on the Bewcastle cross, can best be understood in the light of liturgical developments in Northumbria in the early eighth century.[1] Firstly, I argue that the panels at the foot of the south face of the Ruthwell cross representing the annunciation and the crucifixion (see outline of the iconographical plan of the Ruthwell and Bewcastle crosses, below, p. 147) are best understood in relation to the introduction into Northumbrian liturgical practice of the feast of the annunciation on 25 March, the anniversary of the Crucifixion. Secondly, the panels on the north face of the Ruthwell cross and on the west face of the Bewcastle cross, representing John the Baptist bearing the Agnus Dei and (immediately below) Christ in majesty over the beasts in the desert, are best understood in relation to the introduction of the chant 'Agnus Dei, qui tollis peccata mundi, miserere nobis' into the Roman Mass in the seventh century. The Paul and Anthony panel on the north face of the Ruthwell cross should also, I suggest, be related to the liturgy of the Mass. Thirdly, the erection of the Ruthwell and Bewcastle crosses may have been inspired by the new importance of the feast of the exaltation of the cross stemming from Pope Sergius's miraculous finding of a relic of the true cross in St Peter's in the year 701. I argue that the crosses reflect the keen interest in Roman liturgical developments which existed in early eighth-century Northumbria; and, finally, that the liturgical link between the annunciation and the crucifixion enables us better to understand the relation between the crucifixion poem inscribed on the Ruthwell cross (the ancestor of The Dream of the Rood copied in the tenth century into the Vercelli Book) and the iconography of the Ruthwell cross.

I

Perhaps the most illuminating discussion of the iconographical pattern of the Ruthwell cross is that by Dr. Saxl.[1a] One of the very few weaknesses of his argument is the absence of a convincing explanation for the presence on the cross of a crucifixion panel at the foot of the south face, under a panel representing the annunciation. He explained the crucifixion panel, not in relation to the panel above it, but in relation to the now obliterated panel at the foot of the north face. Saxl speculated that this panel may have represented the nativity, and wrote that "the nativity and the crucifixion. . . signify the beginning and end of Christ's incarnation."[2] Apart from the fact that this statement is not, strictly speaking, true (Christ's incarnation did not end with the cruci-

131

fixion), we do not have to rely on speculation as to what the obliterated panel may have represented to explain the presence and position of the crucifixion panel on the cross. An educated Anglo-Saxon of the early eighth century would have understood the crucifixion panel in relation to the annunciation panel directly above it on the south face of the cross: he would have known that the crucifixion took place on the anniversary of the annunciation, on 25 March. The crucifixion was liturgically celebrated on the moveable feast of Good Friday; but it was also associated with 25 March. For example, in its entry for 25 March, the Calendar of St Willibrord reads as follows: "Dominus crucifixus est: et sancti Jacobi fratris domini: et immolatio Isaac."[3] March 25 was held to be the anniversary of Christ's death as early as the second century: the tradition, which H. A. Wilson characterizes as "historical rather than liturgical in character,"[4] exemplified the principle that "omnia propriis locis et temporibus gessit salvator,"[5] or, as the Beowulf poet put it,

> se geweald hafað
> sæla ond mæla;   þæt is soð metod.[6]

Christ's nativity was liturgically celebrated on the winter solstice of the Julian calendar, 25 December. It followed that his conception took place exactly nine months previously, at the spring equinox;[7] and Christ was believed to have died on the thirty-third anniversary of his conception, exactly thirty-two years and three months after his nativity.

From the eighth century onwards, this tradition was to be overshadowed by the celebration of the annunciation on 25 March; but throughout the Anglo-Saxon period the idea that the annunciation coincided with the anniversary of the crucifixion was a perfectly familiar one. The Old English Martyrology draws an extended parallel between Christ's conception and his death on the cross, in its entry under 25 March;[8] and it is clear that the idea that 25 March was the anniversary of the crucifixion was familiar to the majority of those who compiled the martyrologies which survive from the late Anglo-Saxon period.[9] The tradition long antedated the celebration of the feast of the annunciation in the western Church. The annunciation was slow to find acceptance in the west, largely because the feast was bound to fall almost always during Lent, and so could not properly be celebrated. The Council of Toledo, in 656 A.D., stated the problem in clear terms:

> Si nativitatis et mortis incarnati Verbi dies absque immutatione
> ita certus habetur, ut absque diversitate in orbe toto
> terrarum ab omni concorditer Ecclesia celebretur, cur non
> festivitas gloriosae Matris eius eadem observantia, uno simul
> ubique die, similique habeatur honore?[10]

The explicit statement that the coincidence of the annunciation and of the anniversary of Christ's death was acknowledged "throughout the world" is interesting. The Council of Toledo, however, decided that, since the feast could not properly be celebrated on 25 March because of the concurrence of the Lenten season, in Spain "ante octavum diem, quo natus est Dominus, genitricis quoque eius dies habeatur celeberrimus et praeclarus."[11]

The earliest surviving record of the celebration at Rome of the feast of the Annunciation occurs in the Liber Pontificalis, as part of a biography of Pope

Sergius (686-701). In the Liber Pontificalis account, we are told that Sergius instituted processions to celebrate four Marian feasts: the annunciation (25 March), the dormition of the Virgin (15 August), the nativity of the Virgin (8 September) and the presentation in the temple (2 February):

> Constituit autem ut diebus Adnuntiationis Domini, Dormitionis
> et Nativitatis sanctae Dei Genitricis semperque virginis
> Mariae ac sancti Symeonis, quod Ypapanti Greci appellant,
> letania exeat a sancto Hadriano et ad sanctam Mariam populus
> occurrat.[12]

The Liber Pontificalis does not say that Sergius himself instituted these feasts; only that he gave them a new solemnity. Duchesne concludes "qu'elles ont été établies à Rome dans le courant du septième siècle."[13] The Chronicon Paschale attests that the feast of the annunciation was already celebrated at Constantinople in the first half of the seventh century, and its institution was confirmed, during the reign of Sergius himself, by the Council "In Trullo" held at Constantinople in 691-2.[14] Pope Sergius was born in Sicily, but his family had come from Antioch in Syria.[15] It is natural, therefore, that feasts like the annunciation, which had long been incorporated into the eastern liturgies but had only recently been introduced into Roman usage, should have been emphasized by additional ceremonial during his pontificate. It may be supposed that the arguments which decided the Council of Toledo in 656 to reject the celebration of the annunciation on the anniversary of the crucifixion were not without weight in Rome forty years later; and therefore Sergius's action in ordering the same celebrations for the 25 March as for the other three Marian feasts, though it might not actually have instituted the feast of the annunciation in Roman observance, was probably decisive for its future survival.

Though the annunciation was already established in the eastern church, we can be pretty certain that the feast was not celebrated in England before the pontificate of Sergius - we have seen, for example, that the Calendar of St Willibrord makes no mention of it.[16] Nevertheless, the four festivals of the Blessed Virgin honoured by Sergius quickly became known in England. They are mentioned by Aldhelm, who died in 709;[17] and Abbot Sigbald, who died (after a long abbacy) in 772, introduced the observation of the four feasts into the monastery (dependent on Lindisfarne) which AEthelwulf later described in his poem De Abbatibus:

> sanctam cumque diem sacrauit uirgo Maria,
> qua uolitans caelos meruit penetrare per altos,
> uel qua presenti generata redditur orbi,
> uel qua prepulchrae susceptat gaudia uitae,
> uel qua celsithronum meruit generare tonantem,
> uel quacumque die, cum templi festa coruscant,
> omnibus his laetus nimium per gaudia sancta
> aurea dulcisonae restaurat munera mentis.
> ac fratres precibus mulcet sollempnia festa
> ad letos caelebrare pie genetricis honores.[18]

Thus, in the light of the documentary evidence adduced above, the best explanation for the juxtaposition of the crucifixion and annunciation panels at the foot of the south face of the Ruthwell cross is that the Ruthwell carvers were also familiar with the recently introduced celebration of the annunciation on 25 March, and wished this example of the control of providence over times and seasons to be reflected on the cross. The inscription around the annunciation panel, which is still partly legible, may provide a confirmatory hint that the Ruthwell sculptors were thinking of liturgical practice. It begins "INGRESSUS A[NGELUS]," and is almost certainly based on Luke i, 28;[19] this verse of St Luke's gospel recurs as an offertory antiphon for the feast of the annunciation in the earliest Roman antiphonaries which survive.[20]

II

Panels representing St John the Baptist holding the Agnus Dei occur both on the north face of the Ruthwell cross and on the Bewcastle cross; on both crosses, panels representing Christ being adored by the beasts in the desert occur immediately below the Agnus Dei panels. The recurrence of the Agnus Dei panels on the crosses, and the context within which they occur, can also be explained by reference to a liturgical innovation associated with the pontificate of Sergius. The Liber Pontificalis states that Pope Sergius "statuit ut tempore confractionis dominici corporis Agnus Dei, qui tollis peccata mundi, miserere nobis a clero et populo decantetur."[21] This is the earliest reference to the Agnus Dei chant in the Roman liturgy of the Mass. It is possible that the Liber Pontificalis is over-simplifying the facts, and that Sergius did not so much introduce the chant as give it a new importance;[22] but as Jungmann remarks,

> even if it was not brought into Rome by Sergius himself, a Syrian by descent, still it was during the later seventh century, in the train of that great inrush of Greek clerics from the Eastern lands overrun by Islam, above all Syria; for it is manifestly an element from the Eastern liturgy. In the East it had become the practice since the sixth century to regard the breaking of the species of bread as a reference to our Lord's Passion and death.[23]

The phrase "a clero et populo decantetur" in the Liber Pontificalis is of great importance for the present argument. Professor Michael Dolley has stressed that "the Agnus Dei was very much a chant of the congregation as opposed to the celebrant, so that the innovation is one that could not fail to have been remarked by the people as a whole."[24] The Agnus Dei was just that kind of innovation in public worship which we might expect to find reflected on outdoor, public monuments such as the Ruthwell and Bewcastle crosses. There is good evidence that the Agnus Dei invocation had reached England as part of the Litany of the Saints, by the year 700; and that it was widely copied and became popular in private devotion.[25] In the liturgy of the Mass, as Jungmann remarks, the chant had a clear devotional function; it was "a reverential and, at the same time, humble greeting of Him who has been made present under the form of bread."[26] It was eminently suitable for engaging the attention of the congregation "tempore confractionis dominici corporis;" Jungmann is of the opinion that "originally the one simple verse was repeated as often as necessary,"[27] until the breaking of the species of bread and its distribution in Communion had been completed; it was only later, when the rite of fraction was rendered superfluous by the introduction of unleavened bread and small

particles, that the chant "gradually assumed the hallowed number three."[28]
By means of the chant, the congregation proclaimed their recognition of Christ's
presence under the species of bread; in particular, they proclaimed their recognition of Christ "in the breaking of bread, " as the disciples at Emmaus had
done: "Et factus est, dum recumberet cum eis, accepit panem et benedixit,
ac fregit, et porrigebat illis. Et aperti sunt oculi eorum, et cognoverunt eum:
et ipse evanuit et oculis eorum."[29] It is significant, therefore, that in both
the Ruthwell and Bewcastle crosses, the Agnus Dei panel is juxtaposed to the
panel in which "bestiae et dracones cognoverunt in deserto salvatorem mundi."[30]

The Bewcastle cross emphasizes the theme of 'recognition' in two ways.
First, the runic inscription "+gessus kristus" has been placed on the cross
between the Agnus Dei panel and the panel of Christ and the beasts: the implication is that Christ is to be recognized "in propria figura, " as the beasts
recognized him, and also as the Agnus Dei. Secondly, the panel at the foot of
this side of the Bewcastle cross, which I take to be the unique representation of
John the evangelist standing and bearing his eagle,[31] gives us the scriptural
auctoritas for the Agnus Dei chant. The text chosen for the chant is found, not
in the synoptic gospels, but only in the Gospel according to St John: "Altera
die vidit Ioannes Iesum venientem ad se, et ait: Ecce agnus Dei, ecce qui
tollit peccatum mundi."[32]

The presence on the Bewcastle cross, not merely of a panel representing
John the Baptist carrying the Agnus Dei, but of a panel representing the evangelist who records the recognition of Christ as the Agnus Dei, may reflect a
concern on the part of those who erected the cross that the significance of the
Agnus Dei chant should be clearly understood. This point can be illustrated
by reference to a theological controversy which may perhaps have influenced
Sergius in his decision to introduce the Agnus Dei chant into the Mass. In
692, the Council "In Trullo" (held in Constantinople under the aegis of the Emperor Justinian II) forbade the representation of Christ under the image of a
lamb.[33] Because the canons of the council failed to represent papal interests
in various ways, Pope Sergius rejected them in toto. Louis Duchesne has
suggested that Sergius may have inserted the Agnus Dei chant into the Mass
at the fraction in order to emphasize that no less an authority than St John the
Baptist had hailed Christ as the Agnus Dei: "Il n'est pas défendu de voir, dans
ce décret de Sergius, une protestation contre le canon 82 du concile In Trullo,
qui proscrivit la représentation symbolique du Sauveur sous forme d'agneau."[34]
Here is a theological controversy about religious art which may have had a
direct effect on liturgical practice, and thence inspired the iconographic programme of the Bewcastle cross. Considered as a unified sequence, the three
panels on the cross suggest a clear theological statement, such as "we recognize
Christ at the fractio under the figure of the Agnus Dei (top panel) even as the
beasts recognized him in the desert (central panel); and our authority for this
is none other than John the evangelist (bottom panel)." It is tempting, indeed,
to read in the iconographic programme of the Bewcastle cross a clear statement of adherence to the papal position, and a rejection of canon 82 of the
Trullan council. This temptation should, however, be resisted; even if
Sergius's motive for inserting the Agnus Dei chant at the fraction was a polemical one (and for this we have only circumstantial evidence), the motive of
the Bewcastle sculptors is much more likely to have been devotional and didactic.

They would surely have been more concerned to encourage a deeper understanding of and response to the liturgy of the Mass, than to refute the canons of the Trullan council.

On the north face of the Ruthwell cross, we again find not only John the Baptist and Christ over the beasts, but (at the top of the cross, in a small panel now mistakenly reversed)[35] a representation of St John the evangelist, bearing his eagle, and identified by the opening words of his gospel.[36] This panel, however, appears to have formed a programme consisting of the four evangelist portraits surrounding (on the centrepiece of the cross) either an Agnus Dei panel or a majestas domini (the programme of the north face of the crosspiece is discussed by Professor Cramp, above, pp. 118-130). It cannot, therefore, be argued that the portrait of St John the evangelist stands in the same relationship to the panels representing John the Baptist and Christ over the beasts as on the Bewcastle cross. The devotional significance of the two large panels is, however, clarified on the Ruthwell cross by the Latin inscriptions surrounding them. Of the inscription around the Agnus Dei panel, only one word survives with certainty, [A]DORAMVS: but it directs our attention to the devotional significance of the Agnus Dei chant in the Mass.[37] That the theme of "recognition" was intended by the Ruthwell carvers is made clear by the inscription around the panel representing Christ and the beasts, which emphasizes that the beasts "cognoverunt in deserto salvatorem mundi."[38] Nor do the two large panels stand in thematic isolation on the Ruthwell cross: as at Bewcastle, they are to be interpreted in relation to the panel below the one representing Christ and the beasts. At Ruthwell, this panel represents St Paul and St Anthony, and is inscribed '+ SCS: PAVLVS: ET: A . . . FREGER[VNT]: PANEM IN DESERTO:.'[39] Like the Agnus Dei panel, this Paul and Anthony panel is to be related to the 'confractio dominici corporis' of the Mass.

In the Vita Sancti Pauli, the two hermits break a heaven-sent loaf between them as the solution to a competition in humility: St Paul had insisted on St Anthony's right to divide the bread, as guest, and St Anthony had urged that St Paul, as the senior of the two, should divide it.[40] A passage in Adamnan's life of St Colmcille implies that the "confractio dominici corporis" was, at least at Iona, carried out as a "co-fractio" performed by two priests breaking the species of bread between them, and that this rite was symbolic of the harmony that should exist within a monastic community. Adamnan tells us that a bishop from Munster visited Iona, and humbly concealed his episcopal rank. Thus, when (as visitor) he was invited to celebrate Mass, he called on St Colmcille to assist him at the fractio 'as two presbyters together'; but the saint had perceived that the visitor was a bishop, and insisted on him breaking bread alone, "according to the episcopal rite":

> Nam alia die dominica a sancto jusus Christi corpus ex more
> conficere sanctum advocat, ut simul quasi duo prespiteri
> dominicum panem frangerent. Sanctus proinde ad altarium
> accedens repente intuitus faciem ejus sic eum conpellat:
> 'Benedicat te Christus, frater. Nunc scimus quod sis
> episcopus: quare hucusque te occultare conatus es, ut
> tibi a nobis debeta non redderetur veneratio?' Quo audito
> sancti verbo humilis perigrinus valde stupefactus Christum

in sancto veneratus est. Et qui inerant praesentes nimis
ammirati glorificarunt deum. [41]

It is surely not unreasonable to argue that in this episode Adamnan presented St Colmcille and the bishop from Munster as re-enacting the contest
in courtesy and humility between St Paul and St Anthony. St Colmcille's remarkable insight had found a reason for granting the bishop the honour of
breaking the consecrated bread for the whole community. Besides being evidence for the rite of co-fractio at Iona, [42] the passage implies that the rite
was itself seen as a commemoration of the fraternal virtues of St Paul and
St Anthony, the models for Celtic monasticism. In Adamnan's mind, the co-
fractio of the Mass and the contest in courtesy between St Paul and St Anthony
were associated. For those who erected the Ruthwell cross, the way in which
St Paul and St Anthony "fregerunt panem in deserto" would have recalled the
way in which (at least in Iona and probably in monasteries related to it) the
"confractio dominici corporis" was enacted in the Mass.

The three large central panels on the north face of the Ruthwell cross
form a triptych of thematically related scenes. The central panel of the triptych, Christ over the beasts, represents in propria figura "Iesus Christus
Iudex AEquitatis, " and explicitly states the theme which unifies the triptych:
"bestiae et dracones cognoverunt in deserto salvatorem mundi. "[43] As Saxl
has pointed out, the panels above and below this central panel are related to
it by the theme "in deserto"; but besides being associated with the desert,
and so with eremetic monasticism, the figures of John the Baptist holding the
Agnus Dei and of Paul and Anthony together breaking bread are associated
with the "confractio dominici corporis" in the Mass. The upper panel reflects
the recently-introduced Roman chant for the confractio, "Agnus dei, qui tollis
peccata mundi, miserere nobis"; the lower panel reflects the way in which,
at the identical moment of the Mass, a co-fractio was enacted in some monasteries following Celtic customs.

It is possible to see, in the pattern of the triptych of panels, an eirenic
intention. One element of the devotional meaning of the triptych is surely
that monasteries of both the Celtic and the Roman observance, however differently they celebrated the Eucharist, agreed in recognizing Christ, like the
disciples at Emmaus, in the breaking of bread. Though it may be significant
that the Agnus Dei panel (recalling the new Roman chant) is given the place of
honour at the top of the triptych, this monument on the borders of Northumbria
seems to emphasize what the Celtic and Roman traditions had in common,
rather than what held them apart. Similarly, at the foot of the south face of
the cross, the juxtaposition of the crucifixion and annunciation panels had
emphasized the date, 25 March, which both Celtic and Roman traditions agreed
was the date on which Christ had been conceived and died. [44] The Ruthwell
cross may be taken as evidence that the Easter controversy of the preceding
century was no longer a living issue, and that at least one patron familiar with
both Roman and Celtic liturgical traditions felt it more important to stress
those elements on which the universal Church was agreed, though its rites
might vary - in the words of the Council of Toledo in 656, what "absque im-
mutatione ita certus habetur, ut absque diversitate in orbe toto terrarum ab
omni concorditer Ecclesia celebretur. "[45]

III

It is possible that, in addition to those I have just discussed, a third liturgical innovation associated with Pope Sergius may have influenced those who erected the Ruthwell and Bewcastle crosses - the celebration of the feast of the exaltation of the cross.   In the words of the Liber Pontificalis,

> Hic beatissimus vir in sacrario beati Petri apostoli capsam
> argenteam in angulo obscurissimo iacentem et ex nigridine
> transacto annositatis nec si esset argentea apparente, Deo
> ei revelante, repperit. Oratione itaque facta, sigillum
> expressum abstulit; lucellum aperuit, in quo interius
> plumacium ex holosirico superpositum, quod stauracin dicitur,
> invenit; eoque ablato, inferius crucem diversis ac pretiosis
> lapidibus perornatam inspexit. De qua tractis IIII petalis
> in quibus gemmae clausae erant, mire magnitudinis et
> ineffabilem portionem salutaris ligni dominicae crucis
> interius repositam invenit. Qui etiam ex die illo pro salute
> humani generis ab omni populo christiano, die Exaltationis
> sanctae Crucis, in basilicam Salvatoris quae appellatur
> Constantiniana osculatur ac adoratur. [46]

Once more, the biography of Sergius in the Liber Pontificalis is the earliest evidence we have for the celebration of a feast at Rome; once more, the feast has been brought into Roman usage from the East;[47] and, though the Liber Pontificalis does not say that Sergius instituted the feast, it clearly implies that his discovery of the relic of the True Cross in the Vatican gave the celebration of the feast a new solemnity at Rome.   The feast was soon known in England.   Bede knew and used the Liber Pontificalis, [48] and paraphrased its account of Sergius's find in the Chronicle appended to his De Temporum Ratione, under the year 701. [49] As long ago as 1905, Aloys Brandl suggested that The Dream of the Rood might have been inspired by news of Sergius's vision and the resulting veneration of the Cross; he pointed out that monks from Jarrow were in Rome in 701, so that the news could not have taken long to reach Northumbria. [50] Whatever we think about Brandl's theory about the origin of the Ruthwell cross crucifixion poem (the Ruthwell cross does not provide direct evidence that the poem had the form of a 'Traumgesicht' at this early period), it is not unlikely that the idea of erecting the magnificent stone crosses at Ruthwell and at Bewcastle should have been suggested by an increased devotion to the feast of the exultation as a result of recent developments in Rome.

IV

As Professor Rosemary Cramp has put it, "we must . . . think of the earliest sculpture as a direct reflection of monastic culture."[51] Stemming from such a culture, we might expect the Ruthwell and Bewcastle crosses to reflect the opus dei, the public worship of the monastic community, as well as (or even rather than) devotional themes based on written texts. [52] It is to be expected that Northumbrian monuments of this period should reflect recent developments in the Roman liturgy. Both Eddius Stephanus (the biographer of St Wilfrid), and John, the arch-cantor of St Peter's at Rome, taught liturgical chant in Northumbria in the late seventh and early eighth centuries;[53]

and it is not impossible that ivory or metal plaques, brought from Rome during the many visits of Benedict Biscop, Wilfrid and other Northumbrian monks, provided models for some at least of the panels on the Ruthwell and Bewcastle crosses. [54] St Wilfrid of York had occasion to visit Rome several times, both in his youth and during his troubled episcopacy; [55] while his friend and patron, king Caedwalla of Wessex, was baptized by Pope Sergius and died at Rome. [56] Benedict Biscop, abbot of Monkwearmouth-Jarrow, visited Rome six times between 653 and 686; [57] although Sergius seems to have come to Rome from Sicily as late as the reign of Pope Adeodatus (672-6), and to have been ordained priest as late as June 683, [58] he would already have been appointed "prior cantorum" during Benedict Biscop's last visit to Rome (685-6). [59] Ceolfrid (who succeeded Benedict Biscop as abbot) visited Rome with his predecessor in 678, and was on his way to Rome when de died at Langres in 716. [60] Ceolfrid sent a mission (which included Hwaetberht, who was to succeed him) to Rome in 700-701, to procure from Pope Sergius the privileges for Monkwearmouth-Jarrow which Pope Agatho had granted to Benedict Biscop; [61] and a letter of Sergius to Ceolfrid is extant. [62] Of Ceolfrid's successor, Hwaetberht, Bede wrote (in a passage stressing his suitability for the position of abbot) that

> scribendi, cantandi, legendi ac docendi fuerat non parua
> exercitatus industria. Romam quoque temporibus beatae
> memoriae Sergii papae accurrens, et non paruo ibidem temporis
> spatio demoratus, quaequae sibi necessaria iudicabat,
> didicit, descripsit, retulit. [63]

Hwaetberht was typical of Northumbrian monastic culture, not only in combining an interest in learning with an interest in the liturgy ("cantandi"), but also in seeing Rome as the source from which whatever was necessary for the monastic life was to be learned, copied or brought back to Northumbria.

It is tempting but dangerous to argue that the close contacts between Monkwearmouth-Jarrow and Rome during the lifetime of Sergius prove that the Ruthwell and Bewcastle crosses, which reflect a knowledge and interest in Roman liturgical observance, were produced by monks from Monkwearmouth-Jarrow.   The figure of Wilfrid alone should be enough to remind us that other Northumbrian centres were in close contact with Rome during this period. Nevertheless, Professor Rosemary Cramp's suggestion ("not . . . a proven or even provable theory") that the Ruthwell cross carvers might have been trained at Monkwearmouth-Jarrow [64] fits very well with the argument of the present paper (see also the remarks of Professor Cramp, above, pp. 118-30, and Professor Farrell, above pp. 96-117).   As the Sergian liturgical innovations seem to have spread to Northumbria in the first half of the eighth century, the present argument reinforces the accumulating evidence that the Ruthwell and Bewcastle crosses were erected within that half-century (700-750). [65]

The three liturgical innovations which, I have argued, are reflected in the iconography of the Ruthwell cross do not interfere with the devotional programme of the cross, but instead reinforce and enrich it. [66] The surviving panels of the north face of the cross-shaft all refer to life "in deserto." As Dr Saxl has remarked, "the accumulation of scenes related to desert life on the front of the Ruthwell cross can . . . hardly be ascribed to chance." [67] The inscriptions for the "_Agnus Dei_ triptych" emphasize the theme, and it is continued by the panel underneath the "triptych," which represents Mary and Joseph carrying the Christ-child across the desert of Sinai into Egypt.[68] Awareness of the liturgical associations behind the "Agnus Dei triptych" in fact gives new force to the devotional theme of eremetic life "in deserto" by focussing attention on the central event in the life of a monastic community, one might almost say its raison d'être: participation in the Eucharist. The panels on the opposite (south) face of the cross seem to be unified by the theme of response to Christ. This theme is clearly seen in the panel representing the cure of the blind man; Saxl is surely right in suggesting that "in this miracle is symbolized . . . the divine power of illuminating a believing soul."[69] The panel directly above represents the woman who was a sinner anointing Christ's feet; and it has been generally agreed that this represents the next stage in the Christian life, conversio morum springing from repentance and penance.[70] The panel above, whether it represents the Visitation[71] or, as has recently been suggested, Martha and Mary,[72] clearly continues the themes of response to Christ and the stages of the Christian life; a theme which is brought to moving resolution in the figures of the archer and the bird at the head of the cross (I agree with Professor Farrell's interpretation of these panels, above, pp.96-117). The crucifixion and annunciation panels, at the foot of the cross, fit into the devotional programme of the south side as a whole - provide, in more senses than one, a fitting basis for the programme. The salvation of all Christian souls depended fundamentally on Mary's uncomprehending but obedient reception of Gabriel's message at the annunciation, and on the cross's uncomprehending but obedient bearing of its Lord to his death thirty-three years later: a theme most movingly expressed in the Ruthwell cross crucifixion poem, inscribed in runic letters on the narrow sides of the cross, and in its descendant, The Dream of the Rood in the Vercelli Book (950-1000).

V

I shall conclude this paper by suggesting a close thematic link between the iconography of the south face of the Ruthwell cross and the crucifixion poem inscribed in runic letters on the narrow sides of the cross. In a poem clearly descended from the Ruthwell cross crucifixion poem, The Dream of the Rood, we are explicitly invited to compare the glory given to the cross with that given to Mary:

> Hwæt, me þa geweorðode wuldres Ealdor
> ofer holmwudu, heofonrices Weard,
> swylce swa he his modor eac, Marian sylfe,
> ælmihtig God, for ealle menn
> geweorðode ofer eall wifa cynn.[73]

As I shall argue in another paper,[74] in The Dream of the Rood the crucifixion is presented in terms reminiscent of the annunciation (a link suggested by the coincidence of both events on 25 March). In that poem, Christ does not bear his cross to Calvary: the cross is already standing there when it sees Christ hastening to mount upon it. This departure from the scriptural accounts of the crucifixion is not arbitrary: it enables the cross to dramatize its experience of the crucifixion in terms reminiscent of Mary's incomprehending obedience at the annunciation. Such a presentation is also found in the Ruthwell cross

crucifixion poem.   Like Mary, who was troubled at the Angel's greeting ("tur-
bata est ...", Luke I, 29) and did not understand what the Lord demanded of
her ("Quomodo fiet istud . ...", Luke I, 34) the cross in the Ruthwell poem is
represented as troubled yet obedient: 'þuga (ic ni dorstæ), "[75] "hælda
ic ni dorstæ," Þic pæt al biheald. saræ ic wæs miÞ sorgum gidroefid. "[76]
Isidore, Gregory and Bede saw Christ's action at the annunciation as an heroic
defeat of the powers of darkness:

> De quo propheta in psalmo: Dominus, inquit, fortis et potens
> dominus potens in proelio.   Illo nimirum proelio quo
> potestates aerias debellare et ab earum tyrannide mundum
> ueniebat eripere.[77]

Similarly, in the Ruthwell cross crucifixion poem Christ appears as an heroic
figure, "god almeȝttig, " "modig fore (allæ) men, " "riicnæ kyninc heafunes
hlafard, " who, instead of being led to the cross, approaches it and mounts it
of his own will " Þa he walde on galgu gistiga. " This presentation of Christ is
not at all reminiscent of the liturgy of Good Friday, in either the eighth or the
tenth centuries; but it is remarkably close to Bede's description of Christ's
action at the annunciation. The opinion of Professor Schapiro, that in the iconography of the Ruthwell cross "we find little that pertains directly to the poem"[78]
stands in need of reconsideration. The recently-introduced feast of the annunciation on the anniversary of the crucifixion may have inspired the Ruthwell
carvers, not merely to juxtapose crucifixion and annunciation panels on the
south face of the cross, but to inscribe on the east and west faces part of a
(recently composed?) poem in which the crucifixion is presented in terms reminiscent of the annunciation. Sergian liturgical innovations, indeed, may
have inspired both the erection of the Ruthwell cross and the composition of
the crucifixion poem inscribed upon it; in which case lines 90-94 of The Dream
of the Rood, which explicitly link the cross with Mary, preserve a traditional
interpretation of the poem familiar to the carvers of the Ruthwell cross.[79]
Cross and poem stem from a single milieu: that of monastic devotion within
a liturgical context.

NOTES

1. I wish to thank various scholars who read versions of this paper in type-
    script and who offered me helpful comments on its argument; in particular
    Malcolm Parkes, C.J.E. Ball, Gerald Bonner, John Braidwood, Rosemary
    Cramp, Michael Dolley, W.G. East, R.T. Farrell, Henry Mayr-Harting,
    Alastair Minnis, Jane Roberts and Patrick Wormald.

1a. F. Saxl, "The Ruthwell cross, " Journal of the Warburg and Courtauld
    Institutes 6 (1943), 1-19.

2. Saxl, "Ruthwell cross, "p. 5.

3. The Calendar of St Willibrord, ed. H.A. Wilson, Henry Bradshaw So-
    ciety 55 (London, 1918), fol. 35v (plate III), p. 5 (transcription), and
    pp. 24-6 (notes). Wilson dates the calendar between 701 and 709 (pp.
    x-xi). The reference to Isaac is in another, later hand.

4. Wilson, Calendar of St Willibrord, p. 24. For a survey of the tradition, see V. Loi, "Il 25 Marzo data pasquale e la cronologia Giovannea della Passione in età patristica," Ephemerides Liturgicae 85 (1971), 48-69.

5. Ambrosiaster, Quaestiones Veteris et Noui Testamenti, Quaestio iv, ed. A. Souter, Corpus Scriptorum Ecclesiasticorum Latinorum 50 (Vienna, 1908), p. 100, as quoted in Loi, "Il 25 Marzo data pasquale," p. 53.

6. Beowulf, 1610b-11; Anglo-Saxon Poetic Records IV, ed. E.V.K. Dobbie (New York, 1953), p. 50.

7. See Bedae Opera de Temporibus, ed. C.W. Jones (Cambridge, Mass., 1943), Introduction, pp. 6-7. Bede, who knew that the spring equinox fell on 21 March, nevertheless remarked that many and wise authorities held the other view: "multorum late et sapientium seculi, et Christianorum sententia claret" - De Temporum Ratione XXX, ed. Jones, p. 235.

8. The old English Martyrology. ed. G. Herzfield, Early English Text Society o.s. 116 (London, 1900), p. 48. Celia Sisam, "An early fragment of the Old English Martyrology," Review of English Studies, n. s. 4 (1953), 209-20 (at 217) has argued that this is a Mercian text which circulated in the south of England from the late ninth century.

9. See F. Wormald, English Kalendars before A.D. 1100, Henry Bradshaw Society 72 (London, 1934). Only one of the nineteen caiendars printed by Wormald explicitly indicates the coincidence: Salisbury, Cathedral Library MS 150, fol. 4r: "EQVINOCTIVM. Conceptio Sanctae Marie. Crucifixio domini" (Wormald, English Kalendars, p. 18). Fifteen of these calendars, however, implicitly indicate the coincidence, by noting "Resurreccio domini" under 27 March: see, for example, Oxford, Bodleian Library MS Digby 63, fol. 14v (Wormald, English Kalendars, p. 4). Only three of the calendars printed by Wormald make no reference to the tradition (see Wormald, pp. 32, 158 and 256).

10. As quoted in H. Jugié, "La première fête mariale en Orient et en Occident, l'Avent primitif," Echos d'Orient 22 (1923), 129-52 (at 144); see also H. Leclercq in Dictionnaire d'archéologie chrétienne et de liturgie (Paris, 1907) I, columns 2241-67 under Annonciation (column 2243).

11. Jugié, "La première fête Mariale," pp. 144-5.

12. L. Duchesne, Le Liber Pontificalis, 2 vols. (Paris, 1886-92) I, 376.

13. Duchesne, Liber Pontificalis I, 381.

14. See I. Cecchetti, "L'annunziazione: il racconto biblico e la festa liturgica," Bollettino Ceciliano (Turin) 38 (1943), 46-8 and 98-114 (at 103); see also Leclercq DACL, column 2244.

15. Duchesne, Liber Pontificalis I, 371.

16. Its absence in St Willibrord's Calendar is all the more striking when we consider that the three other Marian feasts mentioned in the Liber Pontificalis account quoted above are all entered in the calendar: see Wilson, Calendar, pp. 21, 36-7 and 39.

17. Aldhelm, "In Ecclesia Mariae a Bugge Exstructa," lines 59-65, ed. R. Ehwald, Aldhelmi Opera, MGH Auctores Antiquissimi XV (Berlin, 1919), p. 17. See H. Mayr-Harting, The Coming of Christianity to Anglo-Saxon England (London, 1972), pp. 189 and 308.

18. AEthelwulf "De Abbatibus," ed. A. Campbell (Oxford, 1967), lines 460-9, pp. 37-9.

19. See E. Okasha, Hand-List of Anglo-Saxon Non-Runic Inscriptions (Cambridge, 1971), p. 111.

20. Antiphonale Missarum Sextuplex, ed. R. J. Hesbert (Brussels, 1935), no. 33, pp. 42-5; see also the Office antiphons printed (from eleventh-century manuscripts) in Corpus Antiphonalium Officii, ed. R. J. Hesbert and R. Prevost, 6 vols. (Rome, 1963) III, nos 3339-40, p. 284, and I, no. 51, pp. 124-5.

21. Duchesne, Liber Pontificalis I, 376.

22. See E. Bishop, Liturgica Historica (Oxford, 1918), p. 145.

23. J.A. Jungmann, The Mass of the Roman Rite (London, 1959) p. 485. J.A. Jungmann, Missarum Sollemnia, 4th ed., 2 vols. (Freiburg, 1958) II, 412-23, gives the references to primary sources omitted in the abridged English edition.

24. M.Dolley, "The nummular brooch from Sulgrave," England Before the Conquest, ed. P. Clemoes and K. Hughes (Cambridge, 1971), pp. 333-49 (at 344). Professor Dolley is here discussing the introduction of the variant dona nobis pacem in the late tenth century, but the principle is valid for the introduction of the chant in its original form.

25. See E. Bishop, "The Litany of the Saints in the Stowe Missal," Liturgica Historica (Oxford, 1918), pp. 137-64 (especially pp. 143, 147-8).

26. Jungmann, The Mass of the Roman Rite, p. 486.

27. Ibid., p. 487.

28. Ibid., pp. 486, 488.

29. Luke XXIV, 30-1; italics mine.

30. See Okasha, Handlist, p. 110, for a full transcript of the inscription.

31. Saxl,"Ruthwell Cross," p. 9, n. 6, states that "for the standing evangelist with his symbol no Mediterranean model has come to my knowledge"; Rosemary Cramp, Early Northumbrian Sculpture (Jarrow Lecture 1965), p. 8, suggests that the Bewcastle carver had adapted a seated evangelist portrait to a standing position. It might be suggested that the reason for this adaptation was to make the lower panel fit better in style with the standing figures of the middle and upper panels on the cross shaft.

32. John I, 29; it should be noted that the precise formula ("qui tollis peccata mundi, . . . miserere nobis") comes not directly from St John's Gospel, but via the liturgical chant, "Gloria in excelsis Deo." See F. Cabrol, in Dictionnaire d'archéologie chrétienne et de liturgie I (Paris, 1907), under Agnus Dei, columns 965-9 (column 966).

33. The eighty-second canon of the council, together with a Latin translation, is available in C. Kirch, Enchiridion Fontium Historiae Ecclesiae Antiquae, ninth edition (Freiburg in Breisgau, 1965), p. 610.

34. Duchesne, Liber Pontificalis I, 381.

35. See R.T. Farrell, above, pp. 96-7.

36. See R. Cramp, above, p. 118.

37. For a recent speculation on the nature of the complete inscription around the panel, see D. Howlett, "Two panels on the Ruthwell cross," Journal of the Warburg and Courtauld Institutes 37 (1974), 333-6 (at 334). I had discussed an early form of the present paper with Dr Howlett in 1971; and he agrees with me that the panel is to be associated with Pope Sergius's introduction of the Agnus Dei into the Mass (pp. 333-4).

38. Okasha, Handlist, p. 110.

39. Ibid., p. 110.

40. St Jerome, Vita Sancti Pauli, PL, xxiii, 17-28 (column 25).

41. Adamnan's Life of Columba, ed. A.O. Anderson and M.O. Anderson (London, 1961), p. 304.

42. The rite of co-fractio was not invariably practised when two presbyters were together; the Andersons, in their edition of Adamnan's Life, p. 124, point out that on other occasions "Columba appears to have celebrated the Mass alone." L. Gougaud, "Les rites de la consécration et de la fraction dans la liturgie celtique de la messe," Proceedings of the Nineteenth Eucharistic Congress (London, 1909), pp. 348-61, has warned against generalizing too widely on the basis of this episode about the general practice of co-fractio in Celtic lands (pp. 360-1).

43. Okasha, Handlist, p. 110.

44. March 25 is usually noted as the anniversary of the crucifixion in early Irish martyrologies. See The Martyrology of Tallaght, ed. R. I. Best and H. J. Lawlor, Henry Bradshaw Society 68 (London, 1931), p. 27; The Martyrology of Oengus the Culdee, ed. W. Stokes, Henry Bradshaw Society 29 (London, 1905), p. 101. The Martyrology of Gorman, edited by W. Stokes Henry Bradshaw Society 9 (London, 1885), p. 63.

45. See above, p. 132.

46. Duchesne, Liber Pontificalis I, 374.

47. Ibid., I, 379; E. Bishop, Liturgica Historica, p. 145.

48. See M. W. L. Laistner, "The Library of the Venerable Bede," in Bede: His Life, Times and Writings, ed. A. H. Thompson (Oxford, 1935), p. 265; J. D. A. Ogilvy, Books Known to the English 597-1066 (Cambridge, Mass., 1967), pp. 193-4.

49. PL 90, col. 569.

50. A. Brandl, "Zum ags. Gedichte 'Traumgesicht vom Kreuze Christi,' ".

Sitzungsberichte der königlich preussischen Akademie (1905), pp. 716-23.
See The Dream of the Rood, ed. M. Swanton (Manchester, 1970), p. 48.

51. Early Northumbrian Sculpture (Jarrow, 1965), p. 7.

52. Such as, for example, the Bedan parallels suggested by Howlett, "Two panels," p. 335.

53. See Venerabilis Baedae Opera Historica, ed. C. Plummer (Oxford, 1896) II, 118-119.

54. See the list of pictures and "sanctarum imaginum" given by Bede, Historia Abbatum, chapters vi and ix (Plummer I, 369 and 373).

55. The Life of Bishop Wilfrid by Eddius Stephanus, ed. B. Colgrave (Cambridge, 1927), chapters v, xxix-xxxii, 1-1v.

56. Bede, Historia Ecclesiastica V. 7; Plummer I, 292-4; II, 278-82; Eddius Stephanus, Vita, chapters xli-xlii.

57. See Bede, Historia Abbatum, ii-vii, Plummer I, 365-71 (text); II, 356-61 (notes).

58. Duchesne, Liber Pontificalis I, 377.

59. Ibid., I, p. 371.

60. Bede, Historia Abbatum, vii, xv and xxi-xxiii, Plummer I, 370, 379 and 385-6 (text); II, 361, 365 and 369-70 (notes).

61. Bede, Historia Abbatum, xv; Plummer I, 380 (text); II, 365 (notes).

62. See Councils and Ecclesiastical Documents relating to Great Britain and Ireland, ed. A. W. Haddan and W. Stubbs, vol. 3 (Oxford, 1881), pp. 248-50.

63. Bede, Historia Abbatum, xviii; Plummer, I, 383.

64. Early Northumbrian Sculpture, pp. 10-11.

65. See A. S. C. Ross, "The linguistic evidence for the date of the 'Ruthwell cross,' " Modern Language Review 28 (1933), 145-55; A. Campbell, Old English Grammar (Oxford, 1959), p. 4 note 2; E. Mercer, "The Ruthwell and Bewcastle crosses," Antiquity 38 (1964), 268-76 (at 270).

66. I agree in general with the interpretations of the iconographic programme put forward by Saxl, "The Ruthwell Cross,"; by M. Schapiro "The religious meaning of the Ruthwell cross," Art Bulletin 26 (1944), 232-45, and by R. T. Farrell, above, pp. 96-119.

67. Saxl, "Ruthwell Cross," p. 5.

68. Okasha, Handbook, p. 111.

69. Saxl, "Ruthwell Cross," p. 3.

70. See Schapiro, "Religious Meaning," p. 237.

71. Saxl, "Ruthwell Cross," p. 4; Schapiro, "Religious Meaning," p. 238.

72. Howlett, "Two panels on the Ruthwell cross," p. 334.

73. *The Dream of the Rood*, ed. M. Swanton (Manchester, 1970), lines 90-4.

74. "Crucifixion as annunciation: the relation of *The Dream of the Rood* to the liturgy reconsidered, "to appear in a *festschrift* to honour Professor Paul Christophersen.

75. The words in brackets in this and the following quotations from the Ruthwell cross poem are not now legible, and have to be reconstructed from the Vercelli text. I have followed D. Howlett, "A reconstruction of the Ruthwell Crucifixion Poem, " *Studia Neophilologica* 48: 1 (1976). I am grateful to Dr Howlett for giving me a pre-publication typescript of this article.

76. For further consideration of this point, see my forthcoming article "Crucifixion as annunciation. "

77. Bede, *Homeliarum Euangelii Libri II*, ed. D. Hurst, Corpus Christianorum, Series Latina 122 (Turnholt, 1955), Homily no. 3, pp. 14-20 (at 15). See also Gregory the Great, *XL Homiliarum in Evangelia*, Book II, Homily xxxiv, PL, 76, col. 1251, and *Isidori Hispalensis Episcopi Etymologiarum sive Originum Libri XX*, edited by W. M. Lindsay, 2 vols (Oxford, 1911) I, Book VII, Chapter v "De Angelis, " 10-11.

78. Schapiro, "Religious Meaning, " p. 232.

79. Rosemary Woolf has argued that "that part of the poem which follows the description of the crucifixion must surely be a later addition by a writer of the school of Cynewulf" - "Doctrinal Influences on *The Dream of the Rood*, " *Medium Ævum* 27 (1958), 137-53 (at 153 note 34). This may be so; I merely believe that later revisers or readers were aware of, and sympathetic to, earlier traditions of interpreting the poem, and attempted to clarify and express the poem's *sententia* in the light of these traditions.

RUTHWELL		BEWCASTLE
South Face	North Face	
Crosshead (now mistakenly reversed) Bird clinging to foliage	Crosshead (now mistakenly reversed) St John the Evangelist and his eagle	Crosshead Destroyed
Transom now lost	Transom now lost	
Lower arm of crosshead: archer, drawing his bow	Lower arm of crosshead: St Matthew and his symbol (?)	
The Visitation (?) or Martha and Mary (?)	St John the Baptist bearing the Agnus Dei (compare Bewcastle, West Face)	St John the Baptist bearing the Agnus Dei (compare Ruthwell, North Face) Runic inscription: + GESSUS KRISTTUS
Penitent woman annointing the feet of Christ	Christ in Glory, adored by beasts (compare Bewcastle, West Face)	Christ in Glory adored by beasts (compare Ruthwell, North Face)
Christ healing a blind man	Sts Paul and Anthony, breaking bread in the desert	Runic inscription
The Annunciation	The Flight into Egypt	John the Evangelist and his eagle
The Crucifixion	Panel obliterated	

VII. GRAVE GOODS FROM FRILFORD CEMETERY

Robert G. Calkins

In November 1972 a group of objects was discovered at Cornell University which proved to be those excavated by Professor George Rolleston at Frilford (Berkshire) in May 1870[1] and sent to Cornell University in the same year. Rolleston published two accounts of his excavations at Frilford in Archaeologia, but only the second made brief mention of the grave-goods which were sent to Cornell.[2] The most complete account of the 1870 excavations appeared under the heading "Recent gifts" in a relatively inaccessible bulletin which contained the announcements of courses and the list of faculty for Cornell University for the year 1870-71, but although he provided a full description of the skeletons and their situation in the Frilford graves, Rolleston gave neither detailed descriptions of the artefacts nor any illustrations of them.[3]

Among these grave-goods were a pair of brooches which have been mentioned in the literature on Anglo-Saxon archaeology and have been illustrated once, but the other objects have not been discussed.[4] An attempt to find the Frilford artefacts at Cornell in 1962 was fruitless, and it was presumed that they were irrevocably lost.[5] It was therefore a striking coincidence that they were rediscovered at the time when preparations were being made for a colloquium to celebrate the 1300th anniversary of the birth of the Venerable Bede, the result of which is the present volume. This report endeavors to present and amplify the record concerning Rolleston's excavations of 1870, and to relate the subsequent vicissitudes of the objects which are now restored and safely housed in the Herbert F. Johnson Museum of Art at Cornell University.[6]

According to Rolleston's account, as printed in the Cornell Register and reprinted in full at the end of this discussion, four graves were excavated at Frilford on 23 and 27 May 1870. Rolleston's interest was primarily in the skeletal remains from these graves and he gave them, together with their attendant artifacts, to Cornell University through the good offices of his friend Goldwin Smith in July of the same year.[7] The skeletons and the grave goods were housed in a "Museum of Zoology and Physiology" in 1871-72, but there is no mention of them thereafter.[8] In response to an inquiry from E.T. Leeds in 1912, Charles H. Hull, Goldwin Smith Professor of American History and Dean of the Faculty of Arts and Sciences, took the pair of brooches and perhaps some other Frilford objects to London or Oxford where they were examined, photographed, and possibly drawn by Leeds.[9] It may have been after the artefacts were returned to Cornell in the fall of 1912 that they were stored away and forgotten until November 1972 when they were found on the top shelf of a cupboard in the Andrew Dickson White Museum.[10] The skeletal remains described by Rolleston had by this time disappeared; only one skull (No. iii, May 23, 1870) has been found in the collection of the Anthropology Department.

The four graves were those of (1) an "old Romano-Briton" male, (2) a "young Anglo-Saxon" male, (3) an "old Anglo-Saxon woman, " and (4) a "little old Romano-Briton" male. The goods from each grave are discussed below in the order of Rolleston's description. [10a]

(1) Two fragments of Roman pottery found near the remains of the old Romano-Briton were not among the objects when they were rediscovered in 1972.

(2) An iron shield-boss or umbo was discovered broken in fragments and wrapped in paper toweling in 1972. [11] Additional pieces were contained in a small birchwood box with the inscription "Fragments of Umbo, May 23, 1870" in Rolleston's handwriting. Temporary reconstruction made by Robert Farrell revealed a gently curved boss of approximately 16.5cm in diameter and 7cm in height (the bottom lip = 2cm; the vertical rise = 2cm; the curving slope = 7cm; and the top projection = .8cm). The boss was restored and treated by Mrs Davidson at the British Museum in the spring of 1973 (plate XIX). The form of the boss, with undercut vertical band blending into the flat rim around the base, a subtly curved upward surface and slightly flattened button on the terminal is similar to that of another Anglo-Saxon boss excavated at Frilford in 1873 and of others from the vicinity of Abingdon. [12] The Cornell umbo appears to have been attached to the shield by at least four, probably five studs, the heads of four of which are still attached to the rim. [13] Two of these studs penetrate through the rim, and around the longest one (shown at the left of Fig. 3) are fragments of wood with the grain corresponding to the radius of the boss. In its low, rounded shape and in the probable use of five shield studs, the Cornell boss is most like fifth-century Germanic bosses and various sixth-century Anglo-Saxon examples which continued these traditions. [14] Rolleston found the boss, and shield studs and handle discussed below over the pelvic area of a yound Anglo-Saxon male. Two flat headed nails were found in 1972 in a birchwood box marked "Shield studs (?) Anglo-Saxon, May 23, 1870. " The largest, apparently complete, is 3cm long with a head of approximately 1.8cm in diameter. The second, with the same size head, is only 1.3cm long. As noted above, four other heads of studs of the same dimensions are present on the rim of the restored boss. A shield handle, found in two pieces by Rolleston was in four fragments when rediscovered in 1972 (plate XX). Approximately 14cm long and averaging about 2.5cm wide, this handle has vestiges of turned up edges along the sides which Rolleston believed wrapped around a wooden support onto which the umbo and handle were nailed (Fig. 4 (b)). Near the neck of both rounded ends of the handle are remnants of wood, the grain of which runs at right angles to the axis of the handle. The remnants of a stud appear in the left end. The handle must have been set off-centre in relation to the boss in order for its ends to line up with the placement of the studs on the rim. [15] An iron knife, found by Rolleston on the right side of the pelvis just above the right hip, measures 11cm in length and 1.8cm at its widest part (plate XX). The blade tapers to both edges, and appears to have been well worn (fig. 4(c)). A lance-head of approximately 18cm in length and 2.5cm at its wides part was actually the first object Rolleston found associated with the grave of the young Anglo-Saxon. The spear-head contains a "V-shaped" slit 5.5cm in length and 1.5cm in diameter at its mouth into which the wooden shaft was inserted. Some vestiges of wood remain in this socket. The shaft

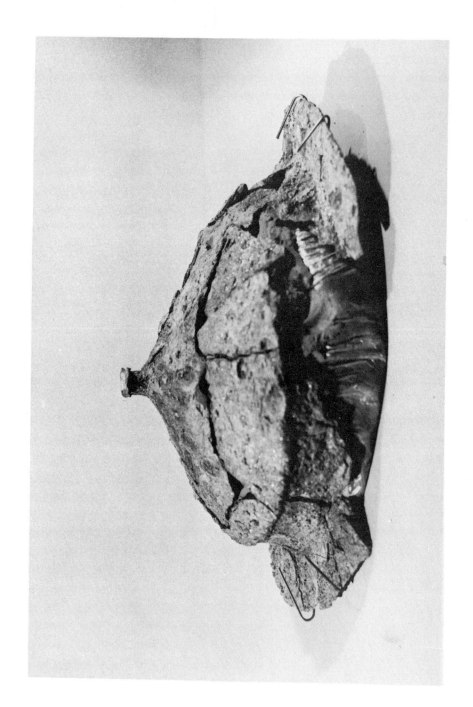

Plate XVIII Shield boss, preliminary reconstruction (from the grave of the young Anglo-Saxon).

Plate XIX   Shield boss after restoration.

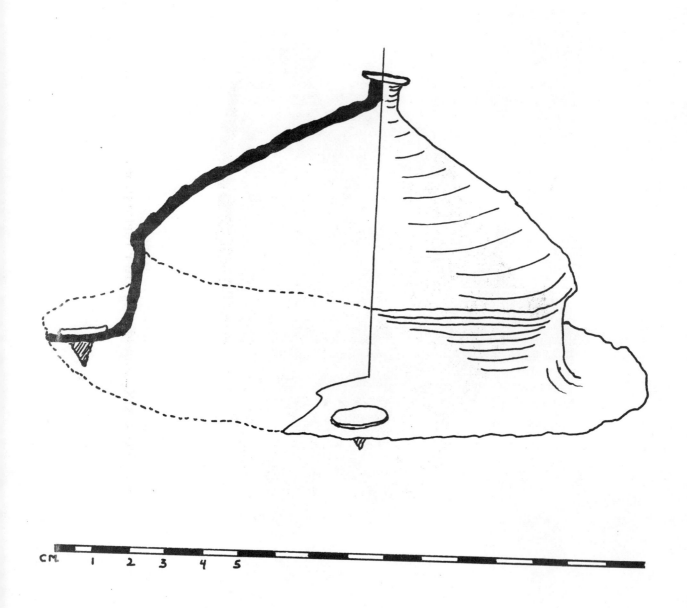

Fig. 3:   Shield boss, cross section

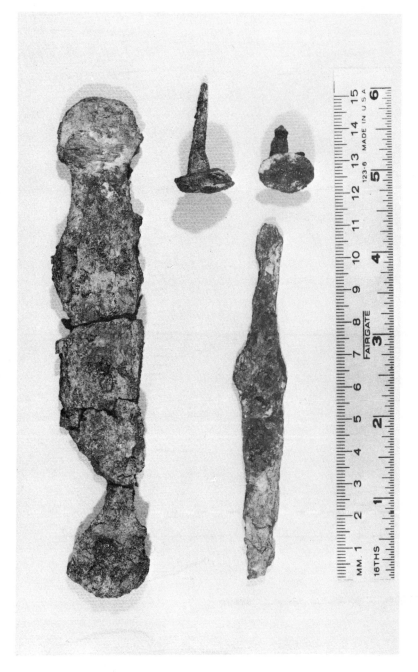

Plate XX   Shield handle, knife and shield studs from the grave of the young Anglo-Saxon.

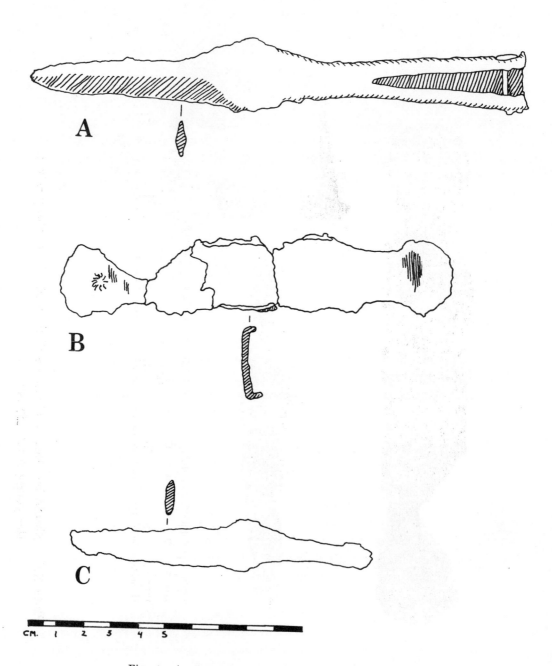

Fig. 4 A. Spear head; B. Spear handle; C. Knife.

was fixed by a rivet which still remains, set approximately 8mm from the open end (plate XXI). The blade is a flattened diamond shape in section (fig. 4 (a)) with a finely demarcated ridge running down the length of each side. A similar lance-head found at Frilford in the excavations of 1869, now in the Ashmolean Museum (No. 1872.2636), is though to date from the sixth century.

(3) A pair of bowed cruciform brooches in cast bronze, 8.5cm in length, were founds by Rolleston in the grave of an old Anglo-Saxon woman (plates XXII-XXIV). These were located at the collarbones of the skeleton (see Rolleston's sketch, plate XXV), together with a fragment of a spear-shaped bronze pin which may have been either the pin of one of the brooches or a shroud pin. In addition, two bronze catches, presumably from the brooches, and a dumb-bell shaped terminal were also found (plate XXII). The catches are made of sheets of bronze and were apparently brazed or soldered onto the underside of the brooches; there is no vistige of an integral catch, which would have been part of the original casting, having broken off (plates XXIII-XXIV). Brooch A (left in plates XXII-XXIV) lacks both lateral bosses, but on the reverse clearly shows the semicircular cast flange behind the headplate upon which the pin was hinged. Brooch B (right in the plates) retained a fully rounded dumb-bell shaped boss on the left, attached to the pin flange beneath the headplate. The loose boss closely approximates in size and shape the one still attached to the brooch. The knob at the top of the headplate is part of the original casting. It is flat on the bottom, as is the remainder of the body of the brooch. There are two horizontal depressions across the surface of the headplate creating a ribbed effect. The foot of the brooches below the bow contains similar ridges, and both terminate in an elongated, subtly modulated snout like a horse's head with flared nostrils. These brooches fall within the stylistic group of early cruciform or "cruciform long" brooches which are thought to date from the last quarter of the fifth into the first quarter of the sixth centuries. But they contain characteristics which place them between Åberg's Class I (with full-round knobs) and Class II (with "half-round knobs, foot without lappets, animal head with scroll shaped nostrils") brooches.[16] The half-round knob at the top, cast in a unit with the body of the fibula, is a Class II characteristic, but the full-round lateral knobs, cast separately and attached with the hinge of the pin to the flange beneath the headplate is even more archaic than the system found on most Class I brooches. In many of the Class I fibulae, the full-round lateral knobs are cast with the headplate, simply abutted against it with a portion of their volumes rising above its surface, as in the Class I brooch from East Shefford (Newbury Museum).[17] The knobs of the Cornell fibulae are set entirely beneath the headplate. In contrast, a typical Class II brooch from West Stow Heath (Suffolk), now in the Ashmolean Museum, has three half-round knobs cast onto the headplate.[18] Another remarkable feature of the Frilford brooches is their compactness in the proportioning of the relative elements. In section they are semicircular, whereas other brooches of this general type tend to be flatter and broader. The headplates are small and lack the lateral extensions or wings of similar cruciform long brooches such as those mentioned above. Thus the head of the brooches, with knobs intact, would have had a more narrow and vertical effect, lacking the balance of a pronounced horizontal axis provided by a wider head and more widely spaced knobs of the East Shefford and West Stow Heath fibulae.[19] Although lacking the lateral knobs, brooches with similar narrow proportions

Plate XXI   Spear head from the grave of the young Anglo–Saxon.

Plate XXII Cruciform fibulae with detached knob and clasps from
the grave of the old Anglo-Saxon woman.

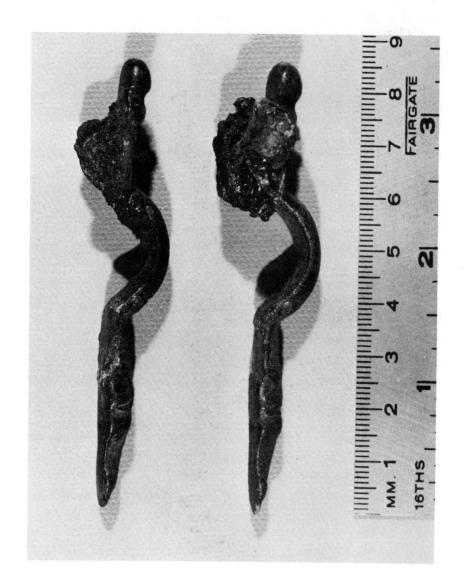

Plate XXIII   Cruciform fibulae, side view.

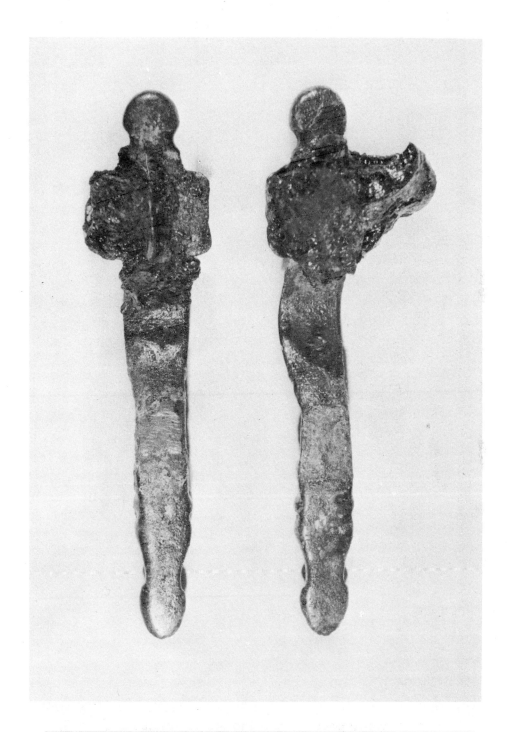

Plate XXIV   Cruciform fibulae, reverse (before cleaning).

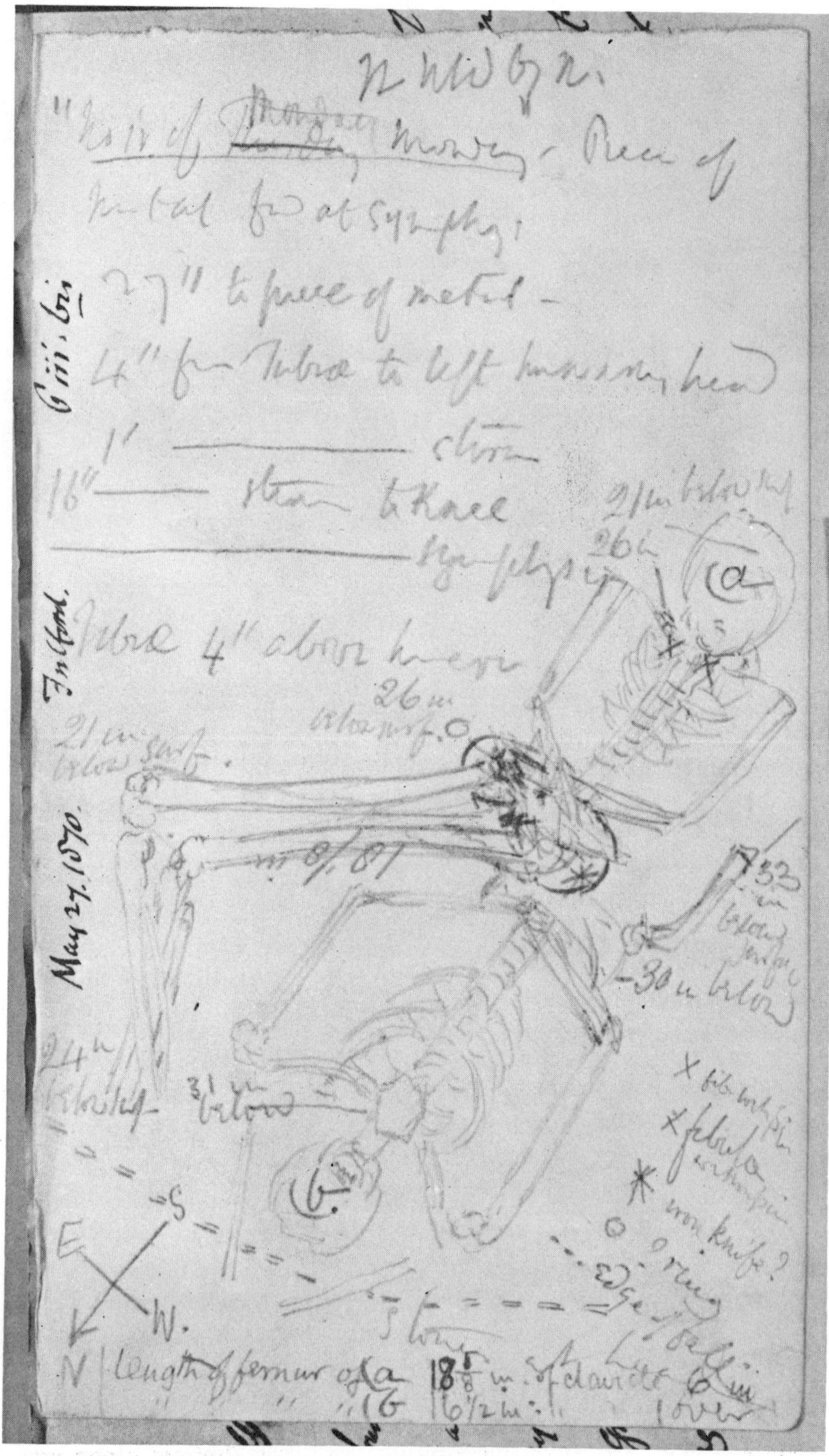

Plate XXV Rolleston's sketch of the graves of the old Anglo-Saxon woman and of the little old Romano-Briton.

were found in Suffolk and at Cesterover near Rugby.[20] No exact continental parallels have yet been found, but in their narrow proportions and in the horizontal ribbing of the headplate and foot, the Cornell fibulae have a general resemblance to some early cruciform brooches from Scandinavia, particularly one from Linkoping (Ostergotland) now in the Statenshistoriska Museum, Stockholm, and with brooches from the Lower Elbe region and Schleswig, the homeland of the early Angles and Saxons. Thus the Cornell brooches constitute important evidence, as Leeds and Evison have noted, of early post-invasion objects indicating the extent of the Anglo-Saxon penetration along the Icknield Way west and south of the Thames in the late fifth and early sixth centuries. [21] Given their unique fusion of different characteristics, particularly with their detached side knobs and integral half knob on top, a date of c. 475 to 500 may not be too far off. [22]

Also found in the grave of the old Anglo-Saxon woman was part of a very worn knife (in two fragments in 1972), 8cm long and 1.5cm broad, and various fragments thought to be the remains of a pair of tweezers. An iron ring which Rolleston found on the left hand (which had been placed across the body to the right hip, see fig. 8), and which was sent to Cornell in 1870, was not found with the artefacts in 1972.

(4) Six large iron nails, four of them bent, were found by Rolleston in the grave of a "little old Romano-Briton" male which was partially underneath that of the Anglo-Saxon woman (see plate XXV). These nails vary in length from 5cm to 3.5cm and have heads of approximately 2cm in diameter. Rolleston suggested that they were coffin nails (plate XXVI).

The site which Rolleston and others excavated in the nineteenth century had changed little by the time Buxton published a map of his excavations at the Frilford Cemetery in 1920, and apparently hardly at all between that time and 1939 when an aerial photograph was taken. [23] Since then, however, drastic changes have occurred. The triangular depression which had been the nineteenth-century quarry (plate XXVII), by the spring of 1973 had expanded eastward almost to the Oxford-Wantage road and southward almost to the small access road by the shed. Entirely overgrown with grass, this hollow is now used as the town dump for Frilford (plate XXVIII).

Unfortunately, the exact location of the graves excavated by Rolleston in 1870 is not known. According to Buxton's map, the Anglo-Saxon graves were concentrated in the south-eastern quadrant of the quarry, between the depression and the road, and the Romano-British ones to the north and west of the quarry face. Considering that the Anglo-Saxon graves dug up by Rolleston overlaid Romano-British ones, these may have been situated in the north-eastern face between the two concentrations, but we cannot be sure. In any event, the Frilford cemetery is remarkable for the unusual continued use of a burial site once used by the Romanized Britons by the later Anglo-Saxons who replaced them.

The Cornell artefacts occupy a special place among the many remains unearthed by various excavations at Frilford. They are thought to be the only Anglo-Saxon grave-goods in the United States from a known grave site. Moreover, since many of the objects found in other excavations at Frilford were widely dispersed by Rolleston, some of them given to institutions in Leipzig, Montreal, Australia and even Mexico, the Cornell artefacts assume an even

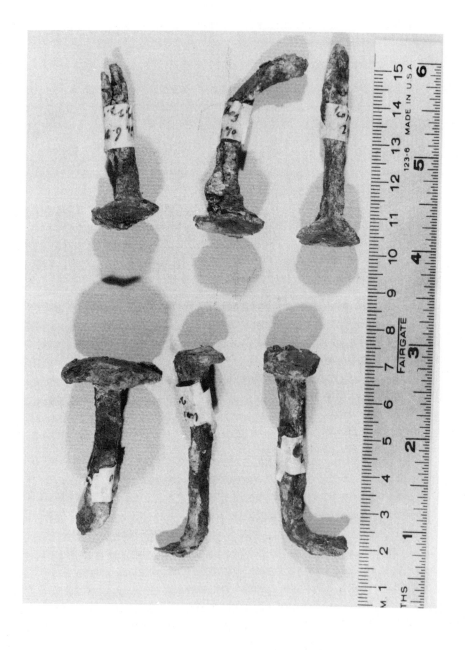

Plate XXVI   Coffin nails from the grave of the little old Romano–Briton.

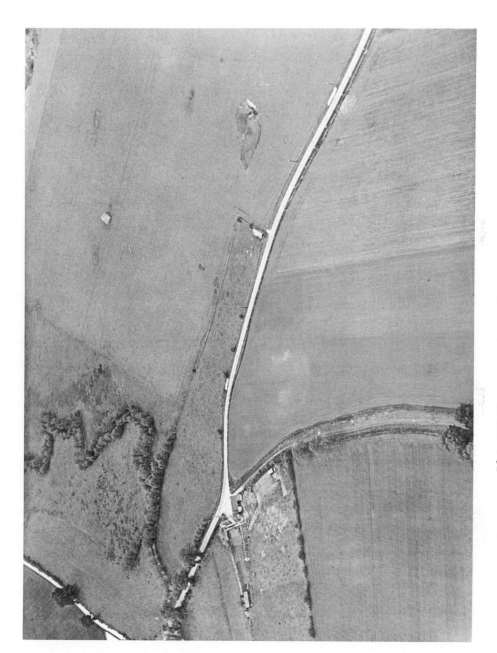

Plate XXVII   Aerial view of the Frilford site, 1939.

Plate XXVIII   View north-east along the north face of the quarry escarpment, Frilford. The triangular sign at the right marks the Oxford-Wantage road (1973).

greater importance as a collection of related objects from each of three specific and typical graves at that site.

GEORGE ROLLESTON'S "ACCOUNT OF SKULLS AND OTHER RELICS SENT TO CORNELL UNIVERSITY"

[1] OLD ROMANO-BRITON Skull "No iii, May 23, 1870," The skull and bones labelled "No. iii, May 23, 1870," belonged in all probability to a Romanized Briton inasmuch as the skeleton of which they formed a part was found in one of the Romano-British graves, described in Archaeologia (42 (1869), 423,) and inasmuch as it was found to have an Anglo-Saxon skeleton (No. vii, May 23, 1870, sent herewith) lying superficially to it by a distance of 18 inches. This skull and the three others all alike came from the Frilford Cemetery described, loc.cit. The skull belongs to the four which I have spoken of under the name of the "Globose Romano-British" type see Archaeologis loc.cit. p. 455 and which I have supposed to correspond with the "Sion Typus" of His and Rutimeyer. I say this to save repetition in manuscript of what the Society of Antiquaries has printed for me in the Memoir sent herewith.[24] The old age of the owner of these remains and the signs of his having been exposed to rough handling (see right clavicle and humerus) are points, as I have thought, not without their significance. Two fragments of Roman pottery were found in the neighbourhood of these bones.[26] The patellae accompanying the other bones showed that the skeleton had lain undisturbed since the burial of its owner.

[2] YOUNG ANGLO-SAXON Skull "No. vii, May 23, 1870." The skeleton to which the skull labelled "No. vii, May 23, 1870" belonged was found lying with its feet at the north and its head at the south, in a grave, therefore, running nearly at right angles to that of the Romano-Briton No. iii. This latter grave was 18 inches deeper than the one containing the bones and other relics of which we are now treating, and as it ran underneath it, must have been dug before it. Now with the skeleton to which skull No. vii belonged were found the unmistakeably Anglo-Saxon relics which I send with it, namely an umbo, a spear-head, and a knife of iron. There would appear, therefore, no possible source of fallacy to beset the conclusion that we have here to deal with an Anglo-Saxon and in the previous case with a Romano-British interment. (For this argument in point and in detail see Memoir on Frilford, p. 7.)[25] The skull was about 24 inches from the surface of the ground. The knees of No. iii underlaid it at a distance deeper by about 18 inches. The femur was about 17 inches long; neither this nor any other of the long bones have been recovered uninjured, the youth of the subject having militated against our obtaining them in the perfect condition in which the bones of No. iii are sent. The umbo was found overlying the pelvis and lower abdominal region. The knife was found on the right side of the pelvis just above the right hip. The spear head was knocked out of the ground whilst we were working out the femora of No. iii, and its appearance was the first hint we had of the presence of an Anglo-Saxon. Consequently we did not discover its exact position relating to the head of the Anglo-Saxon; it was, however, somewhere very near to it. Two broad-headed nails accompany the other relics. I think

they may have been shield studs; one of them was found close by the right ulna. The handle of the umbo accompanies it, in two pieces I am sorry to say. I do not think the Abbé Cochet is right in thinking that the hollow in the handle was intended to receive the fingers of the hand which grasped it; indeed the specimen shows that this hollow was intended to receive a wooden support on to which the umbo itself was nailed. (See Abbé Cochet, Normandie Souterraine, p. 239. pl. viii figs. 2 & 3; pl. xvi fig. 5.) The youth of this young Anglo-Saxon man is significant. See Memoir on Frilford, p. 29. The cranial characters also have an importance. See pp. 43 and 44, loc.cit.[27] I removed, I think, every one of these relics myself, as I did also all those labelled No. iii, with the exception of the skull, which a person present anticipated me in taking up from the bottom of the grave.

[3] OLD ANGLO-SAXON WOMAN Skull "No. iv-a, May 23 and May 27, 1870." The skull and bones labelled "No. iv-a, May 23" was [sic] found with the similarly labelled Anglo-Saxon ornaments, viz., two bronze fibulae, an iron knife, and an iron ring, which are sent with them.[28] The skeleton, like the preceding one, had been placed in a grave which crossed an older grave containing a skeleton of one of the conquered Romano-Britons (No. iv-b, May 23, 1870) lying at a lower level. But it differs from the preceding Anglo-Saxon skeleton, as it belonged to a woman of advanced age instead of belonging to a young man, and as it was buried with the lower limbs bent upon themselves and upon the trunk instead of being extended at full length. [See Rolleston's drawing of these two graves, pl. XXV.] The history of the discovery of this skeleton is as follows. Some quarrying operations had exposed a skull without disturbing it in situ, where a quantity of undermined soil had parted away in what the workmen call a "fall" from the undisturbed, not undermined ground. On either side of that cranium ("No. iv-b., May 23") were seen two flat stones placed as a lean-to, one on either side of the skull. On either side were seen phalanges and torsal bones; and on further investigation the ends of three long bones were also discovered in the neighbourhood of the skull. The coming on of the night of Monday, May 23, prevented us from doing more than find out that these long bones or rather the parts of them which we were able to expose in the vertical face of the ground, at the time very dry and hard, were the distal ends of a tibia and fibula and the proximal end of a humerus. The skull was removed that evening and will have its history given below under heading iv, "No. iv-b May 23, 1870." The problem of the relation of the long bones to this skull was left to be worked out on the Friday following, viz., May 27. On that day Mr. G. H. Morrell, M.A., of Exeter College [Oxford] who was good enough to give his help, worked out that problem to the following effect:- The long leg bones were found to belong to a different skeleton from that of the skull of which had been removed, and which was at a deeper level by from 7 to 4 inches in various parts, the upper grave having varied in depth in different parts. With the more superficially placed skeleton with which we have to deal under this heading ("No. iv-a, May 23") were found the following ornaments characteristic of the female Anglo-Saxon interment in the non-cremation period (of transition, see p. 20, Memoir on Frilford.)[29] First, two cruciform bronze fibulae found at the junction of the clavicles with the sternum, such as may be seen figured, pl. vii fig. 31 of Neville's "Saxon Obsequies," the dumb-bell shaped lateral

166

bosses having been detached in every case, and recovered only in one. Secondly, with the fibula which lay upon the junction of the left clavicle with the sternum was found a spear-shaped bronze pin which may have been possibly the tongue of the brooch: but which probably was the shroud pin (of which I have spoken, see Memoir, p. 56).[30] Thirdly, two small pieces of bronze which were probably the catches of the brooches. Round several of these various pieces and implements of bronze, bits of textile fabric were and still are recognizable.[31] Fourthly, an iron ring, such as Abbé Cochet in his Normandie Souterraine, p. 216, ed. 1, speaks of as having been found by him à satiété même in Merovingian interments but which he says have not within his recollection been figured by Wylie, Smith, Troyon, Lindenschmit, de Caumont, etc. It was found on the left hand, middle finger, (?) and as having no trace upon it of a tongue, was probably not a buckle, but what it is seen to be, namely a ring. Fifthly, a knife, in two pieces, which was found on the left side but a little underneath the left hip, and in the immediate neighbourhood of which a rectangular small piece of the same metal was found, probably from the fastenings of the handle of the knife.

The lower leg bones of the skeleton to which skull "No. iv-a May 23-27" belonged, lay about a foot to the east of skull "iv-b May 23," and they were about 7 in. nearer to the surface of the ground. The long axis of the tibiae was S.E., the patellae were in situ, the legs were crossed, the right being uppermost; the knees were higher by 3in. than the distal ends of the tibiae. The femora ran in a S.W. direction nearly at right angles to the tibiae; their length was 18in. The heads of the thigh-bones were 26 inches below the surface, that is to say, they were five inches lower than the knees. The axis of the pelvis lay East and West, and the trunk again very nearly North and South; the depth at which they lay being 26 inches. The head was raised five inches above the sternum by three limestones which had been placed under it; and probably from having had a stone which was above it forced upon it when the hard ground was being picked down, it had some of the many fractures which it undergone inflicted upon it. But these bones had suffered much as shallowly buried bones have often been observed to do, from water wear, before they were excavated by us. The arms were crossed and the hands folded inwards.

[4] Skull "No. iv, b, May 23, 1870". This skull formed part of the skeleton of a little old Romano-Briton, of some five feet two inches in height, who, unlike the Anglo-Saxon woman buried above him, was buried in a coffin, at least if we may say so upon the evidence of the nails which were found in considerable abundance in the grave. The patellae was not in situ, having probably been disturbed; though none other of the bones appear to have been so, when the Anglo-Saxon body (iv-a) was put in. Between the pelvis of the deeper lying skeleton and that of the other there were only 4 inches intervening; and it was in following up the pelvis of the Romano-Briton that the knife of the Anglo-Saxon woman already mentioned, was come upon, so close together were they. But barring the loss of the patellae,

> It was little he recked as they let him sleep on,
> In the grave where a Briton had laid him.

167

Fragments of charcoal and of bones were found above the skeleton where it was not overlaid by the Anglo-Saxon one. (For this see Memoir, p. 10).[32] The skull is what I should call a transitional form between the "globose" and the "elongated" Romano-British skulls spoken of, Memoir p. 62. For the great age attained to by the civilized Romano-British see ibid. p. 20.[33] The tibiae show a tendency to be platycnemic. I have observed the same in an Anglo-Saxon woman's skeleton, also dug up at Frilford. Some of the bones sent herewith were dug out on Friday, May 27, and hence some are labelled iv iv R.B., for Romano-Briton, May 27, 1870, instead of iv-b., May 23, 1870.

The reconstruction which these skulls more or less needed, they have received at the hands of Charles Robertson, Esq., Demonstrator of Anatomy in the University Museum. G. M. Morrell, Esq., M.A., and I, took out the skeletons and skulls, Mr. Morrell taking out Nos. iv-a and iv-b, and I taking out Nos. iii, May 23 and viii, May 23, 1870.

Oxford, July 4, 1870.

NOTES

1. This discovery was noted by Leslie E. Webster, "Medieval Britain in 1972: I. Pre-Conquest," Medieval Archaeology 17 (1973), 138.

2. George Rolleston, "Researches and excavations carried on in an ancient cemetery at Frilford in 1867-1868," Archaeologia 42 (1869), 417-485; and idem "Further researches in an Anglo-Saxon cemetery at Frilford, with remarks on the northern limit of Anglo-Saxon cremation in England," Archaeologia 45 (1880), 405-410.

3. Cornell University Register (1870-71), pp. 50-54.

4. See E. T. Leeds, The Archaeology of the Anglo-Saxon Settlements (Oxford, 1913), p. 64; L. H. D. Buxton, "Excavations at Frilford," Antiquaries Journal 1 (1920), 96; Leeds, "The West Saxon invasion and the Icknield Way," History 10 (1925), 103; idem, "The early Saxon penetration of the Upper Thames area," Antiquaries Journal 13 no. 3 (1933), 239-242 and Plate 33c; idem, "The growth of Wessex," Oxoniensia 19 (1954), 51; G. J. Copley, The Conquest of Wessex in the Sixth Century (London, 1954), pp. 106 and 109; A. Meaney, A Gazetteer of Early Anglo-Saxon Burial Sites (London, 1964), pp. 46-7.

5. A request for further information concerning the Frilford brooches, sent by Miranda Townsend to Dr. Hencken of the American School of Prehistoric Research, Peabody Museum, Harvard University, and forwarded to Cornell, resulted in the disturbing realization that no trace of the objects could be found. I am indebted to Professor Frederick Waage for making this correspondence available to me. His unearthing of these letters made it possible to identify the objects with certainty within several days of their rediscovery.

6. Acquisition No. 73.84. It was through Professor Farrell that arrangements were made with the British Museum for their restoration, and through him and Thomas W. Leavitt, Director of the Johnson Art Museum that an application was made for necessary funding. Professor Farrell and I gratefully acknowledge that the research on these objects and their subsequent restoration undertaken by Mrs. Davidson of the British Museum was supported by a grant from the National Endowment for the Arts in Washington D.C., a Federal agency.

7. Although it was suspected that Goldwin Smith was responsible for Rolleston's gift, this was not known for certain until I had the opportunity of examining Rolleston's notes at the Ashmolean Museum, Oxford, where I saw the notation in his handwriting " Given to Cornell University through Goldwin Smith." I am extremely grateful to David Brown of the Ashmolean Museum for making Rolleston's notes available to me, for providing me with photographs and copies of correspondence, and for

accompanying me to the site at Frilford. I also wish to express my
thanks to David Miles who made it possible for me to see the Anglo-
Saxon objects in the County Hall Museum in Abingdon. Tania Dickinson,
in her census, has numbered Grave ii, No. 137 and Grave iii, No. 138.
I am indebted to Mrs Dickinson for her helpful suggestions.

Cornell University Register (1871-2), p. 70.

9. Leeds "Early Anglo-Saxon penetration of the Upper Thames area," pp.
    239-40, Plate 33c. Both brooches are shown (the profile view is not
    of the brooch shown in the frontal view).

10. A shoebox containing the objects was discovered by Carol Murray,
    Registrar of the Museum, as the building was being cleared in prepara-
    tion for moving into the new Herbert F. Johnson Museum. The iden-
    tification of the objects as Anglo-Saxon was made by me and confirmed
    by Robert Farrell, but it was several days later before we determined
    that they had come from Frilford (see above, p. 169, n. 5). A prelimin-
    ary report on the Frilford artifacts was made in a paper, "An Anglo-
    Saxon find at Cornell" delivered at the Eighth Conference on Medieval
    Studies, The Medieval Institute of Western Michigan University,
    Kalamazoo, Michigan, in May 1973.

10a. All the Roman and Anglo-Saxon graves at Frilford have been renumbered
     from 1- for republication as part of the Corpus of Anglo-Saxon Graves
     and Gravegoods in the Upper Thames Valley being prepared by David
     Brown. The numbers are:

Cornell no. I iii of 23 May 1870	Grave 234
Cornell no. II vii of 23 May 1870	Grave 239
Cornell no. III iva of 23 and 27 May 1870	Grave 235
Cornell no. IV ivb of 23 May 1870	Grave 236

11. According to a letter written by Professor Hull to E. T. Leeds, dated
    27 June 1912, the umbo had been broken into several pieces by that
    time.

12. Now in the Ashmolean Museum, Oxford (No. 1886.1436). See also
    Leeds and Harden, The Anglo-Saxon Cemetery at Abingdon, Berkshire
    (Oxford, 1936), pl. 19, especially nos. 4 and 69.

13. Several portions of the rim were missing when a preliminary recons-
    truction was made (pl. XVIII). The placement of the studs proceeding
    clockwise from the stud with the longest surviving shank (at the left
    in Fig. 4 here designated "6:00") is as follows: 6:00; 8:30; 10:30;
    (1:00?-conjectural) 3:00. Two additional studs were found loose in
    association with the boss and handle. One of them may have occupied
    the position conjectured above, but the placement of the other is dif-
    ficult to envisage.

14. See Bernhard Salin, Die altgermanische Thierornamentik (Stockholm,
    1935), p. 94 and fig. 227: boss from Selzen, Rheinessen. In addition
    to those mentioned above, other similar Anglo-Saxon bosses were
    found at Barrington (Cambridgeshire; ibid. fig. 229), at Buttsole, Eastry

and Stowting (Kent; G. Baldwin Brown, <u>The Arts in Early England</u>,
III: <u>Saxon Art and Industry in the Pagan Period</u> (London, pl. 22, nos.
2a and 4); and at Fairford (Gloucestershire; <u>ibid.</u>, pl. 23, no. 4).
Two similar bosses from Long Wittenham (Berkshire) are in the British
Museum (nos. 75, 3-10, 27 and 75, 3-10, 24).

15. A likely position would have been between studs at 10:30 and 1:00 (conjec-
tural), in which case the direction of the wood grain would have been
the same as on the stud at 6:00. Thus the profile of the boss as given
in fig. 4, if the handle were held in a vertical position, is along the
East-West axis.

16. Nils Åberg, <u>The Anglo-Saxons in England During the Early Centuries
After the Invasion</u>, Arbeten utgivna med understöd av Vilhelm Ekmans
Universitetsfond, Uppsala, 33 (Uppsala, 1926, pp. 28-29, especially
p. 33.

17. Leeds "Early Anglo-Saxon penetration of the Upper Thames area,"
Plate XXXIV (a).

18. Illustrated in D. M. Wilson, <u>The Anglo-Saxons</u> (Harmondsworth, 1972),
fig. 20b (see pp. 94 and 216), and Åberg <u>Anglo-Saxons in England</u> p. 37,
fig. 59.

19. Other typical examples of this type of Class II fibula are the brooches
from Trumpington (Cambridgeshire: University Museum of Archaeology and Ethnology. See R. Jessup, <u>Anglo-Saxon Jewelry</u> (London, 1950),
Pl. XIII, No. 1 and pp. 105-6) and from Barrington (Cambridgeshire).

20. Baldwin Brown (1915), Vol. 3, pl. XL, no. 4 and <u>ibid.</u>, pl. XLI, no. 1.

21. Leeds "The West Saxon invasion and the Icknield Way," 97-109, especially p. 103; <u>idem</u>, "Early Anglo-Saxon penetration of the Upper
Thames area," pp. 229-251; <u>idem</u>, (1954), 45-60; and V. J. Evison,
<u>The Fifth Century Invasions South and West of the Thames</u> (London,
1965), esp. p. 3.

22. Baldwin Brown (1915), vol. 3, p. 261 considered English fibulae with
separate side knobs to date prior to A.D. 500.

23. Buxton "Excavations at Frilford," pp. 88-9.

24. Rolleston's <u>Archaeologia</u> account (42 (1869), 417-85) was later republished
as an offprint entitled <u>Memoir on Frilford</u>, with separate pagination.

25. These fragments were not with the objects when they were rediscovered
in 1972.

26. <u>Archaeologia</u> 42 (1869), 423-4.

27. <u>Ibid.</u>, pp. 444-5.

28. As noted above, the ring was not with the grave-goods when found in 1972.

29. <u>Archaeologia</u> 42 (1869), 437.

30. <u>Ibid.</u>, p. 472.

31. No fabric was evident when the objects were discovered in 1972.

32. <u>Archaeologia</u> 42 (1869), 425-6. The charcoal and the bones have not survived.

33. <u>Ibid.</u>, p. 436.